Playing with Videogames

Playing with Videogames documents the richly productive, playful and social cultures of videogaming that support, surround and sustain this most important of digital media forms and yet which remain largely invisible within existing studies.

James Newman details the rich array of activities that surround game-playing, charting the vibrant and productive practices of the vast number of videogame players and the extensive 'shadow' economy of walkthroughs, FAQs, art, narratives, online discussion boards and fan games, as well as the cultures of cheating, copying and piracy that have emerged.

Playing with Videogames offers the reader a comprehensive understanding of the meanings of videogames and videogaming within the contemporary media environment.

James Newman is Senior Lecturer in Media Communications and Cultural Studies at Bath Spa University. He teaches, researches and writes about videogames and digital media. His books include *Videogames* (2004), *Difficult Questions about Videogames* (2004), *Teaching Videogames* (2006) and 100 *Videogames* (2007).

Playing with Videogames

James Newman

Routledge
Taylor & Francis Group

LONDON AND NEW YORK

First published 2008
by Routledge
2 Park Square, Milton Park, Abingdon, Oxon, OX14 4RN

Simultaneously published in the USA and Canada
by Routledge
270 Madison Ave, New York, NY 10016

*Routledge is an imprint of the Taylor & Francis Group,
an informa business*

© 2008 James Newman

Typeset in 11/13pt Perpetua by
Graphicraft Limited, Hong Kong
Printed and bound in Great Britain by
TJ International Ltd, Padstow, Cornwall

British Library Cataloguing in Publication Data
A catalogue record for this book is available
from the British Library

Library of Congress Cataloging in Publication Data
Newman, James (James A.)
Playing with videogames / James Newman.
p. cm.
Includes bibliographical references.
1. Video games. 2. Video games—Social aspects. I. Title.
GV1469.3.N47 2008
794.8—dc22
2008005772

ISBN10: 0-415-38522-9 (hbk)
ISBN10: 0-415-38523-7 (pbk)
ISBN10: 0-203-89261-5 (ebk)

ISBN13: 978-0-415-38522-0 (hbk)
ISBN13: 978-0-415-38523-7 (pbk)
ISBN13: 978-0-203-89261-9 (ebk)

Contents

Preface

As I sit at my desk to write the introduction to this book, I find myself surrounded by the evidence of a lifetime of videogaming. Aside from the library of CDs, DVDs, Blu-Ray discs and cartridges, countless joysticks, joypads and handheld systems litter my workspace. My bookshelves groan under the weight of books about every aspect of videogames from artwork, design and production through to scholarly criticism and analysis. Alongside these, decades of archived copies of gaming magazines such as *Edge*, and glossy game guides wrestle for space among an ever-growing collection of lever arch folders stuffed almost to bursting point with printouts of player-produced Frequently Asked Questions (FAQs), and walkthroughs for every conceivable game. On my desk, a bobble-headed Super Mario, a plastic Pikachu filled with curiously flavourless Japanese sweets, and a cuddly Link from *The Legend of Zelda*, are just some of the game-related toys spread throughout my office and home. Each is a gift from a friend or graduating student and each reminds me how much my identity is defined by my professional and personal interest in videogames. My iPod has playlists of Commodore 64 classics from Rob Hubbard and Martin Galway and ensures that I am only ever a few button clicks away from *Kentilla*, *Sanxion* or *Wizball* just as my old cassette Walkman did over twenty years ago. My daily trawl of online news and RSS feeds takes in a number of gaming sites that bring me information and previews of upcoming releases, hints, cheats and tips, as well as the machinations of the games industry and academic game studies community. Oh yes, and I am wearing a *Legend of Zelda* T-shirt.

I paint this picture not because I seek to convince anybody of my gaming pedigree – indeed, it disappoints me greatly to admit that despite my many years of playing, I can only reliably beat my colleague Iain Simons who will surely claim that he lets me win when I am at his house because that is the way a good host should behave. Rather, I want to demonstrate what it means to be interested in videogames. There is more to videogaming than the blips of light on the screen, the sounds pumping through the speakers, or the carefully co-ordinated combinations of button presses and feedback loops of rumbling joypads, Wiimotes and styli. By recognising the existence and importance of game-related music, toys, books, magazines and websites, we begin to appreciate how much more there is to videogaming than playing videogames.

Of course, all of this only begins to scratch the surface of what we might term 'videogame culture'. Among the issues I am particularly keen to explore in this book is the inherently social, productive and creative nature of these cultures that surround and support videogaming. As such, the following pages chart the vibrant and productive practices of the vast numbers of videogame fans and players and the extensive 'shadow economy' of player-produced walk-throughs, FAQs, art, narratives and even games, not to mention the cultures of cheating, copying and piracy, that have emerged. However, despite their preval-ence, and the size of the communities that support them, these activities and practices are all but invisible within academic, and even most popular, writing on videogames and gaming. *Playing with Videogames* is interested in the mean-ings of videogames to players and the myriad ways in which they make use of them besides just playing them – playing *with* them.

At least one of the aims of this book is to challenge some of the taken-for-granted assumptions circulating in both popular and academic discourse by high-lighting the creativity, productivity and sociality of videogame culture. As we will see in the opening chapter, the ease with which videogames can be derided as 'junk culture' that reduce their players to 'blinking lizards, motionless, absorbed, only the twitching of their hands showing they are still conscious' (Johnson 2006 [online]) speaks of an alarmist tendency that is seemingly unaware of the richness and diversity of gaming cultures. This book's investigation of videogame fans' artistic and literary production, the creation of walkthroughs and FAQ texts, the modification of existing games and the development of entirely new fangames, speaks clearly of the complexity of player engagements with videogames and the ways games are reconfigured to increase their life-span and add challenge, for example. Furthermore, online discussion boards and forums dedicated to the scrutiny of game titles or series reveal considerable passion and invention as fans interrogate and consult vast arrays of supporting texts, often in translation, so as to better understand the objects of their fandom, perhaps seeking to make sense of appar-ent inconsistencies in the backstories that weave together two titles in a series, for instance. Where the production of fan art and fiction ably demonstrate the intertextuality of readings of videogames, these investigations into the history of the game's development reveal much of the videogame fans' understanding of the processes of commercial media production including the tensions between creative vision, budgetary constraints, deadlines and technical limitations.

It is my wish that this book will provide a useful and enlightening introduction to these rich communities, cultures and practices. Certainly, even though I count

myself as a gamer, if not a hardcore gamer (as many of my students who frequently engage in marathon gaming sessions spanning many days are keen to
remind me), much of what this research uncovered reveals a culture that is richer
and more intricate than I had previously realised. However, this raises one final
issue. I am not suggesting that the practices that I document and discuss throughout this book are uniformly a part of every gamer's experience of videogame
culture. While some activities and communities such as those that emerge from
playground and watercooler talk are reasonably widespread, others such as
the production of in-depth walkthroughs, fanfiction stories or game-inspired costumes, are altogether more niche. However, even though those engaged in the
production of lengthy stories that expand or repair the incomplete, official narratives of videogames serials might be in the minority, the Internet has made
available these products to a potentially huge audience. Similarly, it is clear that
only a small subset of gamers create the extensive walkthroughs, game guides
we find online at sites such as www.gamefaqs.com, for example, or devise new
challenges that breathe new life into games long after they have slipped off the
retail radar. Yet, these challenges, these new ways of playing come into the hands
of the many thousands who download their works and whose playing is subsequently enriched and enlivened by these newly found resources. My point here
is that while I do not wish to present a situation in which the actions of the
few are made to stand for those of the many, it is important to recognise that
to some degree much of our apparently solitary, personal or private videogame
play is always and already situated within a shared experience of play that locates
us within a complex network of gamers at once staking their claim as experts
and sharing their insight and wisdom with the community at large without expecta-
tion of remuneration. Interestingly, we are perhaps beginning to witness the
mainstreaming of some of this hitherto marginal fan activity. While modding –
the practice of modifying games using officially-supplied tools – might be open
to only a few by virtue of the high levels of technical skill required, games
such as *LittleBigPlanet* make it extremely accessible. *LBP* is essentially a game
predicated around modding in which the construction of the gameworld, and the
act of sharing it with others so that they might play it, *is* the game. In a similar
fashion, we see that the practice of speedrunning – the attempt to 'complete'
a game as quickly as possible perhaps by exploiting its foibles and imperfections but, most importantly, by ignoring its ostensible goals – finds itself built
into the very fabric of *Super Mario Galaxy*. What was once a peripheral 'playing
against the grain' is now a requisite mode of play in one of Nintendo's highest
profile, flagship titles. While we must be careful not to overstate matters, we
should not overlook the role of digital communications networks and services
such as YouTube in raising the visibility and popularity of 'subversive' practices

such as speedrunning so that they become 'legitimised' as part of the gameplay vocabulary of mainstream titles.

And so, although I do not want to suggest that the various practices and ways of playing/playing with videogames that are documented in this book are typical of every gamer's experience, I hope that most gamers will recognise themselves somewhere in the following chapters.

Acknowledgements

This book is one of the outputs of a four-year research project on videogame cultures funded by the HEFCE Capability Fund (UoA 65) Communication, Cultural and Media Studies. Without this funding and the support of my managers and colleagues at Bath Spa University, this book would not have been possible. I would particularly like to extend my thanks to my research assistants Liam Stone and Alice Bonasio, whose sterling work searching through forums and discussion boards proved invaluable and whose archiving and filing more than compensated for my own organisational shortcomings; Rebecca Feasey for reading through the drafts; Susan Dunsmore for remaining calm in the face of technical meltdown; and Iain Simons for keeping me interested in videogames and maintaining his tireless campaign of spamming my inbox with useful links.

I would also like to offer my sincerest thanks to Lucy Newman for her continuing support, good humour and the endless cups of coffee that are the real reason this book got written, and to my daughter, Martha for constantly giggling, smiling and having the decency not to have saved over my draft with the complete jibberish she occasionally typed into my unattended word processor.

And, finally, I am thankful to the legion of gamers whose creativity, inventiveness and imagination provided the material for this book. It is to all the speedrunners, sequence breakers, cosplayers, modders, walkthrough authors, fanfic writers, artists, musicians, fanslators, remixers, hackers and above all, gamers, that this book is dedicated.

Chapter 1

Everybody hates videogames

'Junk culture': the Prince and the paper

Videogames have not enjoyed an easy ride in the popular press which has long concerned itself with the negative influences of their representations and the consequences of play. For many commentators, if videogames are worth considering at all, they can be easily and readily dismissed as little more than inconsequential trivialities. Indeed, so pervasive is this discourse of videogaming as worthless diversion that many gamers recount the experiences to which they devote many hours of puzzling, dedication and creative effort as shameful, guilty pleasures (see Cragg *et al.* 2007). In what may be the apotheosis of this position, Richard Abanes (2006: 11) recounts the influential child psychologist Dr Benjamin Spock's brief and dismissive analysis of videogames as nothing more than a 'colossal waste of time'. Not everybody has been this sanguine in their assessment, however.

More recently, throughout the myriad column inches that have been set aside to investigations of the form, two types of story have come to dominate. The first centres on the apparently universally violent nature of videogames, though the focus is on a small number of key titles such as *DOOM*, *Manhunt* and the *Grand Theft Auto* series. The substance of such stories deals with the putative effects on players' behaviour and psychology that arise from engaging and interacting with the brutal narratives and images contained within these games. Among the more notable headlines this line of enquiry has generated are the recounting of a 'Murder by Playstation' (*Daily Mail*, 29 July 2004) and exaltations to 'Ban These Evil Games' (*Daily Mail*, 30 July 2004). A number of academics and critics have pointed to the lack of a credible basis upon which to make these bold assertions of causation and the absence of any substantive discussion of the mechanism by which gameplay might affect post-play behaviour (see Gunter 1998, Durkin and Aisbett 1999, Griffiths 1999, Harris 2001, Unsworth and Ward 2001; and Heins and Bertin 2002, for example, on the inconsistencies in the empirical research base). However, while it is true that a weak evidential base does not negate the very possibility of a case to answer, scholars of media and cultural studies well versed in the considerable body of active audience and reception theory will, without doubt, be more than a little exacerbated by the voracity with which the media effects tradition is discussed and the lack of criticality in the assumptions surrounding causation and the power of media messages over audiences that underpins the reporting in these stories. It is certainly true that this kind of popular discourse has ensured that effects claims based on fairly crude hypodermic models of media and audience remain some of the most popular lay-theories of media and that videogames have, for some time, been subjected to the kind of panicky responses seen earlier in relation to 'video nasties', 'comic books', or more recently, Internet chatrooms (see Cumberbatch 1998 for a concise history of media panics). It is not within the remit of the current book to tackle the complex issues of media effects and influences, audiences and the making of textual meaning as they relate to so-called 'violent videogames' (the difficulty of arriving at an adequate and transferable definition of media 'violence' is a problematic issue in itself, as Scott 1995 notes). The reader wishing to pursue this subject further would be well advised to trawl the extensive literature in this field both in terms of game-specific studies that attempt to account for the interactivity and participatory nature of videogame play (e.g. Gunter 1998; Jones 2002; Cumberbatch 2004; Newman and Oram 2006) as well as more general investigations of media forms (e.g. Barker and Petley 1997; Johnson 2005).

In this volume, instead we shall focus on the second type of story which, unlike those concerned with the violent and aggressive behaviour that is seen to stem from gameplay and that tend to focus on specific videogame titles deemed to be to blame (such as Rockstar's *Manhunt*, for instance, to which the two *Daily Mail* pieces noted above explicitly refer), treats videogames *en masse*. This second type of story treats these experientially, technologically and structurally identical 'videogames' as both symptomatic of and the partial or even sole cause of social, cultural and educational decline. From standards of child literacy through sociality to imagination and creativity, videogames are seen to exert a singularly deleterious effect. In 2001, Prince Charles summed up the situation succinctly in claiming:

> One of the great battles we face today is to persuade our children away from the computer games towards what can only be described as worthwhile books . . . None of us can underestimate the importance of books in an age dominated by the computer screen and the constant wish for immediate gratification.
>
> ('Prince Battles Video Games' 2001)

Writing for the Telegraph.co.uk, Boris Johnson elucidates while ramping up the vitriol to a most impressive level:

> We demand that teachers provide our children with reading skills; we expect the schools to fill them with a love of books; and yet at home we let them slump in front of the consoles. We get on with our hedonistic 21st-century lives while in some other room the nippers are bleeping and zapping in speechless rapture, their passive faces washed in explosions and gore. They sit for so long that their souls seem to have been sucked down the cathode ray tube.
>
> They become like blinking lizards, motionless, absorbed, only the twitching of their hands showing they are still conscious. These machines teach them nothing. They stimulate no ratiocination, discovery or feat of memory – though some of them may cunningly pretend to be educational.
>
> (Johnson 2006 [online])

The charge here, then, is an oddly counter-intuitive one. Videogames, a form defined best by their interactivity, are accused of reducing their players to a near-deathly passivity. More than that, games appear to exercise a powerful hold over players who play for evidently excessive periods of time in single sessions. The notion of the gamer captivated and absorbed by the game conjures images of obsessives or, as others such as David Grossman (2001) would have it, 'addicts'. The language has made its way into scholarly investigations also with discussions of 'fixes' and allusions to videogame players as cocaine addicts in Klein (1984), Braun and Giroux (1989), and Zimbardo (1982, cited in Klein 1984).

It is worth noting that, because critiques like Johnson's or Grossman's (2001) do not seek to pin the blame on any particular game, their authors are freed from the tyrannical grip of detail, nuance and accuracy and find themselves at liberty to discuss videogames as a homogenous group of experiences that centre on the mindless blasting and zapping of enemies and reduce the player to a soporific state of near trance-like zombification. Here, though, the concern is not the blasting and zapping, *per se*. That the player is engaged in killing is of less importance than the fact that they are engaged in an apparently thoughtless, monotonous repetitive activity that occupies them in the entirety of their being but that offers absolutely no positive benefit. Moreover, because the vision of videogames that is activated in such discussions is one in which a single player plays alone for many hours on end, to distraction and to the exclusion of all other (presumably more valuable) alternative activities, the player not only fails to develop as a social being, but becomes yet more reclusive and isolated. Videogames, then, may be both an antisocial and asocial force that simultaneously encourages violence and aggression against others along with withdrawal and seclusion. In fact, as we begin to see here, while I have separated them out for the purposes of this discussion, the two types of story highlighted here and the version of gameplay and gamers that they trade in often become difficult to disentangle. One can be effectively used to reinforce the other in building a powerful stereotype of the medium and its followers.

Interestingly, the incidence of stories in the popular media that associate videogames and gameplay with cultural decline, falling standards of literacy and educational achievement, and that denounce them as a modern scourge has become more prevalent in recent years perhaps mirroring the increasing penetration of gaming into mainstream popular culture. The most damning of these public whip-pings is to be found in a front-page piece in *The Daily Telegraph* on 12 September 2006. Prompted by a letter from a 'powerful lobby of academics and children's experts', the piece entitled 'Junk culture "is poisoning our children"' details the experts' claims that fast food, computer games and competitive schooling are to blame for a rise in depression. This 'sinister cocktail' of 'virtual play' (sedentary, screen-based entertainment) is evidently intrinsically harmful and a poor sub-stitute for the bucolic simulacrum of childhood that is evoked in the imagery of 'real play'. Among the somewhat confusing and unfocused, scatter-gun attack on junk food and target-based education, videogames find themselves labelled as part of a scarily toxic future whose coming to pass must be fought at all costs by all reasonable people.

Lumping videogames and gameplay in with the consumption of 'junk food' in this wholly undifferentiated manner conveniently constructs a scenario in which both the physical and mental health of young people is systemically threatened by the irretrievably evil products of a faceless, and in this case nameless, cor-porate capitalism. The conjuring of a vision of videogaming that is dominated by mindless routines and something akin to a base, Pavlovian response to stimuli relies on an uncomplicated image of videogames that sees them as carefully mea-sured doses of Huxley's *soma*, satisfying the simple needs of the duped players. The erosion of traditional values and the replacement of the natural and the real with the synthetic and the virtual are accompanied, inevitably, by the col-lapse of standards and well-being. The surprisingly well-balanced and reasoned discussion contained within Richard Abanes' (2006) alarmist-sounding *What Every Parent Needs to Know about Video Games: A Gamer Explores the Good, Bad and Ugly of the Virtual World* concludes its survey of popular concerns and fears with a six-point checklist that seeks to encourage the non-acolyte used only to read-ing about videogames in the popular media to consider them in a fresh light. Point 1 is particularly eye-opening, if not jaw-dropping. 'Video games are not inherently evil, destructive or lacking in positive benefits' (ibid.: 104). That one should even feel the need to write these words, or to address a preconception of this severity and extremity, seems incredible. Were we to read nothing but the popular press, we could be forgiven for thinking that everybody hates video-games. Or, at the very least, that everybody should.

The case against videogames

For all their well-documented popularity and their growing visibility within popular culture, videogames remain the subject of considerable and sustained criticism. In addition to the ongoing debates about the effects of violent media content on post-play behaviour, we can break down the various charges against the medium into four distinct but related categories. According to their detractors, videogames are responsible for damaging effects on sociality, creativity, productivity, and literacy.

Sociality

Videogame players play in isolation because videogames are ultimately a lonely medium. The stereotype of the videogame player is that of a maladjusted, with-drawn 'geek' more at home with engagements with technology than with other people. As Kline (1997, cited in Kline 1999: 19) notes:

> What seems to differentiate the gamer is the absence of friends and altern-ative leisure opportunities; heavy gamers resort to solitary media for dis-traction and entertainment . . . Family and sibling play is infrequent, mostly involves playing with brothers, and is more frequent in the occasional player groups.
>
> (Kline 1999: 19)

The idea of the isolated, socially inept player is so pervasive and so inexorably bound up in the vision of the obsessive, unbalanced, dangerous gamer, that it is often seamlessly invoked in the discussion and reporting of acts of violence and aggression such as the school shootings in Columbine and Paducah (see *Video Nasties*, Channel 4 Television, 2000, for the apotheosis of this position and tabloid journalism at its most scurrilous and unbalanced). The player is not merely socially withdrawn and incapable because of videogames. Rather, their condition is *caused* by videogames.

Creativity

This criticism centres on the fact that the videogame is an utterly inconse-quential activity that neither requires nor develops imagination. We might recall Boris Johnson's portrait of videogame play as endlessly repetitive 'blasting and zapping' that sends players into a 'speechless rapture'. The triviality of this activity is clearly problematic as it offers no stimulation or variation from the reflex response (though Johnson goes on to endorse the principle of iteration and repetition in learning how to write). Pleasures and rewards are offered in spoon-fed fashion and with immediate effect for instant gratification. There is no sense that rewards are earned or that gameplay may involve effort or work, let alone strategy or planning. Indeed, in the assertion that gameplay is dominated by blasting and zapping, we might also note that, at the crudest possible level, the activity described here is literally destructive. Gameplay, then, is concerned with destroying what has been created by another.

Productivity

If we are to believe the image of players transfixed by the events on-screen, all but comatosed by the hypnotic stimuli and wholly absorbed in an unbreakable loop of mindless and inconsequential reflexes and twitches, then it will come as no surprise to learn that videogame players are unproductive sorts. We have already learned from Dr Spock that gameplay offers nothing of any consequence in and of itself and is, at best, a colossal waste of time. However, we also know that videogames are seen to exert a considerable hold over their players who play with an apparently unhealthy frequency and for lengthy periods of time. We might then assume that this is time that could be better spent participating in more valuable and enriching activities especially those that encourage activity rather than the 'passivity' that characterises engagements with interactive media (see also Kirriemuir and McFarlane 2004, on the fear that videogames may supplant other activities).

Literacy

The criticisms of videogames we have noted at the beginning of this chapter trade in a somewhat limited definition of literacy that concerns the written word and that does not concede the possibility or value of other kinds of skills or competencies. Similarly, the argument forwarded by Boris Johnson, the letter writers to *The Daily Telegraph* and Prince Charles implies that videogame play not only supplants reading in young people's lives but is wholly incompatible with it. To play videogames appears to be to reject books as they sit in stark, polar opposition in this argument. The desperate nature of this situation is compounded yet further if we think of the game as a closed system that ends when the console or PC is switched off. Just as the gameplay itself is meaningless, it offers nothing to take away that can be of use or value beyond the contained world of the game.

In the call to promote books over videogames we note the putative link between reading and writing, consumption and production. To read is to promote literacy and to encourage the creation of new texts. This is presumably why apparently solitary activities such as book reading are preferred and valorised. Ultimately, videogames offer no opportunity for creativity and present no raw materials for creativity, imagination and productivity to be developed.

It will be clear to most players of videogames that the nature of the criticisms outlined here are greatly flawed and trade in grotesquely parodic versions of videogames, gameplay and players. However, the voracity of the criticisms is considerable and the continued currency of the stereotypes in the popular media means a corrective is still required. This is particularly true given that, as Livingstone (2002) and Facer *et al.* (2003) note, the research agenda in this field is largely set by the popular discourse. Given that videogames have become increasingly subject to scholarly scrutiny, it is useful to briefly consider the ways in which these various academic perspectives might assist us in better appreciating videogames and tackling the presuppositions and misapprehensions of the naysayers we have encountered.

Game Studies and beyond

While even a cursory knowledge of the history of moral panics might leave us unsurprised to learn that the popular press has all but abandoned videogames, rejecting them as a near-constant source of harm, what is most interesting to note is that videogames have found a new and loyal, if perhaps unexpected, ally. The academy has become home to a body of critics and commentators who, though by no means apologists for videogames, are among the keenest supporters and advocates of the form. As Rutter and Bryce (2006: 1) correctly observe, while some scholarly research into videogames has been conducted for some time, there has been a surge in publications in the last few years and a more visible and sustained effort to investigate the form has emerged. Espen Aarseth similarly notes that it was not until the early part of the twenty-first century, many decades after the first videogames broke out of university research labs and into arcades and living rooms across the world, that the form shifted from '*media non grata* to a recognized field of great scholarly potential, a place for academic expansion and recognition' (2004: 45). Certainly, recent years have seen a rapid warming of the relationship between academics, particularly those in the arts and humanities, and videogames. Countless conferences across the world such as the *DiGRA International Conference* (Digital Games Research Association) and *Women in Games* are dedicated to exploring various aspects of cutting edge research into electronic entertainment, while the publication of numerous books, journal articles, and even journals (e.g. *Game Studies* and *Games and Culture*) all manifestly demonstrate the ways in which academics have begun to embrace video-games – or at least have begun to publicly admit to embracing videogames.

The diversity of what has become known as the discipline of 'game studies' is quite impressive. Enquiries range from investigations of the economics of the videogames industry (e.g. Kerr 2006) through large-scale ethnographic surveys of online communities and Massively Multiplayer Online Role-Playing Games (e.g. Taylor 2006; Castranova 2005), to interrogations of the representations of gender in games (e.g. Cassell and Jenkins 1998) as well as more general intro-ductions to the field (e.g. Newman 2004; Carr et al. 2006; Dovey and Kennedy 2006) and readers that attempt to bring together a range of diverse perspect-ives sometimes combining academic and practitioner approaches and commentaries (e.g. Wolf and Perron 2003) in a refreshingly and helpfully multidisciplinary manner. While each piece of work treated individually does much to advance the understanding and appreciation of the richness of videogames as a form, by drawing attention to the intricacy of narrative structures and representations or by foregrounding the simulation that is activated and mutated by the act of play-ing, it is when we consider these studies collectively, as a body of scholarship offering differing analytical and methodological techniques that draw upon a wide range of scholarly traditions, that we see the way in which game studies can present a considerable rejoinder to the accusation that videogames are nothing more than a waste of time.

Space does not permit us to undertake a thorough survey of the range of game studies literatures here, but it is perhaps useful to highlight a few key issues in order to advance our discussion. In particular, we might single out the work of educational researchers who have recently attended to videogames and who have begun to ably and eloquently demonstrate the role that videogames play in skills development and how they may be effectively harnessed by edu-cators (e.g. Aldrich 2004, 2005; Kirriemuir and McFarlane 2004; Shaffer 2007). Facer et al. (2003) identify a series of specific competencies that together form a 'game literacy'. These skills include, for instance, the ability to operate multimodally. That is, to process information arriving in visual, auditory and haptic forms simultaneously, at great speed and, most importantly, to be able to act meaningfully as a consequence. The ability to respond in a measured man-ner and act in a way that not only makes sense within the rules and objectives of the game but that also advances the player relies on developing the capacity to filter the vast array of multi-sensory stimuli, stripping out the extraneous material and leaving only that which is of importance at that moment. This focused attentiveness – what Malone (1980) has referred to as 'flow' – that is aware of the task at hand and that actively develops and operates strategies to discern between valuable and superfluous information even when these are presented in a deliberately confusing and chaotic form paints a picture of the videogame player that is far from the twitching, barely conscious dupe, blasting and zapping as a matter of reflex as conjured in the popular discourse.

At an even more forensic level, researchers such as Marc Prensky (2006a) examine the structures of games for evidence of the ways in which designers and developers have, perhaps even unwittingly, constructed them as highly effective learning environments (see also Prensky 2006b, 2007; Gee 2003). While the motivation, challenge and reward structure of a given game may be expressed among designers and players alike in terms of 'gameplay', 'level design' or 'puzzle design' rather than in the terminology of learning, the principles are essentially similar. Explaining the mechanisms of a game, the rulesets, what is allowed and disallowed within the virtual world, and gradually unpacking the often complex capabilities and capacities of the player's avatar, character or presence in the world, without recourse to didacticism – or worse still, the printed instruction manual – are skills that the finest videogame developers, as facilitators of players' active learning, have in abundance. We are well used to the ways in which narratives reveal themselves in the telling. Twists and turns, detours and dead ends unravel creating an ever richer tapestry of events, characters, situations and consequences. In a videogame like *Super Mario 64*, however, it is not only a storyline that unfolds but also the place, role and, importantly, capabilities of the player-as-Mario within the narrative. More than revealing aspects of a character, *Super Mario 64* slowly reveals the full extent of Mario's skills. The performative repertoire is not revealed or available in its entirety at the beginning of the game but rather is developed and expanded through time. Mario's full capacity is drip-fed to the player with vital skills gradually unlocked or revealed at strategic moments throughout the early sequences of the game until the complete set of tools is at the player's disposal. For Warren Spector, it is the game's ability to allow, encourage and support learning through exploration and experimentation that are the keys to its success:

> Mario has, like, ten things he can do and yet there's never a moment where you feel constrained in any way. No game has done a better job of showing goals before they can be attained, allowing players to make a plan and execute on it.
>
> ('The GameSpy Staff' 2001 [online])

As such, the game is learned and mastered through practice and experimentation without ever being explicitly taught. Drawing on Jones' (1984) work, Provenzo (1991: 34) notes that 'Video games are literally teaching machines that instruct the player using them in the rules of the game as it is played.' Similarly, the 'meeting of minds' that Turkle (1984) describes as the player comes to understand the scope of the game's rules and their capabilities within the game system is achieved through seamlessly integrated tutorials that encourage the player to put newly acquired skills and knowledge to the test. The videogame may be seen as an active learning, or perhaps Problem-Based Learning (PBL), environment where solutions are deduced and tackled through systematic experimentation, evaluation and the use of the tools at hand. The game developer creates an environment in which the player takes an active role in and ownership of the learning process (see Savin-Baden 2003; Savin-Baden and Major 2004 for more on PBL; Sandford and Williamson 2005; and Papert's (1980) discussion of 'hard fun').

Nintendo's *Metroid* series approaches the issue of teaching the player how to play in a slightly different manner. *Metroid Prime* follows other titles in the series with the player adopting the role of a fully-equipped Samus Aran, replete with body armour, missiles and the ability to morph into a ball to access parts of the world impenetrable to the full-sized combatant. The player is afforded a good sense of the range of potentials and capabilities during these opening moments of the game but no sooner have they become accustomed to the situation than a catastrophic episode sees them stripped of all but the most basic skills. The remainder of the game is spent in search of these once-glimpsed but now lost powers. Many of the puzzles within the game are structured in a manner that effectively signals to the player that a particular set of skills or capacities will be required and so the availability or otherwise of these powers becomes an implicit mechanism for shaping the narrative of the experience. Creating a puzzle that seems *almost* impossible, an object that is seemingly out of reach, a maze that seems insolvable, or an enemy that appears invincible, while motivating the player sufficiently to know that a solution is not only possible but within their grasp is the true skill of the game developer. As Jamie Fristrom, technical director of Torpex games and creator of the Spiderman series for PS2, Xbox and GameCube, states, while game developers might not use the language of learning and teaching, the issues at stake are precisely the same as those facing educators. Discussing the design in *Half-Life 2*, Fristrom observes that:

> These puzzles are at the perfect level of difficulty for a mass-market computer game: difficult enough to be nontrivial and make you feel somewhat clever for solving them, but not so difficult that many people are likely to shelf-level-event on them. I never had to consult gamefaqs to complete it.
>
> (Fristrom 2004 [online])[1]

From even this briefest sampling of the available work in the field, it is clear that, while tackling such issues head-on may not be their stated intention, game studies researchers and members of the development community are amassing a compendium of research, insights and observations that begins to powerfully challenge the taken-for-granted assumptions about videogames and players we have seen above. Detailed investigations of specific titles such as those offered by Grossman (2003), or the analysis of specific styles or forms (e.g. Montfort 2005), for instance, help greatly in understanding the mechanisms by which videogames are structured along with their puzzle orientation. However, there is a potential limitation. In their analysis of the present state of game studies, Crawford and Rutter (2007) note:

> The research trope that appears to be developing around much of the study of digital games has emphasized the spectacular (e.g. King and Krzywinska 2002), the out-of-the-ordinary (e.g. Kennedy 2002), the place of digital games in the canon of 'art' (e.g. Jenkins 2005a), or possible links to aggressive and violent behavior [sic] (Bryce and Rutter 2006).
>
> (Crawford and Rutter 2007: 271)

As such, for Crawford and Rutter, while it has been the primary focus of cultural studies-inspired approaches to media audiences, the 'everydayness' of videogames and, in particular, the consumption of games through the routine practices of play, is not well represented in the game studies research canon. Moreover, while the coverage of the discipline of game studies might be diverse in terms of its approaches and perspectives, there is a further limitation. Many extant studies have tended to focus on formal or sometimes aesthetic analyses of the games themselves. This privileging of the game as text – or even as simulation model – has the dual consequence of centring our attentions on the game rather than the player. Where the player is included in the analysis, they are frequently positioned not as members of a community or constituency of players in the manner of a mass media audience, but rather as an individual player engaged in an experiential or even cybernetic relationship with a game-as-technology via a process of 'interaction'.

> The textual (often narratological) emphasis commonly evident in work on digital games along with a focus on the disruptive possibilities of games technologies has meant that rather than being understood as an 'audience,' much of the literature on gaming continues to situate gamers as individual players.
>
> (Crawford and Rutter 2007: 272–273)

In fact, this call for approaches more sensitive to the patterns of play is not a new one. Some 14 years previously, Henry Jenkins noted that investigations of videogames must be more attentive to the experience of playing games rather than simply interpreting their surface features. We need to situate them more precisely within their social and educational contexts, to understand them more fully within their place in children's lives.

(Jenkins 1993: 69)

It is my hope that this volume will make its contribution to the discussion of videogames by foregrounding these practices of play in and around the game. The consequence of the situation in contemporary game studies that Crawford and Rutter describe is that many of the most vibrant and richly creative *uses* of videogames have gone unrecorded and are presently under-researched. Even the most basic level of talk and discussion, of sharing hints, tips and strategies, or even of playing together online or offline in multiplayer games reveals the poverty of approaches that fail to recognise the socially-situated nature of much videogame play as well as the fact that the actual act of playing games is only part of what is involved in being a gamer and being enmeshed in the culture of videogaming or to be part of what Crawford and Rutter might call the *audience* for digital games.

Videogame players will know well that to fully understand videogaming, one needs to appreciate not only what the game is as a formal structure or mechanism but also what happens to it, what can be made with it, in the playing – how it is made real, transformed, used and abused. As such, the transformative practices and performances of play are a vital element of any game studies. However, to complicate matters, as we shall see later, playing is not a singular or even necessarily predictable activity. There is considerable variation in the ways in which different players play. Indeed, there is considerable variation in the ways in which the same players play over time. Moreover, because playing videogames is not an activity undertaken in a vacuum but rather is one that is informed by and situated within the contexts of other players and their analyses and playing, such variations are not invisible. In fact, as we shall see, via digital networks, magazines, fanzines or even word-of-mouth, these different performances, perspectives and insights are frequently and widely publicised and, thanks in no small part to the world wide web, are highly available. The online connectivity of the current cohort of videogames consoles makes accessible not only other players to play and converse with, but also makes accessible material such as videos of expert players tackling games or in competition with one another. That these playing masterclasses are seamlessly available from within the games console itself speaks eloquently of the way in which gameplay practice is permanently enmeshed within a wider, increasingly global context and culture of other players playing and performing. As such, even where a game is played by an individual player in apparent isolation rather than as part of a large group of players operating simultaneously as a clan, for instance, this 'solo' play is always and already located within a community-authored set of meanings, readings and interpretations and the collective knowledge of players, commentators, critics and fans alike who have contributed to this very public understanding and evaluation of the game through public performances, readings of previews, and reviews, for example.

As such, while the game – whether conceived and analysed as text or simulation – is certainly an important element in the picture we should paint in game studies, it is only one element. As Crawford and Rutter (2007) and Jenkins (1993) intimate, the investigation of the cultures of play and gaming is another potential string to the bow of game studies and there is clear room for a more systematic consideration of the situatedness of gameplay and these collective meanings and practices. Additionally, I argue that in order to present the most persuasive and comprehensive challenge to the popular discourses we have briefly outlined at the beginning of this chapter, we need to make visible the range of highly productive activity that surrounds and supports gameplay, and the often unexpected and unanticipated creative work of modifying, transforming, adapting, making sense of and understanding videogames. This complex of socially-situated practices that impact upon, but that go beyond *playing* videogames, is what I refer to here as playing *with* videogames.

About this book

The aim of this book is to chart the vibrant and productive practices of the vast numbers of videogame fans and players and the extensive 'shadow economy' (Fiske 1992) of player-produced walkthroughs, FAQs (Frequently Asked Questions), art, narratives and even games, not to mention the cultures of cheating, copying and piracy, that have emerged alongside videogames. For many years, dedicated gamers sometimes working in teams, have been designing and developing their own games, modifying commercial products and writing eloquent and insightful analyses of games that shed considerable light on the pleasures of play and the nature and parameters of cheating, for example, and which are used to negotiate and communicate identity within these communities of fans. However, despite their prevalence, and the size of the communities that support them, these activities and practices are all but invisible within the majority of academic, and even most popular, treatises on videogames and gaming. Importantly, while this book moves some way from the typical game studies path in being concerned not just with playing videogames, many of the 'invisible' practices we shall investigate, such as walkthrough production and use, super-play, tool-assisted speedrunning, and sequence breaking for instance, profoundly inform and reveal much about the act of play and its varied pleasures. We uncover much about the wildly differing pleasures of videogame play in online forum discussions of the legitimacy of certain tactics espoused by some players or groups that are sometimes derided as 'cheating', for example, just as we learn about the pleasures of puzzle-solving versus performance in discussions of the use of walkthroughs, FAQ lists, and solution guidebooks. As such, it is my contention here that the act of playing a videogame cannot be adequately analysed or appreciated without a deep understanding of the ways in which this performative practice is enmeshed within and informed by the cultures and communities of gamers contributing to the collective knowledge of videogame culture.

In this book, I hope to build on some of the emerging work on gaming fan cultures and practices (e.g. Consalvo 2003a; Lowood 2005, 2007; Newman 2005; Burn 2006a, 2006b; Schott and Burn 2007); in order to challenge many of the taken-for-granted assumptions we have seen to be circulating in both popular and academic discourse, by highlighting the inherent creativity, productivity and sociality of these wider videogame cultures. The investigation of gamers' artistic and literary production, the creation of walkthroughs and FAQ texts, the modification of existing games and the development of entirely new games, speaks clearly of the complexity of engagements with videogames and the ways games are reconfigured to increase their life-span and add challenge, for example. Furthermore, online discussion boards and forums dedicated to the scrutiny of game titles or series reveal considerable passion and invention as gamers interrogate and consult vast arrays of supporting texts, often in translation, so as to better understand the objects of their fandom, perhaps seeking to make sense of apparent inconsistencies in the backstories that weave together two titles in a series, for instance. This may involve imaginative theorising and the concoction of new narrative elements to fill in the missing details in officially sanctioned materials that accompany the game, but interestingly, may also involve considerable investigative work on the part of the fan, searching through interviews with developers during the processes of pre-production or even, in some extreme cases, disassembling the code of the finally released game to unveil remnants of unfinished graphics or level designs unintended for public viewing through which to speculate on potential directions of development. Where the production of fan art and fiction ably demonstrate the intertextuality of readings of videogames, these investigations into the history of the game's development reveal much of the videogame fans' understanding of the processes of commercial media production including the tensions between creative vision, budgetary constraints, deadlines and technical limitations.

As we have already noted, in contrast to many studies in the burgeoning field of game studies, the present volume is only partly concerned with actually playing videogames *per se* and, even then, the interest lies in what this teaches us about the playfulness that characterises many of the engagements with this most pervasive of new media forms so as to challenge the presuppositions and mis-understandings we have seen in the opening sections of this chapter.

In addition to, and sometimes in place of, playing the game 'as intended' or as indicated by the accompanying instruction book or in-game tutorials, players are frequently to be found inventing new challenges that reveal not only the plasticity of the game as material for play but also the sophistication of their under-standing of the underlying rule systems and simulation model. Moreover, while this knowledge typically extends to a detailed understanding of the lim-itations of the simulation model both in terms of its experiential potentiality, in terms of where it is possible or impossible to travel in the gameworld, what can and cannot be done, for example, it very often covers the technical imple-mentation of the simulation. That is, players explore and probe the boundaries of what the game will do to destruction, exposing and exploiting the glitches that slip through the quality control systems and that, *in extremis*, may crash the game outright. More interestingly, many of these glitches or limitations in the simulation, allow access to new, perhaps unpredictable, techniques and capab-ilities or to unravel the sequence of the game-making levels or abilities avail-able out of order. As such, gamers not only modify their engagement with the game, but also remodel the very simulation that enables and powers the game. In this way, the game is reinvented in the hands of the dedicated gamer and afforded increased longevity as continued replay is encouraged.

The essential premise of this book, then, is that videogames provide a complex and varied suite of materials for gamers that encourage flexible and creative play, talk, discussion and the production of supporting texts that are exchanged and valued within the myriad fan communities that exist, especially online. Moreover, while in no way intended as a criticism of studies that centre on the game as struc-ture, narrative or simulation, my assertion in this book is that it is the investiga-tion of the cultures and practices that emerge from videogames and that sustain, surround, support and inform gameplay, that we find perhaps the most effectively persuasive way of demonstrating the poverty of detractors' claims that video-games stifle creativity and sociality. While my focus in this book is on the practices of playing and, more precisely, *playing with* videogames, it should be noted that it is the mutability of the videogame, its openness to modification through perform-ance, hacking/cracking or the exploitation of its technical inconsistencies, that makes possible many of these activities we shall see in the following chapters.

This book is split into three main parts that each deal with games in a dif-ferent manner. In itself, this structure speaks of the mutability of videogames that may be variously seen as media texts, technologies or simulations. This book, then, is neither a ludological or narrativist account, *per se*. Rather, it attempts to illustrate the myriad ways in which different players and player communities respond to videogames:

Part 1   Videogames as representational systems
Part 2   Videogames as configurative performances
Part 3   Videogames as technology.

In Part 1, the analysis centres on those responses that illustrate the textual qualities of videogames. Andrew Burn (2006b: 92) has noted that, 'most authors of
fan fiction largely ignore the game system and concentrate on the narrative'. Here,
the 'gameness' of the videogame, its interactive or experiential pleasures and
qualities, its structures and formal design, are of less significance than the potential of the narrative or aesthetic to be developed. In Part 2, we focus on those
gamers whose work and activity are enabled by and draw attention to the ludic
potentialities of the game. Here, it is the plasticity of the simulation model and
its inherent mutability that facilitate modification and transformation through
innovative and inventive patterns of performance and play. The concept of gameplay as configurative practice is central to the analysis. As Moulthrop (2004:
64) observes, videogames offer 'the chance to manipulate complex systems within
continuous loops of intervention, observation, and response . . . that develop
in unpredictable or emergent ways'. Finally, in Part 3, we examine those practices that take advantage of the videogame as machine. Here, attention is focused
both on the game code and on the software and hardware composition of the
platforms upon which they run. Play here is centred on perhaps the most fundamental systems of the game whether they are routines and DRM (Digital Rights
Management[2]) that are bypassed to enable unauthorised games to be run, or
modifications to the rule systems of a given game in order to increase or decrease
its difficulty, for instance, or simply to change its graphics or sound.

This book's structure is partly an artifice that exists for the purposes of
clarity and organisation and there is some overlap between the categories but,
in general, the intention is to allow a consideration of how games may be
variously understood and investigated as continuations and extensions of other
media and that may support and encourage similar audience/fan responses as
film, television and literature (Part 1); as experiences that may be transformed
and mutated through acts of play and performance to create unexpected, perhaps highly personalised outcomes and that support and encourage the production
of materials and texts that assist in the modification of the game through play
(Part 2); and as pieces of code, slithers of silicon and slabs of plastic that may
be tinkered with and altered to create new and different systems whether intended
or sanctioned by their original creators or otherwise (Part 3).

Players, fans, Otaku: some notes on terminology

The desire to move beyond accounts centred on the interpretation of the surface features of games or those investigations that privilege gameplay over the

range of other non-gameplay activities such as walkthrough production, the development of game mods, or game-inspired fiction is not a trivial one. One consequence of this shift in analytical focus away from the game as something to be played to something to be played with is that while our object of study might remain 'the videogame', we are no longer dealing with a singular means of engaging with it. Theorists keen to differentiate videogame play from spectatorship, viewing or reading, have long struggled with the terminology of 'player' (see Perron 2003; Giddings and Kennedy 2006), but to complicate issues, no longer do we necessarily offer primacy to the player – whether this be an individual or a team waggling their collective joysticks and controllers, or rhythmically gyrating on dancemats. Rather, the scope of this book and its desire to account for the array of activities that take place within the broader cultures of gaming mean that at various points in our analysis the videogame is subjected to a variety of differing engagements and interactions by individuals and groups acting sometimes as players, sometimes as readers of games as texts, and sometimes executing technical and technological interventions and modifications.

As we have already seen, the videogame is capable of supporting a range of relationships with users and may be encountered on a number of different levels. Some of these may even stand in stark contrast to one another by privileging different aspects of the game. Different groups may derive pleasure from the mutability of the game system's simulation model, rules and the performative potential or conversely from the narrative potential of the setting, characters, and plot, for instance. Indeed, individuals may move between these different positions and relationships as they variously play and play with the videogame.

The flexibility and openness of the videogame are interesting from an analytical perspective, but the situation is problematic as it leaves us struggling to find a term to describe the individuals and groups that engage, in these vastly different ways, with the games. Even a brief consideration of the range of activities and perspectives under discussion in this book should reveal to us that the notion of the videogame 'player' is something of a caricature. 'Player' is clearly inadequate for our purposes here as it privileges the act of performance and engagements with the game system which represent only part of what we are interested in investigating. A number of other terms are available but each brings with it its own unwarranted baggage or fails to adequately accommodate the variety of relationships and pleasures. Many of the activities that we will be examining in this book seem to be located squarely within the frame of media fandom, for instance. However, as most scholars of fan studies are quick to highlight, while many fan communities have long since recuperated the term, 'fan' still frequently carries with it many negative associations outside these circles. There is no need to rehearse the discussion of the problematic connotations of the term fan (instead, see Jenkins 1992; Hills 2002; Sandvoss 2007, for example) though it is interesting to note that the term is often used pejoratively within the cultures and communities of gaming with those gamers seen to offer overly partisan accounts, often displaying putatively excessive loyalty to a hardware platform, derided as 'fanboys' (though even this term is recuperated by some, note Joystiq's 'PSP Fanboy' and 'Xbox360 Fanboy' news sites, for instance). Instead, it is useful to note that 'fandom' is helpful in communicating a sense of community and coherence as an audience that 'player' tends not to and is effective in drawing attention to qualities such as productivity, creativity and sociality which are more than evident among the many walkthrough and fiction writers, artists, musicians and poets, of the gaming fraternity. However, the association with obsessiveness, a putatively unhealthy interest in the objects of fandom, and the extraordinary nature of this kind of media use and relationship makes the term problematic for our purposes here. Moreover, if we consider the use as a generic term, the participatory culture of Jenkins (1992) and Hills (2002) is some way from the practices of gameplay that we will see in superplay, speedrunning and sequence breaking, for example, or what Sue Morris (2003) has called the co-creativity of media production through play and performance, making 'fan' a poor fit here.

Among popular accounts of gaming communities and cultures, the term 'Otaku' has become somewhat commonplace (Lamarre 2004). In its original Japanese usage, the Otaku refers to a particularly excessive and obsessive form of fandom often associated with anime or Manga and is typically a derogatory term (see Eng 2002). As it has been adopted in English-speaking anime, Manga and videogaming cultures (the 'Otakon' convention, for example), Otaku's meaning has softened considerably. It has adopted a meaning not dissimilar to the recuperated 'geek'. As Facer *et al.* (2003) note, many young people have reappropriated hitherto derogatory terms associated with heavy computer use and interest, though note also King and Borland's (2003) assertion of the popular binarism in the subtitle for their *Dungeons and Dreamers* book: 'From Geek to Chic'), as well as Coppa's (2006) discussion of the complex stratifications of 'geekdom' as exemplified in Sjöberg's (2002) 'geek hierarchy'. While Otaku is commonly used in gaming culture (the gaming blog 'Kotaku' is a play on the word, for instance) and in magazines such as *Edge* in the UK to refer to those interested or participating in videogame culture in its widest sense, its use in this book is problematic for many of the same reasons as 'fan'. Additionally, its use in anime and Manga cultures and communities robs it of a specificity in relation to videogames. To some extent, then, the Otaku may be understood as broadly interested in Japanese culture, of which videogames may be a significant part but it is important to remember that videogaming is not the totality of Japanese media culture and that Japanese videogames and gaming are only a subset of the wider, global culture of gaming.

It is because of the partialness of the terms above that I have settled on the use of 'gamer' in this book. Gamer seems useful in being specific to videogames in a way that fan, Otaku, or for that matter audience or reader, are not. Importantly, unlike 'player', gamer does not imply or exclude play as a performative practice. As such, gamers' agency may be expressed through the transformations and performativity of play and through engagement with what Andrew Burn (2006b) calls the 'game system' of rules and simulation even though this play may take expected or unexpected forms and have unpredictable and non-predicted outcomes. Similarly, the gamer may draw pictures and write music inspired by videogames, or fashion hardware and software hacks and cracks that modify the ways videogames operate for other players or their own future play. The gamer, then, may be player, fan, fanboy/girl, audience, Otaku, reader and writer. And any given gamer may be some or all of these at different times and in different social and cultural contexts. Where appropriate, these more specific terms such as 'player' may still be used, but only where they accurately describe that particular relationship or mode of engagement under scrutiny. Gamer is, in essence, the collective noun though it comes with a similar caveat to that offered by Bacon-Smith (1992) in relation to her designation of 'interest groups' that emerges more from the need of the theorist to classify rather than the community to define itself. The discussion that follows in the remainder of this book seeks to draw out the variety of relationships and positions that can be adopted by gamers as they play (with) videogames.

Part I

Videogames as representational systems

Chapter 2

Talking about videogames

Playing together: videogames and talk

Writing *Videogames* in 2003 (Newman 2004), I commented on the pervasiveness of what I termed the 'myth of the solitary videogame player' and the claims that videogames not only appealed to but were actually responsible for creating socially withdrawn individuals (see also Jessen 1995). As we saw in Chapter 1, some five years on, the notion of the gamer as an isolated loner remains a staple of the popular discourse and is even activated among gamers, albeit in a rather more ironic way, with talk of 'Otaku' and 'fanboys'. It is not my intention to retread the ground covered in my earlier book, but it is useful to briefly recap some of the key points so as to provide a base upon which to expand our analysis here.

The charge that videogames are socially problematic is a fallacy for two distinct reasons. First, it assumes that the videogame is exclusively, or at least predominantly, a solo experience. This is, quite simply, untrue. Second, it utterly refuses to entertain the possibility of the existence of the videogames cultures of talk, discussion, sharing and collaboration that are evident in the emerging studies of game fandom and that form the evidential basis for this book. Before we explore the extent and complexity of these rich cultures of talk and social interaction in this chapter, it is useful to dedicate a little time here to considering the nature of gameplay itself and, in particular, the impact of the developments of the past five years on the social contexts of gameplay.

Perhaps the most persuasive challenge to the charge that videogame play is a solitary lone experience is to note the prevalence and popularity of multiplayer gaming. The current crop of games consoles, the Wii, Xbox 360 and PlayStation 3, each support the simultaneous connection of at least four controllers, thereby facilitating physically proximate multiplayer gaming. That is, multiplayer gaming where all players are co-present in a given space. While the design of Nintendo's DS and Sony's PSP handhelds might seem to preclude any more than single-player engagement, their Wi-Fi connectivity allows players to construct ad-hoc networks to share their gaming experiences with one another. Importantly, this technical capacity for multiplayer gaming is not left as an under-exploited feature and the majority of contemporary titles offer some form of multiplayer mode that encourages co-operative (e.g. *Lego Star Wars*) or competitive (e.g. *Virtua Fighter 5*) collaboration. To some extent, LAN-parties, the large gatherings of (usually PC-based) gamers who assemble temporary computer networks ('Local Area Networks', hence the soubriquet) in order to play against one another either individually or in teams ('clans'), are the apotheosis of this kind of physically proximate multiplayer gaming. The important point of note here is not that sociality automatically emerges from gaming experiences that happen to pit two or more human players against one another rather than challenging the artificial intelligence of an automated 'bot' (computer-controlled character). Rather, the gameplay, regardless of whether it takes place in a living room or LAN-party, is surrounded by and suffused with talk, conversation and discussion. Indeed, according to both Swalwell (2006) and Jansz and Martens (2005), the sociality of these events is frequently cited by players as one of the prime reasons for attendance. Here then, we begin to get a sense of gameplay as an activity that takes place *within* a social setting. Indeed, as I have noted elsewhere (e.g. Newman 2002b), even games designed for single-player control may be tackled by collaborative teams of players who take on specific roles. Thus, to stretch our terminology here, while a videogame such as *Tomb Raider* or *Metal Gear Solid* may recognise the inputs of only one 'player', there may be many 'gamers' participating in the processes of map-reading, puzzle-solving, and guiding Lara or Snake to their respective goals.

The sense of gaming as a social practice is even more keenly felt if we look online. As Kerr (2006) correctly notes, videogame play occurs in a wide variety of different contexts and online multiplayer gaming has become an increasingly significant feature of the contemporary medium. Each of the three current consoles and both handheld platforms offer Internet connectivity as standard though, at the time of writing, Nintendo has remained rather reticent to reveal its plans for online play on the Wii console. Elsewhere, however, Sony, Microsoft and Nintendo with the DS, have embraced online play with the former companies building the facilities into the very fabric of their platform strategies. Both Microsoft and Sony have developed dedicated gaming networks in 'Xbox Live' and the 'PlayStation Network' respectively. These systems offer a range of functionality including downloadable game demos, videos or additional content as we will learn in later chapters. Importantly, though, the embedded nature of these networks means that online multiplayer gaming is at the heart of console gameplay and design. Accordingly, console gaming is beginning to acquire some of the game styles and performance practices that previously were limited to PC gaming. This is particularly true of Xbox Live which is somewhat more developed for online gaming than Sony's network and it is interesting to note that Microsoft bundles a microphone and headset with all but the basic Xbox 360 package. As one would imagine, this device facilitates in-game talk as well as communication outside of play. For some games, in-game talk may be a vital part of the play mechanic as battalions of troops are ordered around or team members co-ordinate their tactics, for instance. In this way, talk can be seen to be added to the performative repertoire of players alongside their buttons, keyboards and joypads. However, in-game talk, whether console or PC-based, is not always focused solely on directing performance and should not be understood as simply representing an extension of the control system. The importance of this talk in shaping the meaning of the game and the experience of play should not be underestimated. In their work on players of the online First-Person Shooter (FPS) *Counter-Strike*, Wright *et al.* (2002) observe:

> The meaning of playing *Counter-Strike* is not merely embodied in the graphics or even the violent gameplay, but in the social mediations that go on between players through their talk with each other and by their performance within the game. Participants, then, actively create the meaning of the game through their virtual talk and behavior.
>
> (Wright *et al.* 2002)

Studies of MMORPGs (Massively Multiplayer Online Role-Paying Games) (e.g. Kelly 2004; Castranova 2005; Taylor 2006) similarly point to the widespread nature and importance of both in-game and out-of-game talk, whether this be verbal or textual, in creating the meaning of the game for gamers as well as providing a key motivation for play (e.g. Burn and Carr 2006 on 'communal motivations' in *Anarchy Online*). As if to recognise the importance of non-playing experience in gaming cultures, Sony has developed an online service for the PlayStation 3 entitled 'PlayStation Home' which is oriented largely around social interactions, talk and community with little emphasis on gameplay (see Chapter 7 for more on PlayStation Home and Sony's vision of 'Game 3.0').

Playgrounds and watercoolers: talking about videogames

As we noted above, even though we can find ample evidence of gameplay as social practice, we should not confine our discussion of sociality and videogaming to just the sessions of play themselves. Videogaming exists within, just as it creates, cultures and contexts of talk and discussion that take place outside of play. Crawford (2005) reminds us that gaming does not take place in a vacuum and players' responses to their experiences of play frequently spill over into other contexts, when recounting the story of a *Championship Manager* player waking up sleeping members of a friend's household with his exuberant victory celebrations. However, videogame talk extends further than expressions of success or failure. Just as a television programme, film, work of literature or music might stimulate discussion, analysis during or most importantly after being engaged with, and may even create (or perhaps even weaken) bonds between members of their audience, so too do videogames. The process by which texts may be engaged with and experienced in isolation but then become the focus of communal consideration at a later date is well documented in relation to media such as television (e.g. Whetmore and Kielwasser 1983; Jensen and Pauly 1997; Baym 2000; Hill and Palmer 2002). In fact, so widely known is this concept that the phrase 'watercooler moment' which describes those scenes or questions within a given text around which such conversation, debate and gossip coalesces, has passed into everyday parlance. Such watercooler moments might be prompted by the actions or motivations of a character, a series of questions raised or, in the case of serial texts in particular, by a creative and imaginative desire to deduce the narrative progression from clues revealed thus far (and providing excellent evidence of the active reader guessing the endings from the beginnings, for instance). Indeed, the narrative arc of television serials such as *Lost* and *24* appear designed to fashion a predictable number of watercooler moments so as to ensure continued buzz and interest in the show throughout its course. If viewed like other media texts, videogames have many of the same qualities that encourage post-viewing/playing talk and it should not surprise us to learn that gaming experiences would be the stuff of office and playground chatter. However, there is a complication. Just as the advent of timeshifting (see Cubitt 1991) and spaceshifting (the process of converting media content so that it may be consumed on different platforms) might be seen to weaken the possibility of the collective watercooler moment as viewers fill and watch from their PVRs at different times thereby disrupting the rhythm of the schedule, so videogames are and perhaps cannot be played in a predictable manner. They will unfold differently for different gamers precisely because their skill levels vary, the amount of time they commit to playing varies, or even that the decisions they take alter the way the game branches revealing and concealing different parts of the whole. Even if a classroom of gamers rushed out and bought a game on the same day and began playing at the same time, it is almost inevitable that they will each progress through at different rates, with some racing to the end and replaying, others getting stuck and yet others giving up and playing something else. What chance a collective watercooler moment with this incoherence of audience caused by the near-infinitely fragmented experience of play?

At the simplest level, talk about videogames might comprise discussion, comparison and criticism of favourite games or perhaps even favourite sequences or levels from games. The brand-loyalty instilled in gamers through the practice of platform-exclusives provides another possible impetus for conversation and critique as the relative merits of each manufacturer and their hardware are analysed and debated. After-school game clubs provide a formalised context for play, sharing and discussion. Surveying fifteen of my undergraduate game studies students revealed that most had belonged to, or even formed, clubs dedicated to gameplay while at school. While these forums were of varying degrees of formality, their former members identified them as important means of honing their skills, learning more about their games and gaining access to other games and gaming experiences through a network of peers. Many still belonged to similar clubs and societies in their university days and most saw these social practices of learning about gaming through talk and analysis occurring in their gaming with friends and other peer networks. Indeed, videogaming can be seen to be clearly located in the practices and cultures of computer use that Seiter identifies:

> Friendships, kin networks, and work relationships are crucial to the successful adoption of new technologies such as computers (Douglas 1988). Computer use often involves borrowing software, troubleshooting problems, trying out new programs, boasting or discussing successes.
>
> (Seiter 1999: 123)

It follows that, while we might think that it would render collective discussion harder as gameplay takes markedly different trajectories for different players, the mutable structure of videogames is precisely the aspect that makes talk and analysis all the more likely. It is this differential in the experience of and access to the game that drives conversation. If we consider the videogame as a puzzle and in terms of the performative demands it makes (see Krzywinska 2002, 2006), we note immediately, that it presents the player with a challenge to be solved, whether this solution is arrived at through deduction or through excellence in performance. We have noted already in our discussion of the research on videogames and education (e.g. Gee 2003; Kerr 2006; Prensky 2006b, 2007) that videogames may be understood as particularly effective learning environments and that developers often adopt the tacit role of learning facilitators gently encouraging gamers to consider and utilise the skills and competencies they have acquired and earned. However, this is not to say that all facets of the game are revealed in such an open and inclusive manner. Many videogames overflow with hidden secrets or 'Easter Eggs' as they are sometimes termed.[1] As such, there are parts of the game that are deliberately obscure and difficult to find, spaces that can only be accessed under certain conditions, characters and capabilities that are unlocked in specific sets of circumstances. Experimentation and variations in gameplay styles are just some of the mechanisms by which secrets may be uncovered and, as we shall see in Chapter 5, there is much productive work in formalising these knowledges into new texts. Solutions and information about successful techniques and strategies are rendered valuable commodities and it is the knowledge differential between gamers that can be seen to drive the videogaming equivalent of the watercooler moment as the non-adepts learn from the masters. In my earliest research, I observed players sharing tips and strategies gleaned from personal experience or brought to them via other players' wisdom. Saxe (1994) noted a similar process at work in the videogame arcade where crowds of spectators would often gather around expert players in the hope that they might acquire knowledge of the game or insight into technique. Regardless of the means by which it is attained, this information is readily commodified and complex series of trades and barters are commonplace as titbits are swapped in playgrounds and offices and among the groups and networks of gamers that form as a result of the puzzle-orientation of the game.

If we further consider the structure of videogames and their feedback mechanisms, we notice that the portioning of games into discrete sequences (e.g. levels, tracks, rounds, bouts, stages, etc.) and the ready availability of data such as scores or progress ratings, only serve to encourage comparison of performance with others. We could observe, then, that the very structure of the videogame into a series of levels and the presence of high scores and completion statistics presents gamers with a raft of indicators of achievement that assist in comparison with others' performance while the expansiveness of the gameworlds and sheer range of sidequests and ancillary challenges almost presupposes collaboration with others to reveal its innermost complexities.[2]

The development of gaming networks such as Xbox Live has formalised these processes of display yet further through the introduction of 'Achievements'. Achievements are badges of honour awarded to players for successfully performing specific (usually unstated) acts within a given game. They may be associated with relatively predictable aspects of gameplay such as the attainment of a score in excess of a specified threshold, or may be altogether more obscure and counter-intuitive such as *Geometry Wars*' 'Pacifist' Achievement that is bestowed upon those players who manage to survive the first 60 seconds of this frenetic shooting game *without* shooting. Importantly, unlocked Achievements are proudly displayed on each Xbox Live user's public profile or 'Gamecard' thereby ensuring that skill and commitment are broadcast throughout the community. Not only do Achievements offer gamers another mechanism to manifestly display their progress and prowess, the mystery of their attainment also encourages the exploration of games and the sharing or trading of knowledge among the community.[3]

Magazine culture

As we have seen above, just as videogame play does not take place in isolation but is frequently located in one of a variety of social contexts that may include other players and other games, neither does the acquisition of knowledge about the games played occur solely as a consequence of the act of play itself. A number of other agencies are implicated in shaping the meaning of gaming, providing information about games, and even granting access to elements of games that might otherwise remain hidden. These agencies may include the kin networks of families and friends that Seiter (1999) and Douglas (1982) identify, but it is useful to consider another vital but curiously overlooked contribution. Since the earliest days of electronic games, specialist games magazines have occupied a central role in the culture of videogaming yet they remain largely absent from studies of gaming or critical examinations of magazines and periodicals (e.g. Hermes 1995; McLoughlin 2000; Jackson *et al.* 2001; Benwell 2003; Gough-Yates 2003; McKay 2006).

At the most fundamental level, the specialist gaming press performs the function of manufacturing the sense of a wide community of gamers. While we have learned that social play is commonplace, familial and friendship networks necessarily remain comparatively narrow. This is particularly true of the pre-Internet age before accessing the thoughts, opinions and even performances of other gamers became a relatively trivial matter. We shall return to online communications below but, for the moment, it is useful to consider the role that traditional paper publications have played and continue to play. As Brooker (2002) notes of the activities of fans of the *Star Wars* movie trilogies, the specialist videogaming press fosters a sense of belonging among readers. Given the way in which the practice of gameplay is so often devalued and debased (even within the family as Giacquinta *et al.* 1993 note with mothers often disapproving of the representations of masculinity and violence), magazines provide considerable reassurance that other like-minded gamers exist. Moreover, the editorial tone of periodicals such as Future Publishing's *Edge* (1993–present) has played an important role in communicating that this is not simply a community of cultural dupes, wasting their collective time on inconsequential trivialities but rather has encouraged the gamer to appreciate videogames as valuable cultural objects like film, literature or art and the playing, discussion and criticism of videogames as legitimate cultural practices. Without doubt, *Edge* has played a particularly important role in managing UK gamers' perceptions of videogames with its high production values, the quality of its material form, and through the richness of its editorial content. That it manifestly takes videogames and gaming seriously contributes to establishing the validity of the form within popular culture. Its lavishly designed and produced special editions such as *The Art of Videogames* (April 2007) and

The 100 Best Videogames (July 2007) similarly add weight to the notion of the videogame as a criticisable object.

In addition to this symbolic function, the specialist videogames press has been an influential channel through which information about games has flowed. Most obviously, magazines provide a source of news and information about developments in videogaming. This is particularly important when we consider some of the dimensions of the global games industry. While it may be global, technical and marketing restrictions such as region-coding and differential release dates ensure that gamers around the world do not enjoy equality of access to developers' output.[4] In fact, in addition to staggered released dates, many games are never released in all territories. Of course, for some gamers, such titles are imported and gain nothing but an additional exotic value as they are played in their original languages and on hardware similarly imported at often great expense or modified in breach of manufacturers' instructions (see also Newman 2004). This situation prompts some gamers to enact extraordinary feats of ingenuity and care such as translating titles that are not officially localised (this is particularly evident in Japanese RPGs such as early instalments of *Final Fantasy* or perhaps most famously *Seiken Densetsu 3*, see Chapter 7 for more on the process of 'fanslation'). For those less willing or able to extent their efforts to such lengths, magazines provide a means of accessing a fuller picture of the global videogames culture and marketplace and allow gamers to reach into gaming experiences they may never know at first hand. Interviews with members of development teams offer further insight into the processes and practices of designing and creating games thereby enriching gamers' appreciation of the videogames industry, drawing out similarities and differences with other creative endeavours and helping to elevate some designers to celebrity status. The range of magazines and their coverage is significant also in helping to shape the cultures and trajectories of videogaming.

The sheer number of titles available on newsstands speaks clearly of the desire for information among the community of gamers as do readership figures.[5] However, it is worth considering also that the number of titles not only reflects but also communicates a powerful message about the significance of gaming in popular culture. Of these many titles, we can identify two principal categories: multi-format and platform-specific. While the remit of the former extends across all hardware, the latter type centres its attentions exclusively on a single manufacturer or more usually, a single hardware device. As such, PlayStation magazines tend to focus on a specific model such as the PS3 or PlayStation Portable (PSP) but not both though there is some inevitable overlap especially where titles take advantage of connectivity between the two. The consequence of platform-specificity in the videogame magazine sector has been to continue and even promote a rivalry between platforms. Exclusive titles are lauded and paraded while games available for a variety of platforms are typically described in terms that make the version running on the chosen platform appear preferable. While some of the criticism of competing platforms can be somewhat lacking in maturity, there is little doubt that the partisan nature of the coverage does much to further encourage a sense of belonging within a coherent community – albeit a community of millions of gamers who have purchased one console over another (assuming that they do not own more than one themselves). The coverage of the magazine even at this most fundamental level, in the way that it exalts the games and capabilities of one platform over another, plays an important role in forming and maintaining the identity of the gamer within the wider, and ultimately unknowable, imagined community of gamers.

Perhaps the most immediately obvious function of the videogames press, however, is performed by reviews of the current crop of titles. While each publication differs in the detail of its approach, most UK magazines conform to a pattern that affords the majority of page space to a combination of screenshots (images captured during gameplay) and a textual description of the key features of the game. The conclusion of almost all reviews sees a number of formal and aesthetic traits separated out and individually rated with an overall rating for the game completing the picture. Typically, this matrix of formal and aesthetic qualities will allow separate grades for 'graphics' and 'sound' though some publications include rather more nebulous categories such as 'replayability', 'longevity' or even 'addictiveness'. It is interesting to note the durability of this model of review which has been in evidence from *Zzap! 64* in the 1980s to the present day. It is small wonder, then, that we find that this institutionally accepted means of criticising and evaluating games has spilled over into the non-professional writing of gamer communities (see below). Reviews are clearly an important part of videogame magazines as signalled by the fact that they are typically grouped together into a coherent section that can be easily located and by the way in which the reader is directed to them from the front cover. Covers will typically include references to a number of reviews contained within or even, as was the case with the first issue of the Commodore 64-specific magazine *Zzap! 64* (May 1985), *the* number: 'over 50 pages of reviews', it proudly boasted for all to see. Certainly, exclusive reviews (that is, the first review of a given title) are flagged heavily, often claiming the dominant image also. Given the prominence of reviews, the videogames magazine could be seen as little more than an editorialised 'Buyer's Guide' and, indeed, many magazines include a section of mini-reviews of all currently available titles that serve just that purpose. However, to view them as such is to under-appreciate the uses and value of magazines within gaming culture.

For the purposes of our analysis in this book, I want to focus on two further qualities of videogames magazines. First, their participatory nature and, second, in the next section, on the way they address the imminent future rather than the present. One of the most effective ways that videogames magazines build a sense of belonging and membership of a community is through their letters pages and competitions. From the days of *Zzap! 64* and *Crash* to the present, readers have been encouraged to submit questions to resident experts and, most importantly, demonstrate their gaming skills in front of the community. Competitions and challenges remain a staple feature of gaming magazines though their methods have changed somewhat. In the 1980s, when screen capture devices were not available to most gamers, evidence of prowess was often sought in the form of a photograph of the screen showing score or level attained. Leaderboards published each month would further encourage gamers to contribute and provide a mechanism to gauge one's own performance whether or not one had formally entered the competition. Though video capture techniques differ, the principle remains the same in today's magazines.

The publication of hints and tips that range from cheat codes that enable level select features or invincibility, for instance, to elaborate maps and serialised guided tours or 'Player's Guides' serves also to position the magazine as kindly, supportive benefactor – a member of the community of gamers – providing help and assistance and sharing knowledge among the group. In this way, there is a sense of interactivity that is fostered between magazine and readership as questions may be asked of the journalists who are self-identified 'expert players', their advice is given, competitions and challenges are set, and responses performed, recorded and submitted by gamers for evaluation and ranking within the community.

The lure of the imminent

While competitions and challenges and the publication of hints and tips centre attention on the 'now' of play, it is interesting to observe that the focus of videogames magazines is usually set some way into the future. Similarly, even though it is generally (exclusive) reviews of games currently available for purchase that are foregrounded on covers, a great deal of the editorial content of the magazine itself is devoted to previews of forthcoming titles. This may take a variety of forms that range from dedicated 'Preview' sections such as that in *Edge* that present editorialised discussion of progress and screenshots and that take a form very similar to the magazine's reviews, to interviews with developers and features on studios or publishers who talk about their upcoming, in-development work. If we couple these materials with the news sections that similarly tend to highlight future events and releases alongside documenting and reporting things past, we build a picture of magazines that have their sights set predominantly on the horizon, on the imminent future rather than the present.

Examining a selection of titles from September 2007 is revealing. The over-whelming majority of articles and features focus on previewing forthcoming titles that are still in development, many of which have no confirmed release dates and some of which may never see a release if history is a precedent. In *PSW*, some 77 per cent of the articles centre on previews of games in development while for *Xbox 360 World* the figure is 85 per cent, with *Nintendo: The Official Magazine* opting for something akin to futurology in dedicating 90 per cent of its non-advertising material to discussion of as-yet-unreleased games. Indeed, its preview of the forthcoming *Resident Evil: Umbrella Chronicles* is presented under the banner, 'The Next Best Game in The World Ever is . . .' highlighting the temporary nature of this accolade and the inevitability that a new game will claim the title next month. Moreover, reflecting the pleasures of immersion in this culture of the imminent release, 'XBox World 360' includes an 'Anticip–O–Meter' ™ with most of its previews as an index of the excitement the gamer is, or should be, feeling.[6]

In a sense, we might see the gaming press in a similar way to Facer *et al.* (2003) who identify computer (games) magazines as belonging to and helping to create an 'upgrade culture' that situates the user/gamer within a web of consumption, identifying new peripherals, updates and upgrades, for example. Certainly, we could postulate that at least part of the reason for this fetishisa-tion of the imminent could be found in the videogames industry's desire to maintain interest in, commitment and loyalty to its products. By promising an ever-more golden, feature-rich, photorealistic future, the gamer is assured that this is a pastime of great longevity and whose most exciting days are yet to be seen. We could suggest that this is a manifestation of the videogames indus-try's well-documented concern over its status and that gamers might desert the fold in a moment of realisation.[7] However, fixing the gaze on the just-visible horizon serves another purpose also. It serves to rid the videogame of any lasting cultural value. The most exciting videogame is always the next one, the one we haven't yet played. We might rightly question why the videogames industry would wish to encourage such a perspective given that it seems to be at odds with any desire to create artworks of lasting cultural value. The answer becomes clearer if we stop thinking of the videogames industry as one that markets its products as media texts or works of art and instead view it as a series of hardware and software companies releasing updated products and ser-vices. The key concept here is 'obsolescence' though the term is not one that the videogames industry uses. Each console, graphics card and, most especially, each game implicitly renders that which went before instantly obsolete. This is particularly true of games in series which are immediately resigned to the bar-gain bin of history. Just as 'Windows Vista' supersedes 'Windows XP' and 'Office 2007' replaces its predecessor with new features, so *Virtua Fighter 5*, *Ridge Racer*

7 and *Halo 3* soon become the only games in town. The story is typically centred on technology. Improved game engines, graphical capabilities and larger
levels each question and demote the value of the progenitors. The release of
Half-Life 2 was particularly interesting. Fêted as a genre-defining experience and
lauded for its design and narrative structure, the original *Half-Life* was not pushed
to the back of the cupboard and forgotten as is often the case.[8] Instead, the
developers took the decision to re-release the original game, though not in its
original form. Instead, *Half-Life* became *Half-Life: Source* and was treated to an
upgrade that took advantage of the new game technologies that powered the
sequel. What might be seen as an attempt to generate dewy-eyed feelings of
nostalgia instead may be read as part of the inculcating of the ideology of con-
stant and unstoppable technological progress. Half-Life was still a great game,
Valve would not be re-releasing it unless it was, but time had evidently not
been kind to it and the relentless march of technological progress had inevitably
reduced it to old and inadequate. As Dovey and Kennedy (2006) correctly note,
this is not a teleological argument *per se* as there is no imagined, perfect implementation that games are developing towards. Without doubt, however, there
is an irresistible sense of 'progress' and the new is always unproblematically
'better' than that which it replaces. Moreover, the seeds of *Half-Life 2* can be
seen in *Half-Life*. As Lister *et al.* (2003: 48) note, 'The present is understood
as being prefigured in the past and the culmination of it.'

The discourse of technological improvement suffuses the language that the
videogames industry uses to talk to gamers. For example, while Nintendo finally
opted for 'Wii', the in-development soubriquet for the console – which was used
extensively in public discussion – was the rather less inclusive 'Revolution'. As
of November 2007, Nintendo's official US website hosts a page explaining the
Wii monicker under the heading 'Revolution has a new name' (Nintendo 2007).
The vision of inevitable technological progression that the videogames industry
trades in reminds us of Paul Duguid's (1996) concept of 'supersession' (see
also Giddings and Kennedy 2006, on the 'technological imaginary'). Duguid
identifies supersession as one of the key tropes in discussions of new media.
The reductive idea that each new medium subsumes and replaces its predecessor is similarly challenged by Henry Jenkins who argues that:

> History teaches us that old media never die – and they don't even neces-
> sarily fade away. What dies are simply the tools we use to access media
> content – the 8-track, the Beta tape . . . Delivery technologies become obso-
> lete and get replaced; media, on the other hand, evolve.
>
> (Jenkins 2006: 13)

As we shall continue to explore throughout this book, the position of supersession does seem at odds with the cultures of videogaming, play and fandom

in which gamers place great cultural and historical value on games. Moreover, they engage in a variety of practices that keep them alive long after their developers and publishers have moved on to bigger, better, more technologically advanced things. However, it is interesting to note the dual role that magazines play here. Gaming experiences have become so intrinsically linked to the technologies that enable them that it is difficult to disentangle the 'media' from the 'delivery technology'. *Half-Life 2*'s gravity gun is a consequence of technological developments made in the Source game engine and its physics modelling just as the experience of *Wii Sports* is bound up in the motion-sensing capabilities of the Wii remote. The 'media' here, to some extent, incorporate the delivery technology. The two become yet more difficult to separate if we consider that the accepted and institutionalised means of evaluating videogames focus so clearly on those qualities that are irreducibly linked to silicon, graphics engines and software engineering. By emphasising and ranking games with reference to the characteristics and qualities that are indivisibly keyed to the delivery technologies, magazine reviews might be seen to assist in normalising the supersession. It is worth noting also that games journalism has been subjected to some harsh criticism in recent years. In a series of influential articles, Chris Buffa (2006a, 2006b, 2006c, 2006d) called into question the standards and practices of professional writing on videogames and, in particular, reviewing which was led, he argued, by PR. In a similar vein, Kieron Gillen's calls for a 'New Games Journalism' centre on the poverty of existing approaches (e.g. Gillen 2004).

However, these criticisms notwithstanding, there is a particularly interesting consequence of the prevalence of previews and the publication of material about unreleased games. In these features, interviews and write-ups, gamers are presented with an extraordinarily rich array of documentary evidence through which they can trawl for clues as to the direction in which their soon-to-be-favourite games may be headed. Gamers, then, do not simply soak up the PR-approved messages of developers and publishers in a soporific daze as they obediently await the release of the new game. Rather, they embark on a process of imaginative and playful sleuthing. Naturally, previews reveal only those aspects of the game that developers and publishers are willing to put into the public domain. Non-Disclosure Agreements preclude journalists from deviating from the acceptable PR message. However, nothing stops gamers poring over published interview transcripts and screenshots for morsels.

The following postings to an online forum in response to a preview of the GameCube launch title *Luigi's Mansion* (Lake 2001) are typical of the scrutiny of published materials:

> Looking through a Japanese game magazine today, an old friend is looking to join Luigi in his quest through the mansion. Toad will be making an appearance in the game. What he'll be doing exactly is unknown . . .

but if he follows his N64 duties in Mario 64 . . . he'll act more like a guide.

('Billy Berghammer'; original ellipses. See Lake 2001 [online])

I read your update of Luigi's Mansion, and it got me thinking. You mentioned that there was a clock on the screen in the game, and that this might be a hint that the game may have a day and night aspect to it, like Majora's Mask or Pikmin. You also mentioned the old rumor of the Luigi game actually being one disc in a 2-disc set of Super Mario Bros. games, the other disc being a Mario game. I then thought of the games that were removed from Nintendo's game list on their site, and specifically, Mario Sunshine. I think it may be a possibility that Luigi's Mansion and Mario Sunshine be the two games in the rumored 2-disc set. Luigi's game would have the creepy, night atmosphere, while Mario's disc would have the daytime or 'sunshine' feel to it. Then, by completing certain tasks, you could access the daytime hours in Luigi's Mansion and the dark hours in Mario Sunshine, adding tons of replay value and depth to each game. I could be, and most likely am, way off in my prediction, but it was just a though I wanted to share with you guys.

('Philip Halverson'. See Lake 2001 [online])

Here then we see a number of important issues. Most obvious is the scrutiny of Japanese gaming magazines for the most up-to-date information and detail on the unreleased game(s). We should also note the way the speculation draws intertextually on knowledge and experience of other games and notably the previous work of the game's auteur designer Shigeru Miyamoto (Super Mario 64 was the launch title for the Nintendo 64 console, the hardware that preceded the GameCube upon which Luigi's Mansion would debut). Gamers have come to know Miyamoto through his many magazine interviews as well as through playing the products of his development.

There are numerous similar and well-documented examples of gamers scrutinising published materials in magazines for clues. Screenshots published in Japanese magazine Famitsu of the unreleased Super Mario Galaxy that showed a new Princess character prompted considerable speculation about her role within English-speaking forums and involved members in translations of Japanese Kana characters for clues (see NeoGAF 2007). Perhaps even more unlikely, pack shots of the then forthcoming 80GB PlayStation 3 box sent the rumour mill into overdrive as the packaging appeared to picture a SIXAXIS controller (the system's joypad) with an unfamiliar red light/button. This was taken by some to indicate a new unit replete with the rumble function that had been dropped from the PS3 controller (Doerr 2007).

Although these online comments are representative of the countless conversations and debates that take place offline throughout gamer communities, they raise an important issue in themselves. In the past few years, the printed page has been joined, and in some cases, challenged and transformed, by the Internet. As we see here, the printed page still holds considerable value as a source of information though it is only one source in a diverse media environment of streaming video and downloads. As Holmes (2006) and others have noted, magazine publishers and content creators are still struggling to develop strategies to compete with or offer complementary web-based services. In relation to the specialist gaming press, we can identify two key issues. First, the Internet challenges the magazine as a source of information and, second, as a forum for members of the gaming community to talk, theorise and speculate. In one sense, much of what we see online mirrors that which magazines have long since offered but writ large and with a richness of media and immediacy. The following sections explore these two aspects of the Internet and its impact on the ways gamers talk about videogames and the resources they can access and deploy.

Direct feed: cutting out the middleman

The Internet has had a profound and palpable impact on the transmediality of communications strategies used by videogames publishers and developers. Nintendo's US corporate website (accessed July–August 2007) is a case in point. It hosts much of the material the eager gamer might expect to find in a print publication (indeed, the site's homepage runs an advertisement for *Nintendo Power* magazine which proudly boasts that it is 'packed with the previews, reviews and breaking news you crave' to underscore the message). In addition, a number of webgames related to Nintendo characters or franchises vie for attention alongside downloadable wallpapers, 'Instant Messenger' buddy icons and ringtones. Of particular interest to us here, however, the website also offers a host of streaming video clips. These are embedded in game-specific mini sites with new clips highlighted on the front page via the 'Theater'. Some clips replicate TV advertising campaigns, but the majority are footage of gameplay. As at August 2007, the 'Theater' hosts clips of *Picross DS* (Nintendo DS) and *Pokémon Battle Revolution* (Wii) among others. These clips are particularly notable in that, unlike the TV spots that are created as discrete, self-contained packages with the expected framing and explanation, they are raw, unadulterated gameplay. It is just as if one were watching somebody play the game before you. There is no commentary, no audio narration or textual overlays. There is no paratextual explanation as to what is being viewed, why the clip has been selected or even what it has been designed to illustrate. In the case of *Picross DS*, it is not even entirely clear what is happening, particularly if one is unfamiliar with the basis of the game.

As the video shows only the contents of the dual screens and gives no indication of the interface or controls, it is not easy to deduce the game mechanic. Not easy, but certainly fun. We have already seen in the previous section, the pleasures that gamers derive from theorising and speculating on games. In contemporary gaming culture, alongside the interviews and screenshots of magazines (and websites), raw gaming footage is added to the list of resources to play with, interrogate and investigate.

Increasingly, we see developers and publishers communicating directly with gamers in this way. Through their online presence, they offer not just gameplay video from current titles, but rich media of as-yet-unreleased games. Email alerts straight to the inboxes of gamers provide inline materials and links to the latest content situating the gamer within an extensive and immediately accessible operating context and in an intimate relationship with the developer. In addition to this connectivity between the developer's PR department and the gamer's inbox, the proliferation of gaming-related video online is such that we have seen the emergence of hubs such as 'Game Videos.com' that aggregate and collate 'Video game trailers, clips, walkthroughs, teasers, downloads, commercials, upcoming XBOX 360, PS3, previews, footage'. Where direct mail usually requires signing up and, thus, a positive decision to choose to follow specific titles, sites such as Game Videos, accumulate material from as wide a variety of sources as possible. Game Videos does this under a banner that underscores the gamers' sleuthing instinct and desire to interrogate the imminent release: 'Watch Now, Play Later'. The breadth of sites such as Game Videos offers the opportunity to stumble upon material that might otherwise slip below the radar. This is facilitated by the cross-referencing and rating of material by community members. That the community tags and reports on the videos helps communicate a sense of what is deemed important by building a collective intelligence that rates and ranks content while simultaneously serving as a navigational tool to chart a path through the bewildering variety of available video.

The gameplay footage collected at Game Videos is similar to that found at the Nintendo site in that it is not necessarily framed or explained but rather appears as direct feeds from consoles, PCs or conference and expo presentations. As such, it is not only the fact that these are audiovisual materials that separates them from what we might expect to find in print publications. The absence of any framing critical commentary, and its replacement with only the most basic of captioning, signal the removal of the interpretative skills of the games journalist from the process. To some extent, this mirrors the practice in community sites such as Digg.com and Slashdot where the emerging etiquette appears to demand links to original material and looks unfavourably on links to 'blogspam' (links pointing to blogs that redirect to the original material, for instance). While one layer of interpretation might be seen to disappear, the comparatively unfiltered footage provides a rich source for gamers keen to glimpse upcoming titles and encourages the honing of new analytical skills that discern, for example, the control methods when controllers are not necessarily shown or discussed. The built-in Internet connectivity and online stores of PS3, Xbox 360 and Wii also open up opportunities for platforms holders and publishers to use their gaming networks to distribute video footage of new and forthcoming games and even playable demos. Similarly, many print magazines distribute a cover-mount disc with video or playable sequences in an attempt to replicate some of the online sites' cachet in this regard. Game Videos, however, is interesting also in that it is designed as a forum and community hub. Key to its operation in this regard is the facility for gamers to upload their own gameplay footage (or even reviews, for instance) in much the same manner as YouTube. As such, the site is an intriguing mix of material to speculate with and clips of existing games where gamers demonstrate a particular facet, feat or even flaw.

Konami's handling of its *Metal Gear Solid* series is curious in that it displays an unusually public engagement with the gamer community and their feedback and criticism suggesting a rather more dialogical relationship between the two that may have arisen as a result of this more direct means of communication. First introduced in *Metal Gear Solid 2: Sons of Liberty*, Raiden surprised many gamers. His identity was not revealed until some way into the game confounding many players who assumed they had adopted the role of the previous title's hero, Solid Snake. If Snake is a rough and ready, hypermasculine caricature loosely modelled and partly named after Snake Plisskin, the protagonist in the film *Escape from New York* (see Kent n.d. [online]), then Raiden is his exact opposite. In interviews, *Metal Gear* director Hideo Kojima spoke of the need to surpass the original *Metal Gear Solid* title and ' "betray" people's expectations in a good way' (Kojima 2002 [online]). For many gamers, the betrayal was not positive. Raiden's androgyny and sensitivity made him an unsuitable and problematic hero and forums spilled over with a vitriol that spoke both of their passion and of a latent homophobia present in certain sections of the (gaming) community.

> Yeh the biggest reason why no-one likes Raiden is that you should have been Snake. I hate Raiden, he's queer! Any way Tanker was the best part of MGS2
>
> (posted 2006)

> why do ppl hate raiden? Don't get me started. He looks like a shemale, talks like a small boyscout 'I don't smoke' lol, he has semi long blond hair (omg grilish) and he takes the place of the coolest game hero ever (Solid Snake). So Raiden is about the second greatest mistake ever in the world of gaming (the greatest being Wizardry8). Hope we never see him again.
>
> (posted 2007)

The reaction was not dissimilar to that of many *Star Wars* fans to Jar Jar Binks (see Brooker 2002). However, Konami's response was rather different to Lucasfilm's. *Metal Gear Solid 3: Snake Eater* included parodic elements that deliberately mocked and ridiculed Raiden. In what may have been pandering to the criticism over the character's femininity, it was implied that the character Major Ivan Raidenovitch Raikov, who was suspiciously similar in appearance to Raiden, was the secret gay lover of Colonel Volgin. Kojima explained that these self-aware jokes were 'purely for the fans' (Huhtala 2005). More recently, trailers for *Metal Gear Solid 4: Guns of the Patriots* again address the Raiden issue. In one comedic video revolving around musical chairs, Snake is shown acrobatically and violently disposing of a group of enemy soldiers in a hail of machine gun fire. As the camera moves in, he pulls back his rubber mask to reveal . . . Raiden. The more recent video again allows Raiden to reveal himself only after a display of extraordinary Ninja-inspired aggression and destruction. By his own admission, Kojima is clearly engaged in a playful dialogue here and one which, in an interesting twist afforded by the ease with which audiovisual materials can be disseminated and gamers' feedback, commentary, critique (and disgust) can be expressed via digital communications networks, is played out during the development of the game. While it is still Kojima and his development team who direct the trajectory of the game, there is a palpable sense here that the disadvantaged position from which fans typically operate (see Jenkins 1992, for instance) is changing as the gamer is afforded a means of directly accessing materials and directly making their opinion heard.

The influence of the gamer has been felt elsewhere also. During the 2007 'E3 Microsoft Press Conference', *Assassin's Creed* was demonstrated by producer Jade Raymond. The game was still some way from its final release and was shown in beta form. The nature of beta code is that it will inevitably contain some bugs or glitches that will need to be ironed out in the final stages of development and code frequently undergoes optimisation and fairly rapid improvements in its final run-up to retail release. Footage of the live demonstration were broadcast via a number of websites and made available to gamers eager to catch a glimpse of this much trailed and hyped title (see Daniel 2007). The demo ably showcased many aspects of the game that the developers were keen to highlight and a carefully choreographed playthrough demonstrated the interactive environments and crowd dynamics and AI. However, gamer reaction centred on some apparently poor collision detection and, above all, the moment where an enemy dispatched and pushed from a rooftop failed to fall to the ground but instead floated in mid-air. The episode was a very small part of a larger demonstration but it was greeted with an extremely negative response among certain gaming communities who claimed that the game had, even in its unreleased incarnation, failed to live up to the hype and was a disappointment. The

strength of the reaction forced Raymond and the publishers into damage limitation mode and follow-up interviews went to great lengths to communicate that
these kinds of glitches were entirely expected at this stage in the development
cycle and had already been fixed in debugging. However, to some extent, these
assertions appeared rather like trying to force the toothpaste back into the tube.
What is interesting about this occurrence is that it highlights the potential problems associated with allowing the gamer to peer into the development process.
Journalists become well used to preview code that is often considerably more
problematic and buggy than the beta of *Assassin's Creed* and have learned to read
around the limitations and shortcomings. To an uninitiated audience with unre-
alistic expectations for unreleased beta code, the game simply looks poor. The
ability of direct feed video to generate buzz is not in doubt but, in this case at
least, it was far from what the publishers had intended. There is only one thing
worse than being talked about and that's everybody saying your game is buggy.

Internet talk: a community at the digital watercooler

As we have seen, one important function of specialist gaming magazines has
been to create the sense of belonging and a wider community of gamers beyond
any individual gamer's own networks of friends and family. Where this could
be considered a by-product of the print magazine, it is the *raison d'être* for online
forums and discussion boards. Similarly, where the magazine's rhythm of,
typically, monthly publication creates a hiatus, with online forums, there is no
equivalent restriction and the publication of posts, comments and theories can
follow their own trajectory.

The complexion of sites varies greatly with some such as 'GameFAQs' acting as a hub for gamers and hosting many thousands of gamer-produced walkthroughs, FAQ lists, as well as discussion forums (for more on walkthroughs
and FAQs, see Chapter 5), while others such as 'Eurogamer' offer professional
reviews, previews and news and replicate many of the features of a print magazine as well as offering an online video service ('Eurogamer TV'). Each site,
however, offers a variety of means by which gamers can participate directly.
This may be through forums (essentially large discussion boards where different talk is arranged and structured by 'topics' or 'threads' or the ability to comment on stories, features or postings. In fact, the official sites of platform holders,
publishers and developers are usually replete with forums that gamers can sign
up to and share their experiences with like-minded individuals. A number of
developers even maintain their own personal blogs offering news on their work
and perspectives on the state of gaming culture and the industry (see Jamie
Fristrom's 'GameDevBlog' and 'Raph Koster's Website', for instance).

Regardless of the detail of their implementation, whether blog, forum, wiki, or comments list, participative communication is key to these online spaces in which dialogue, discussion and argument are the lifeblood. As Quiggin (2006: 483) notes, 'In many cases, a blog post serves more to initiate a conversation, held in public view, than as a discrete piece of communication from author to reader.' It is not within the remit of this book to explore the fine detail of the various sites and structures though we will examine some in detail as case studies in later chapters (e.g. GameFAQs). Here, it is important to appreciate the sense of kinship that is fostered in the ability to communicate, with directness and immediacy, with the members of the gaming community. Indeed, as Quiggin goes on to note, the sense of location and context is further heightened by links to other sites and, in the case of blogs, a 'blogroll' of related sites that serve to locate this community with one yet wider.

This potential for collaboration and manifest connectedness is among the most important affordances of the forums, blogs and message boards that gamers have access to. We have already begun to see that the sleuthing and theorising that accompany the posting of news or the revelation of a screenshot is a cumulative, collective process in which posters build on, incorporate, develop, challenge or refute ideas. As Jenkins (2006: 4) notes, 'Consumption has become an increasingly collective process . . . None of us can know everything; each of us knows something; and we can put the pieces together if we pool our resources and combine our skills.' Jenkins likens this situation to what Pierre Lévy (1997) has called 'collective intelligence' and there are shades of Surowiecki's (2004) 'wisdom of crowds' also. What is important here is not simply that forums, community sites, blogs and blog commenting reveal the existence of a community of gamers who share an interest, it is that these online spaces are structured and designed to encourage gamers to share their insights and perspectives, giving rise to a collective knowledge that interrogates, theorises and critiques videogames in an open, rigorous and accountable manner. We should not pretend for a moment that all online or offline communication generates the kinds collective meanings and collaborative authorship celebrated by Jenkins, Lévy or Gee (2007) (whose 'affinity spaces' are somewhat similar in their consequences). Certainly, the transcript below ably demonstrates the complexity and thoughtfulness of the theorising, the 'intensive knowledge' (after Gee) of individual contributors and the collaboration between members of the community who arrive at a shared meaning and understanding. However, for each exchange like this, we should be assured that there is a post that has no comments, or a post that descends into a flamewar (the online equivalent of name-calling). Throughout this book, as with most investigations of marginalised, under-represented and under-researched groups, we must be mindful not to let the minority speak as the majority. My point here is not to overstate the extent of these practices but rather to draw attention to their existence at all as they are largely absent from the popular and academic account of gamer cultures.

The following exchange was posted to a forum dedicated to Nintendo's *The Legend of Zelda* series. Of particular concern to gamers is the ambiguous and potentially contradictory timeline of the series. Gamers have long sought a means of reconciling the place of the many titles in the series through means of split timelines that play with ideas of parallel and alternate universes. This exchange from 'The Hylia' (2007) illustrates the formulation and refinement of one such theory and begins with a question on the status of specific games in the timeline.

— **SuperGanny**

Do you think the FS [*Four Swords*] games count?

I do. They're the first three games in mine. You?

— **GameFreak**

I think if anything FSA [*Four Swords Adventure*] counts more. I don't really know a lot about FS but I think if it didn't end up being part of the time-line it wouldn't really matter. It does have a link to ALttP [*A Link to the Past*] if I'm not mistaken though. . . .

So are the FS games part of the timeline? Yes.

— **hisak**

Right now? No. There has been no attempt by the writers to fit it into the timeline, and until they do, I'll see it as a separate timeline. It obviously takes place somewhere in the timeline, but until they're actually relevant to the story, I think it's best not to try to put it in a timeline (not that I'm discouraging people from trying).

— **EzlosApprentice**

FSA is about as close to a true connection as the FS games have come to the main series, and for that reason it now sits quite nicely in my timeline theories, pretty much around the time of ALttP.

TMC [*The Minish Cap*] is, as is tradition for most, at the start of the game (and for more than the hat thing), while I'm a little unique by putting FS after MM, featuring the Hero of Time.

— **rew**

FS, FSA, and MC? Yes, they count.

WoG, FoE, and ZA? No, they don't. [*The Wand of Gamelon, Faces of Evil* and *Zelda's Adventure*]

— **SuperGanny**

But, FSA seems to come after FS, featuring the same Link. And you would think he would know who Ganondorf is, if he fought him in the future. [I'm not a splitist, but I'm looking at it through your point of view] And, besides, since you follow Aonumas statements, didn't Ganondorf 'do something outrageous' in the past, which led up to his failed execution scene in TP?

— **EzlosApprentice**

Seems to, but isn't stated. What is stated (in the manual for FSA) is that Link is Zelda's childhood friend. I just feel like that friendship could stem from OoT [*Ocarina of Time*]

The events of FS could come after Ganondorf has been sorted. And FSA hints at a new Ganondorf. If TP's [*Twilight Princess*] finale shows the death of one Ganondorf, then we are led to this next one.

The exchange continues throughout the remainder of this thread and is further debated and refined as new theories are suggested and new materials are encountered that problematise or shed light on events. As yet, there is no real consensus among the group. Rather, what we see here is a serious and determined attempt to reconcile the seemingly impossible overlaps and inconsistencies in the various, much-loved and respected titles. What strikes the reader of the many threads and posts in this forum is the extraordinary care and attention to detail displayed by the various contributors here. Where Hodge and Tripp's (1986) study of children's uses of television noted a tendency to present extremely sparse and partial accounts of the backstories of characters or the detail of events in order to fit a personal predilection, for instance, here the scholarship and investigation are nothing if not thorough and subject to criticism if they display undue partiality or incompleteness. In the creation of this collective intelligence there is a process akin to peer review at work in which the suggestions and postulations, the evidential basis, premise and grounds are assessed and evaluated. References to external materials such as the wikipedia entries on alternate and parallel universes are offered for perusal and to gain familiarity with the distinctiveness of each formulation as well as references to existing scholarship and vernacular theory in the field with links to previous posts. It is insufficient to simply concoct an imaginative story that brushes away the inconsistencies. What is required and sought here is an elegant solution that is sensitive to the events of the games.

Much of what we will see throughout this book centres on groups, teams and communities of gamers working in collaboration to produce artefacts, performances or technological systems that further support and sustain groups, teams and communities of gamers. Lévy's concept is extremely useful in highlighting not only the sociality of gaming culture but also its inherent productivity. The discussions of timelines here and the speculation over rumbling controllers and light and dark *Super Mario Bros.* speak of the imagination of gamers and of the ability of videogames to fire those imaginations even when they are not being played. The speculation, theorising and creative endeavour we have observed in this chapter centre on scrutinising the narratives, potentials and even packaging of games. These are imaginative exercises based on groups piecing together fragments of information and offering their own specialised, 'intensive' insights and knowledge, some, but not all, of which is based on experiences of play. Above all, in these examples we see powerful evidence that videogame cultures do not necessarily centre on playing games and are impossible to disentangle from their social contexts.

Chapter 3

Videogames and/as stories

Reading videogames

The popular conception of videogames is that they are audiovisual spectacles. Certainly, as we have seen, the format of game reviews and the special attention that they pay to graphics and sound help solidify this sense as does the prevalence of marketing and advertising materials that foreground the graphical prowess of specific games or the capabilities of the hardware platforms (see *PSW* magazine's September 2007 discussion of the next-gen power of the PS3, for instance). It comes as something of a surprise to non-acolytes, then, to encounter games such as *Final Fantasy*, *The Secret of Mana*, *Chrono Trigger* or even *The Legend of Zelda*. While each of these titles has its own unique and well-developed aesthetic in terms of graphics and sound and while each makes use of controls, inputs and outputs in distinctive and sometimes innovative ways, what is perhaps most striking about each of these titles is the sheer amount of text they present. Line upon line of dialogue come together to form truly epic scripts. Importantly, in each of these games and series, and countless other besides, few if any of these lines of dialogue are spoken aloud. For all the talk of interactive movies that the games industry and commentators enjoy indulging in, a great many videogames and, in particular, Role-Playing Games (RPGs) diverge significantly from the cinematic aesthetic. Throughout the first nine instalments, every line of the dialogue in the *Final Fantasy* series was rendered on screen as white text in a blue box which is overlaid onto the richly drawn backgrounds and characters and which is underscored by an elaborate soundtrack (see Morris and Hartas 2004a, for more on RPGs). It is worth recalling the criticisms that videogame play is inferior to reading and the implication that play and reading are incompatible either because the pleasures of gaming are visceral and centre on audiovisual sensory bombardment or because one activity simply replaces the other with gaming dominating in young people's lives. As Smith notes:

Dialogue in Final Fantasy VII is read, not spoken. During game play, the player hits a key, and a character's lines appear on the screen (with the speaker's name). Dialogue lines usually appear when two characters are physically close to each other, and a conversation occurs with multiple key presses, each bringing up a character's single utterance. Occasionally the player is given the opportunity to choose between two possible verbal responses, but usually key presses are simply used to make sure the dialogue appears as quickly or slowly as the player desires.

(Smith 2002 [online])

This is not to say that there are not videogames that make use of voice acting. In the most recent incarnations of the *Metal Gear Solid* series, for example, just like *Final Fantasy X* onwards, characters enjoy extensive voicing and the depth of expression that is brought by the roster of invisible actors can significantly enrich the atmosphere of gameplay. Similarly, there are many games in which characters are barely voiced at all regardless of whether this is presented in written or audible form (e.g. action games such as *Super Mario Bros.*) However, titles such as *The Legend of Zelda* series continue to present the entirety of their lengthy dialogue exchanges in text panels and use the written word to impart essential narrative information. At least part of the reason for this is technological. Even with today's consoles and PCs using storage formats such as DVD and Blu-Ray that potentially make available many gigabytes of data, space is at a premium. Graphics textures, program code, engines and models, video sequences, music and sound effects all vie for the available space on the disc. Discussing the development of the Xbox 360 driving game, *Project Gotham Racing 4*, 'Ben', a member of developer Bizarre Creations' staff, highlighted the problem:

You won't see different times of day per city because this involves recreating all the textures again (one for day and one for night). Whilst this wasn't a problem for our dev team, it was a problem fitting all this data onto a single DVD. So we've worked around the problem by providing different lighting models per city. For example, Macau is always in the daytime, but if you play it during a storm everything looks darker and more foreboding. If you play during a blizzard then things are slightly tinged blue and everything seems more frozen. Of course, playing this track in sunshine will make everything appear bright and yellowy.

('Ben' 2007 [online])

The *Project Gotham Racing* series, in common with most driving games, is not known for its extensive dialogue and yet the limits of the storage medium are already met or even exceeded. The sheer volume of data storage required for audio files for a dialogue intensive game such as an RPG is a serious overhead. In the days when cartridges dominated and when total storage capacities were measured in megabits, spoken dialogue was simply not an option. Moreover, even if the space were available, it is only relatively recently that console sound chips and processors have been capable of dealing with the digital audio sample playback that is presupposed. The built-in sound devices of consoles and PCs in the 1980s and early 1990s (e.g. Commodore 64, Nintendo NES and SNES, Sega MegaDrive) were of varying degrees of sophistication but each was optimised for musical playback rather than speech whether through sampling or synthesis. As such, the RPG has developed as a genre in which on-screen textual dialogue has become part of the aesthetic. In this way, we might note again the difficulty of disentangling the 'media' from the 'delivery technology' in relation to videogames.

The important point here is that many videogames, and indeed whole genres of videogames, are hugely reliant on players reading text and should not be understood only as audiovisual spectacles (see also Aarseth 2004 on the dominance of the visual as a trope in videogame studies). Moreover, by presenting dialogue in this way, not only is the textuality of the game further heightened but also the player's attention is explicitly drawn to the narrative and characterisations. In some sense, these RPGs may be thought of as lavishly illustrated literary texts. We should draw parallels here with other non-electronic games such as table-top or board games like Gary Gygax's *Dungeons and Dragons* or Steve Jackson and Ian Livingstone's *Fighting Fantasy* books which rely similarly on dense text and create rich and complicated narratives.[1] Like Smith (2002), we do not undermine the significance of the audiovisual spectacularity or the pleasures of the interface, but we should recognise that the narrative and the richness and complexity of the dialogue exchanges and characterisations in role playing videogames are vital elements of this most literary of genres. In common with the *Fighting Fantasy* reader or the *Dungeons and Dragons* player, the videogame RPG player has to work extremely hard to traverse the text (see Aarseth 1997) and the interpretative skills demanded by such games are considerable. These are far from the caricatures of players mesmerically engaged in a stimulus-reflex relationship. Not least of the literacies required is discerning the structure and trajectory of interchanges by learning the conventions of dialogue attribution in each game (e.g. the physical placement of dialogue boxes or the tagging of boxes with the speaking character's name).

We will return to the matter of Japanese RPGs in Chapter 7 to learn how the presence of complex narratives and copious text has compounded the problem of differential regional release schedules and the determination of gamer communities to overcome institutional sloppiness or indolence through hacking and translation. Before that, however, it is important to appreciate the richness and density of videogames like *Final Fantasy VII* and their foregrounding of the written word as a means of communicating narrative and character. In particular, it is important to note the way in which RPGs create the bond between videogames and other literary forms.

Official novelisations

To further strengthen and enrich their narratives, a number of videogames have been adapted, supported and extended by official novelisations. In some cases, as with *Resident Evil*, for example, these novelisations follow the storylines of the games and serve to offer deeper insight into the motivations of characters. The introduction to the novels presented at the 'Resident Evil Fan: A New Blood' fansite notes the status of the novels and indicates some possible uses and pleasures particularly in the hiatuses between game releases:

> While the storylines follow the games to some degree they also expand on the content of them, providing a deeper insight to the character's personalities and motivations. The novels aren't considered the 'official' Resident Evil story, but like all fiction they take you on a different path, and explore what could have been. Each one is a nice addition that complements the Resident Evil series, and if you're looking for more Resident Evil while you await that next game release then the novels might be enough to satisfy that 'hunger'.
>
> ('Resident Evil: The Novels' (n.d.) [online])

While the official *Resident Evil* novels add depth to the games and largely serve to elevate the status of the games as the primary texts in the narrative canon (see below for more on 'canonical texts'), those that emerge from the *Halo* universe perform a different function. *Halo* novelisations are interesting for a number of reasons. First, the game is perhaps not the first that springs to mind as a candidate for novelisation. As an FPS (First Person Shooter), *Halo*'s gameplay is unsurprisingly centred on gunplay. There is, however, an unusually rich and complex narrative concerning alien invasion that plays out over the game series (see Accardo (2001) for more on the original game's narrative) and the novelisations play an important role both in providing further detail about the storylines and characters and, importantly, expanding the universe. Unlike *Resident Evil* in which the videogames remain the primary objects that are enhanced by the additional 'subordinate' texts which retain the relationship common to 'licensed' tie-ins (see Jenkins 2007, for instance), the *Halo* novelisations contribute to a larger, coherent narrative world within which the videogames are wholly consistent components. Authorised by the *Halo* game developer Bungie and thereby gaining an 'official' status in the *Halo* mythos, the novelisations precede, move on from and connect the portions of the narrative presented in the games. With the publication of the novelisations and, latterly, graphic novels, *Halo*, then, has become an example of what Marsha Kinder (1991) termed an 'entertainment supersystem' but which is more recently, and vogueishly, called 'transmedia storytelling' (see Jenkins 2003a, 2003b; Dena 2004, 2006, 2007) in which the narrative is revealed across a range of different media. Interestingly, as well as reflecting the synergistic relationship of media organisations and the desire to offer multiple 'entry points' for consumers, as Jenkins has noted more recently (e.g. 2007), transmedia storytelling offers further invitations to play with and extend the narratives of texts. *Halo*'s transmediality encompasses not only novel-isations but also action figures that facilitate yet further playful, personalised performances and encourage us to enmesh and embed ourselves more intimately within these narrative worlds:

> We might also see performance taking centre stage in the release of action figures which encourage children to construct their own stories about the fictional characters or costumes and role playing games which invite us to immerse ourselves in the world of the fiction. In the case of *Star Wars*, the Boba Fett action figure generated consumer interest in a character who had otherwise played a small role in the series, creating pressure for giving that character a larger plot function in future stories.
>
> (Jenkins 2007 [online])

This invitation to engage in creative exploration is key and we should note the way in which the transmediality of videogames such as *Halo* and *Resident Evil*, to name but two popular series, operates both as a clarion call to gamers to produce and create their own texts and narratives and as legitimisation of these endeavours. For Jenkins, the transmedia narrative is a 'textual activator' that demands not only engagement but also assessment, production and archiving and is a form that is ideally suited to the collaborative social structures of 'collective intelligence' that we have seen characterising gaming cultures. It follows that the official novelisation, just like the action figure and the videogame itself with their performative potentialities, may be understood as parts of a mechanism by which gamers are given permission to play with videogames. Andrew Burn has noted that fans tend to have to match their output to the resources they have at their disposal.

> Games are multimodal texts in the sense that they use visual design, anima-tion, music, speech, writing and so on . . . this combination of modes is unavailable to fans, so we should expect to find that they will carry out

their work of remaking and appropriation as a series of transformations into the modes available to them . . . largely writing and drawing.

(Burn 2006b: 89)

However, if we factor in the centrality of on-screen text and the demands for extensive and attentive reading that are made of the role-playing gamer in particular, and consider the richness and complexity of the narratives that are woven in and around these games, we can see that it is almost natural that we arrive at a videogame culture in which narratives and characters are played with, further developed, and made denser and richer through gamers' own written production. In this way, we might see that the privileging of the written word in games such as *Final Fantasy* lessens the magnitude of the transformation from game to fan novel.

In the remainder of this chapter, we will examine the way in which gamers' productive activity is channelled into the production of original works of fiction before proceeding to an investigation of costume, musical composition and the creation of works of visual art in the following chapter.

Welcome to fanfic

The production of fan fiction (fanfiction or simply fanfic) is commonplace across a range of media fan communities and is well documented in general terms (e.g. in Jenkins 1992; Hills 2002; Gray *et al.* 2007), as an online phenomenon (e.g. Hellekson and Busse 2006), in relation to gender (e.g. Bacon-Smith 1992; Bury 2005), and even specific texts and series (e.g. Brooker 2002, on *Star Wars*). Given the centrality of fanfic as a productive endeavour in media fan cultures, it should come as little surprise to find that gamers are similarly motivated to create their own original fictional narratives based upon and around videogames. Indeed, while much fiction is available through fansites dedicated to specific videogames, series or even platforms (e.g. 'Zelda Guide' and 'PlayStation Pro 2'), many online repositories for fanfic host videogame material alongside that created in response to film, television programmes, anime/Manga, and cartoons. There is little benefit in rehearsing the arguments outlined in this body of work on the inherent intertextuality of fanfic or the various ways in which texts may be rewritten by shifting genres or recontextualising, for instance (Jenkins 1992). Instead, here, we shall turn our attention, first, to the ways in which the Internet has provided a forum for the exchanging, sharing and collaborating on the production of fanfic, before moving onto a discussion and closer analysis of some specific examples of videogames fanfic so as to draw out its qualities and characteristics, and its differences and similarities to fanfic inspired by other media texts and forms.

For Burn (2006b), videogame fanfic is particularly interesting in that it is potentially different from fic that responds to other forms of media text. As we have seen earlier, in drawing attention to the multimodality of the videogame, Burn argues that, as fanfic writers have at their disposal only a comparatively limited range of resources, their production is seen as a process of transformations that privilege or discard certain aspects, or modes, of the videogame. Importantly, according to Burn, the game system is one of the modes that is necessarily discarded by the fanfic writer who, instead, concentrates on the representational or narrative modes. The argument here certainly works to explain Burns' chosen examples of fan writing, the 'spoiler', in which the plot of the videogame is retold in purely written form. Burn explores the writer of a *Final Fantasy VII* spoiler who recounts the twisting events that befall the game's protagonist Cloud Strife as a literary narrative. In his analysis, Burn points to the way in which this piece of writing effectively undoes the link between the game and narrative systems, pulling the two apart and separating them like egg yolk and white. In fact, this is understood as being an extension of a separation that already exists within the game and Burn notes that it is a common technique to extend the narrative in videogames through FMV (Full Motion Video) cutscenes. The cutscene is notable for its lack of interactivity and, as such, experientially different from other elements of the game where the performance of the player is privileged. If we assume that narrative in *Final Fantasy VII* is seen to flow mostly in these cutscenes, ultimately, the fanfic writer may be seen to be responding less to a videogame and more to an animated movie.

Even in relation to spoilers, we might nuance this reading. It is a common trope in academic, popular and practitioner discourses to bemoan the separation of 'game' and 'cutscene' and the deleterious effect cutscenes might have on player engagement and immersion (see Newman 2004, for more on differing approaches to cutscenes). However, regardless of one's attitude toward them, it is difficult to locate 'narrative' solely within the confines of the pre-rendered FMV sequence as Steven Poole (2000) does, for instance. Though they may be experientially and even aesthetically different in some cases, we must understand that the meaning of cutscenes is made in the context of playing with the 'game system' just as this play and its meanings exist and are made in the context of other cutscenes. This is not to say that the videogame is indivisible and Burn is right to note that many players skip FMV sequences (though this is often not possible in RPGs like the one he describes), but rather that we perhaps cannot easily portion it up into 'narrative' and 'game' modes (see also Schott's 2006 discussion of *Oddworld* gamers for whom the cutscenes and game interact in rich and interesting ways).

Moreover, if we examine the wider narrative output of fanfic writers rather than just spoilers, we note that much of the detail regarding characterisation, locale and setting and, most pointedly, the capabilities and capacities of characters, for instance, is revealed through the act of performing and playing as them and not only through viewing their action in pre-rendered cutscenes. As such, the performative or co-creative (Morris 2003) aspects of the game convey much of value to the fanfic writer, as do elements of the game's mechanic such as its magic systems and Materia combining methods which are learned through play and transformed into literary narrative by the fanfic writer. While the fanfic writer responding to a videogame may not have a different range of tools to draw upon in their production work from a writer responding to a film or Manga text, the range of experiences they can draw upon is different and includes both the narrative and game systems, the representational and the performative (see also Krzywinska 2002, on this duality in game studies as a critical practice).

Reading and writing: collaborating and betareading

Although fanfiction is hosted on numerous sites across the web, 'FanFiction.net' is perhaps the single largest community for fanfic writers. Among its many services, the site provides hosting for authors who may upload their stories, often produced in episodic form and unravelling over many months or even years, and reach a potentially enormous audience. To aid readers, material is rigorously categorised and classified. At the top level, fics are classified according to the medium of the text that inspire them. Seven categories cover 'Anime/Manga'; 'Books'; 'Cartoons'; 'Comics'; 'Games'; 'Movies'; TV Shows, while an eighth 'Misc' predominantly houses 'X-Overs' or crossovers whose focus is on combining the characters/locales/scenarios/narratives of different texts, sometimes from different genres and media. Below this top level, stories may be filtered in a variety of ways to suit the viewer/reader (e.g. by genre, date, author). The top level structure of the database is illuminating in that it speaks of the containedness of much of the writing. That is, most of the fanfic to be found here limits itself to a single title or series. While this does not mean that intertextuality is verboten, it is interesting to note the separation of X-Overs from the bulk of the production and their classification under the somewhat inauspicious 'Misc' category. This designation of 'Crossover' fanfics as a distinctive sub-genre of writing can be noted elsewhere also. The 'Halo Fan Fiction Competition' run at the 'Halo Wars Heaven' fansite includes specific rules on the acceptability of crossover entries:

> Crossovers *Are* allowed. This may be for humorous or serious purposes, ie: MC [Master Chief, the player-character in *Halo*] having a duel with Darth Vader. This of course would be humorous, for it would not be . . . very good as a serious plot.

If doing a crossover, make sure to include information on how such a crossover happened. If this info is not given, serious Canon and Creativity points will be docked.

('AvidWriter' 2007 [online])

The very existence of FanFiction.net as well as the prevalence of 'Fan Fiction' sections on gaming fansites such as 'Halo Wars Heaven' not only reflects the popularity of reading and writing fanfic, but also gives rise to a greater degree of production and a heightened awareness of the form among potential readers (see Green and Guinery 2004, on the Internet and 'Harry Potter' fanfic). We should be careful to note that while it might seem obvious that the Internet and fanfic hub websites dramatically increase the potential audience for fanfic beyond the paper-based zines that Jenkins (1992) observed, and render trivial the distribution of the material on a global basis, there is more than just audience building and a comparatively open and easy dissemination mechanism at work here. Importantly, FanFiction.net, like the many game-specific fansites, does not merely provide a means of accessing fanfic, but also facilitates patterns of collaborative working. What we see most clearly at FanFiction.net and across the wider fanfic community is Lévy's collective intelligence writ large. It is useful to focus on a few of the services and qualities of FanFiction.net to illustrate the point.

Reviews

While there is no reason to assume and certainly no requirement that fanfiction be written collaboratively, a number of features, of which the reviews are the most immediately obvious, unfailingly locate the authors' work in the context of a community of readers and other writers. Reviewing generally takes place once a piece is submitted rather than during the writing process though given that many writers are engaged in the production of longer 'novels' comprising many chapters or episodes that are published and reviewed separately, there are circumstances in which this feedback may inform the trajectory of the ongoing work. The following examples of feedback on the first episodes of a *Tetris* fanfic and a story based around *Ecco the Dolphin* respectively are typical (see below for more on *Tetris* and playful fanfic writing). Note that the first reviewer is careful not to simply correct what are seen to be problems, inconsistencies or even errors, but rather draws the writer's attention to them and suggests alternatives. This is wholly in keeping with the guidance for Beta Readers outlined in Elizabeth Durack's (2000) widely distributed article and echoes the sensitivity, tenderness and constructive criticism that Schott (2006) observes in the *Oddworld* community:

This has potential. I don't know where you're going with this, but I will stick around to see how it shapes up. I have a couple of suggestions. One, you have a few grammatical errors. Two, it seems like you rushed the pace a bit in certain places. For example, the second chapter starts with the girl reading the note and alerting her mother of her father's disappearance, but a few paragraphs later it mentions that she'd been thinking about her father's disappearance for a week. It might read better if you noted the time shift somehow. Breaking up the argument scene with the statement about her father's disappearance would do the trick nicely. Well, that's about it. Please continue.

('Peace Flower' 2005 [online])

Ive always had the Ecco games and adored the series and i thought more people would also love them too. You can imagine my dismay when I saw the small amount of Ecco stories. So, here I came, fully expecting that I wouldnt find any stories worth reading. But this story is surprisingly good!

I love how you made the connection between Tides of Time and DotF. Two completely different storylines now make sense. And the dolphin world and their interactions is totally believable, every part of it. The original characters each have their own personalities and are easy to reonize.

The connection between Alden and Lucreta and the Eclipse Pod was nicely done. I had no idea what the end of Chap 1 and the beginning of this chapter had anything to do with each other until i read on. Its nice to know that Lucreta and Alden formed their own pod. I'm still wondering how the Eclipse pod, Neria's marking from the Heavens, and Ecco will all be connected, but I suppose I'll find out in later chapters.

('Serengeti Lioness' 2006 [online])

Even where critical feedback on the narrative, characterisation or writing style is not especially forthcoming, the community frequently offers encouragement and support:

This is the best story I have read in a long time!! You are a very talented writer! I can only dream of writing like you ^^
congratulations :D

('Criskah' 2006 [online])

This is great! Amazing! This is the first Ecco the Dolphin fic that I read and I think its one of the best on this site! Pleease update! Im desperate to know what happens!!

('dark-dragon101' 2006 [online])

As the reviews are addressed directly to the author, there is an immediacy and intimacy about the relationship that is fostered here. Feedback is usually constructive and supportive if not always positive and while not all readers post reviews, that some do serves to shift them from remote and unknowable to followers, perhaps even fans, of the author's work and a specific rather than imagined audience to produce for.

Forums

To further cement the sense of FanFiction.Net as a community, each game has its own forum(s) in which more general discussion takes place. Topics frequently cover issues of process, technique and writing style where the collective group wisdom is drawn upon to solve problems or suggest strategies for successful writing. Many sites include guidance for writers or links to other tutorial materials on the web (see the 'Writing Tips' (n.d.) [online] at NintendoLand.com, for instance). Calls for inspiration are also commonplace and may revolve around settings or new and interesting pairings of characters that may spark new dynamics or narrative potential. Indicative of the community spirit of collaboration, more experienced authors often openly offer their services to other writers or even readers whose writing skills may not match the ambition of their imaginations. For example, under the topic heading, 'Dead Plot Bunnies?', 'Black Light Princess' poses the following:

> Maybe you were writing a fic and couldn't finish it, well I'm here to help with that. Maybe you have an idea that you can't or don't want to write, post it and someone will want to use it.
>
> ('Black Light Princess' 2005 [online])

There is a clear attempt here to manage one's identity within the group and establish oneself as an expert writer and sagely fixer. However, the group's response is open and does not interpret the offer negatively or as an attempt to aggrandise. The forum thread continues as posters contribute to the discussion.

> Name: Resident Evil X
> Plot:
> Just a quick thing that I came up about a year ago. It involves Chris investigating a former Umbrella head when he announces that he has developed something to re-stimulate dead cells.
>   Of course, something goes wrong but it has something mainly to do with revenge.

Status: Currently cancelled due to lack of reviews (last one was the tenth of July). Plus, slight writers block and being focused on other projects.

('Dawley' 2005 [online])

I have an old RE fanfic, the first in what my best friend and I wanted to be a three part series, based on two fictional UBCS members that attempt to make their way through Raccoon, but what I'm having a problem with is revising it and continuing with it. Basic jist of the story is this:
Title: Resident Evil UBCS: Ground Zero
Basic Summary: Two fairly new recruits to the UBCS are assigned to help clean up the Raccoon City infestation brought about by the release of the T-Virus. With their team wiped out by the monsters, the two men must fight their way through the infested city in an attempt to escape with their lives, while trying to discover just what caused the infestation.

Rating: Either Teen or Mature, depending on how far language goes and how much detail is put into the gruesomeness.

Basically I just need an idea on how to rewrite the story since it was originally a joint piece between my best friend and myself. I'm open to any suggestions.

('Keizer Xilian' 2006 [online])

This forum exchange illustrates that the collective intelligence of the fanfiction community goes further than reviewing and commenting on the work of others. Here, we see evidence of writers actively soliciting the views of potential readers and responding to their ideas. By drawing on the invention and creativity of the community, the impetus for a new fiction may be arrived at. Once writing is underway, we might be forgiven for thinking that the writer disappears into the solitude of their virtual garret and emerges at some later date with a piece of writing to upload for the community. However, the process of collaboration frequently continues throughout the process. Will Brooker (2002) has rightly called the fanfic community a supportive environment and nowhere is this more ably demonstrated than in the practice of 'betareading'. In the words of 'ariblack':

Basically, a beta-reader is a person who reads a work of fanfiction, with the aim of improving spelling, grammar, punctuation, etc. as well as pointing out plot-holes or inconsistencies. A beta-reader will usually also give an opinion on the characterization, believability (I know that's not a word, sorry), style and flow of the piece, as well as helping stay in 'canon' or double-checking movie-verse, facts, etc.

('ariblack' 2007 [online])

As Jenkins (2006) has noted, the writer–betareader relationship is an open and nurturing one. For Karpovich (2006), the intimacy of the bond makes it unique even when compared with the apparently similar relationships between writers, literary agents and test audiences not only because they act voluntarily but also because their substantial investment and involvement in the project may elicit significant and substantive changes in the direction or form of the text. Interestingly, trawling the literature on fan theory, Karpovich identifies the practice of betareading as one that accompanies the movement of media fandoms online and finds no reference to the activity in scholarly texts such as Jenkins (1992) or Bacon-Smith (1992), fan glossaries such as Southard (1982) or Sanders and Brown (1994) or fanfic histories such as Verba (1996). We might also consider whether the recursivity and exploratory nature of electronic writing that Facer *et al.* (2003) ascribe to the affordances of the word processor may lead to the practices of fanfic production becoming a collaborative continual work in progress.

The parameters of betareading are fairly well inscribed in shared custom and practice. Across the wider fanfiction community, it is understood that the betareader should not position themselves as an expert and should be aware and forthcoming about their limitations and shortcomings. Those responding to ariblack's (2007) post above are quick to point out their own grammatical pedantry, for instance, or their penchant for identifying and plugging inconsistencies in plot. This openness perhaps also goes some way to explaining the responsiveness of the community to Black Light Princess' offer of assistance we saw above.

Aside from the creativity and inventiveness of the productions themselves, the most striking feature of the fanfic community is its supportive nature. There is a true sense of collaboration and a desire to improve the overall quality not just of one's own work but of others also. Tolerance is exercised in order to encourage those whose writing ability does not match their imaginative capabilities (the judges of the 'Halo Wars Heaven' Fan Fiction competition note that they will go easy on grammar and spelling as the storytelling is privileged). To help raise the overall standard and nurture new talent, skills are shared and new writers are mentored formally by betareaders and informally in reviews and forum discussions. While each story is attributed to an individual author, it is clear that most of these productions are clearly located within the context of readers and writers who offer their support, guidance and encouragement. As a consequence, as Lévy suggests, the fanfic community is greater than the sum of its parts.

In the next section, we shall turn our attention to the actual work of these fanfic writers and communities and, in particular, to the complicated ways in which imagination, invention and innovation are both encouraged, rewarded and idealised, and simultaneously contained and policed.

Invention and containment: the canon

In some senses, the production of videogame-inspired fanfiction is no different from that celebrating and triggered by non-videogame media texts. We have seen that the community judges the quality of contributions and typically plays an assistive role in improving the overall standard of writing and invention. This may range from advice and guidance on spelling, grammar and writing style, through informal suggestions for plot developments or changes in pacing, to the formal betareading arrangements that forge close relationships between participants in the community. What is interesting to note is that in addition to the supportive critique on writing and judgements on the creativity of individual pieces, the community also assesses and scrutinises the quality and value of contributions in terms of their compatibility with the established 'canon'. The canon describes those titles that are considered to contain the legitimate material of the series and it is upon the characters, scenarios and narratives enshrined and described in these canonical texts that the fanfic writer can draw. As such, fanfics are judged both on their own creative merits and in terms of their compatibility with the events, characters, situations and narratives already encoded with the 'canon'. Those materials falling outside the canon may retain interest value but they do not possess the status of canonical texts and neither bind the writer in the same way nor offer resources that may be unproblematically utilised. Will Brooker (2002) offers a useful discussion of the relationship between the canon and 'Expanded Universe' in *Star Wars* and the playfulness of Lucasfilm's 'Special Edition' remakes that incorporate and therefore canonise elements previously located outside the sanctioned suite of texts. This example speaks of the fluidity of the canon which is modified and redefined with each new text that is added, making new material available and potentially disallowing older certainties that become inconsistent or contradictory. Indeed, Capcom's (2006) *Resident Evil Archives* proudly proclaims to document the interconnected stories that play out across many games in the series while adding to it and enriching it, thereby simultaneously containing and embellishing the limits and boundaries.

The boundaries of fanfic are, thus, somewhat problematic as invention and creativity are rewarded but only within certain boundaries that are set out by agencies beyond the control of fanfic writers. An interesting dynamic is revealed here in which fan communities produce texts whose very purpose is to push at the boundaries of the game while simultaneously any such contributions are judged in terms of their compatibility with the canon, and the integrity of these newly constructed borders is policed most vehemently. The rules of the 'Halo Wars Heaven' fanfic competition we saw earlier illustrate the point. Contributions are rated for their 'creativity', 'character development' and 'correct canon data'.

Given its significance as a binding set of resources, it is surprising to note that the designation of the canon is often a matter of considerable debate prompting much analysis on forums and discussion boards. Indeed, defining and delineating the canon demands a significant amount of investigation and presents yet further evidence of the collective intelligence of the fanfic community. The inclusion of a specific text within the canon is a complex issue and is not a simple matter of aggregating all of the individual games in a series or identifying the presence of recurring characters. Very often, the status of a game is not governed by its content but rather is contingent of matters of production. Typically, the role of the development studio or even key development personnel is critical. Accordingly, as it is commonplace to find the development duties on a videogame series shared out among different development teams or even different studios, we arrive at a situation where certain titles are considered canonical and others rejected to languish in the extended universe that surrounds but is subordinate to the canon. What we note in the delineation of the videogame canon is that many of the defining characteristics are not widely publicised and require considerable investigation and the kind of collective intelligence and cumulative knowledge that we have already noted at work elsewhere in the community.

The *Sonic the Hedgehog* (1990–present) canon is illustrative. Released in 1990 on the MegaDrive, *Sonic the Hedgehog* was a 2D platform developed by one of Sega's internal development teams who would become known as 'Sonic Team'. The Sonic character and game became a virtual mascot for the MegaDrive and, more broadly for Sega, in the fight with Nintendo and *Super Mario* for console supremacy during the early 1990s. Capitalising on Sonic's popularity and brand value, a number of additional games have been developed and Sonic continues to appear in new games at the time of writing. Titles range from sequels (*Sonic 2, 3* and *Sonic and Knuckles*), through jumps into 3D action adventure with *Sonic Adventure* and its sequels, to pinball in *Sonic Spinball* and combat *Sonic the Fighters*. According to the community assembled at the now defunct 'Sonic the Hedgehog Area 51' forum, however, not all of these titles are necessarily canonical. The *Sonic the Hedgehog* canon does not automatically encompass every official game release from the publisher Sega. Rather, according to the forum members, it is not the presence of Sonic characters, situations or locales, or even the eponymous hedgehog himself, that define a title worthy of inclusion and, by inference, authentic and valuable, but the involvement of the originating developers.

Responses to theorising about the Chaos Emeralds that appear throughout the Sonic series, which appeared on 'The Mobius Forum' message board, reveal much about the delineation of the canon and the dynamic that at once encourages creativity and productivity but insists that it be constrained within carefully defined parameters:

Tsk, tsk. Haven't you learned yet? Only games that Sonic Team developed count in the storyline. That is Sonic 1, Sonic CD (if you wonder why, it's because Ohshima directed it), Sonic 3, Sonic Adventure and Sonic Adventure 2.

Also note, it was Sonic Team who had started development of Sonic R, but had left the programming duties to Traveller's Tales due to time constricitons (Yuji Naka was still producer mind you), so it "counts". In my mind, the only legitimate "non-Sonic Team" game was Sonic the Fighters. Though it was developed by AM2, Naka thought the idea was a hoot and was behind the project all the way. I don't think the same can be said about ANY other games.

('Pepperidge' 2002 [online])

Elsewhere in the analysis of the same issue, fans return to what they consider to be trustworthy 'original' sources (that is, the Japanese manuals that accompany the canonical games that are provided in translation by one of the community who lends his intensive knowledge to the group). The authority of these materials supersedes even the official Sega of America (SoA) and Sega Europe materials which are discarded as disloyal as they frequently invent new narratives and explanations rather than faithfully translating and duplicating the canonical Japanese materials.

This is indicative of a common complaint encountered in much of the discussion in gamer forums who tend to denigrate the official localisations and translations. There is a shared feeling that those involved with the official translations either take liberties with or are simply insufficiently well versed in the minute detail of the canon to produce a sensitive English language version. This dismissive distrust manifests itself in a number of ways and it is clear that the lack of care in preserving the continuity and integrity of the canon as envisioned by the originators aggravates these gamers. Given the amount of time spent analysing details of in-game events and building a consistent frame within which to understand the games, and the reverence reserved for Yuki Naka and his Sonic Team, it is hardly surprising that these gamers should treat with short shrift those introducing inconsistencies into the universe.

Publicity interviews indicating the age of Sonic in the various games in the canon prove particularly contentious, prompting theories including time travelling so as to make the apparently incompatible ages of Sonic and the time elapsed between games marry. However, further investigation into the origination of the assertion rendered any apparent controversy inconsequential and the need to modify the accepted wisdom unnecessary:

Psh, this is a quote from a guy from Sega Europe . . . They're even further out of the loop than SoA [Sega of America], and we all know how much stuff they've pulled out of their asses that doesn't correspond with Sonic Team. I wouldn't automatically assume this guy's words to be gospel just cuz he's on Sega's payroll. The guy who called Amy "Sally" in Sonic CD was an "official Sega person" too . . .

Turner was probably exaggerating anyway. Either purposely making the difference 10 years to emphasise that it was Sonic's 10th anniversary, or just off-handedly calling him a "five-year-old" to suggest he was less mature back then, not literally five.

Note that Sonic Jam (1997) explicitly states his age as 16. Yet according to this theory, Sonic's age changes between the three games on Jam (not to mention he'd presumably be 11 in Sonic World?).

Nah, Sonic's always been portrayed as a teenager (even if they can't nail down the exact age . . .). No use changing that assumption based on an obscure quote from a PR guy in an old magazine

('The Virus AJG' 2003 [online])

Importantly, what we note here is not a simple rejection of material that does not fit with the existing schema. Throughout the complete thread, we see at first an acceptance as this is apparently official material originating from a Sega employee and an attempt to theorise away the inconsistency this creates, before further investigation and a collective evaluation of the authority of the information renders it out of step with the canon and unworthy of incorporation into the knowledgebase. Ultimately, what we see here is a collective intelligence that operates critically on new materials, testing and evaluating them, interrogating them and their origination before either accepting or rejecting them.

Filling the gaps

The example above centring on Sonic's age highlights a common area of concern among fanfic and gamer communities. Inconsistencies in the narratives of the various texts that comprise the canon are a rich source for gamers and provide an ideal focus for their creative and discursive activity. Rather than attempt to hide or gloss over such narrative defects, we find that gamers are only too keen to highlight them. At least part of the reason that puts gamers in this potentially contradictory position that at once valorises and identifies the shortcomings of the game, is certainly a desire to signal their intimate knowledge and mastery of the games. However, it is not sufficient to leave these plot holes and gamers go to considerable lengths to remedy the situation.

In the exchange below that took place on the now inactive 'Sonic the Hedgehog Area 51 Messageboard', one gamer attempts to justify the unexplained change in locale that occurs between two games in the *Sonic the Hedgehog* canon.

Specifically, the localised US conversion of *Sonic & Knuckles* (S3&K) was set on the planet 'Mobius', whereas its sequel *Sonic Adventure* (SA1) was set on Earth. This case is interesting for a number of reasons. First, it is clear that the invention and research here are considerable. Moreover, this gamer has put their technical skills to work to produce their own game based on this theory to link the two canonical titles and explain the anomaly. Burn (2006b) notes that fans usually do not have access to a wide range of 'modes' and their production work typically undergoes a series of transformations into, for instance, art or a literary text. However, the availability of gamemaking tools such as Mark Overmars' 'Game Maker', or 'Unity', or even Macromedia 'Flash', make available a far greater range of modes to programmers and non-programmers of varying abilities. We might see that the act of game making is a natural extension of fanfic and is simply an example of gamers working in different modes in their responses to videogames. We will return to the matter of game production in the analysis of 'modding' in Chapter 7.

> The plot of my fangame, "The end of the Millenium", takes place in the time between S3&K and SA1. The just of the plotline is, In one quick boring summery, Mobius will expode at the end of the millenium due to a 2000 year old curse from the echidnas. Tails finds out about this and they search for a planet that can sustain life, they find earth, they go there, start SA1 storyline. There a lot more to it then that but I'm not about to give away the whole plotline.
>
> ('Miles McCloud' 2002 [online])

However, as is usual in the highly critical community, such theorising does not go unchallenged and further posters rigorously interrogate the validity of the ideas so as to validate or refute their authority. In doing so, these fans demonstrate a remarkably thorough knowledge of the minutiae of the various *Sonic* titles and demonstrate the supportive yet thorough and unapologetically critical environment that characterises gaming culture. In response to a criticism of the geographical integrity of the proposed game's world in relation to the Sonic canon, the creator defends the creation:

> I considered that. After it rises from the Mystic Ruins it floats out of Earth and to Mobius.
>   It is possible – play Sonic3&Knuckles as Knuckles and beat it with all the Emeralds. If you watch carefully in the ending the Island floats up quite high, **almost** (but not quite) into space. The island is likely to have lots of energy surrounding it after it was created and that excess energy could have propelled into space and beyond.

> Anyway I have found some evidence that both supports and discredits the interview.
>
> ('Miles McCloud' 2002 [online])

Further postings highlight the possibility of the apparent inconsistency being a localisation issue where in-game and supporting text is translated for different territories (in this case, from the original Japanese to English). Here again the fans' awareness of the processes of production includes translation of in- and out-game materials such as instruction manuals, backstories and even interviews. In support of the rationale for 'The end of the Millenium' [*sic*], other forum members contribute their thoughts on the validity of materials translated by those potentially insensitive to the minutiae of the canon. As we have seen elsewhere, gamers frequently value translations of original language materials that emerge from within the trusted community of gamers rather than those of regional marketing departments:

> Might I point out that Naka-san is Japanese, and Sega has a way of translating things from Japanese to ENglish to suit their whims. (This isn't just Sega; any large corpration will change certain things like that) Naka may have said something different in relation to a planet name, and Sega may have simply used "Mobius" in its place.
>
> ('Ryoga Masaki' 2002 [online])

Explaining away the flaws in or in between the revered canonical texts appears to be partly motivated by a desire to imprint oneself onto the canon thereby becoming closer to the game and its creators – as a virtual co-author (or co-creator of the game as Morris (2003) might have it). However, while the fanfic writer or theoretician may wish to join the canonical authors, there is an ambivalence here as there is also evidence of a desire to validate the vision of the Sonic Team and Yuji Naka in particular. We might argue that to leave a narrative inconsistency unexplained would be to admit the imperfection of the Sonic mythos. Again, the task of the gamer here is a dual one that pushes and explores at the edge of the canon, expanding, modifying, enriching, while also preserving, policing and remedying. Theorising, whether or not it becomes encoded in fanfic, forum discussion or even a fangame as we see below, is a crucial part of the creation of the collective intelligence upon which gamers collectively contribute and draw upon in future work as the group's lore is established and shared within and across forums who frequently interlink and refer to one another's postings and ideas.

Forum crosstalk is not always quite so positive, however, although even where squabbling or more serious criticism takes place, it often gives rise to creative production in defence of the position, canon or group. As such, some of the theorising and collective recuperation of the canon may be read both as an attempt to maintain or restore perfection in the canon and as a means of protecting the object of the gamers' interest against the charges of detractors that this series is inferior to others, for example. This rivalry is particularly prevalent across gaming platforms with gamers demonstrating allegiance to a given hardware system and thereby to particular games, series, collections of characters or even development houses or individual designers. Again, the case of *Sonic the Hedgehog* is useful here as, until Sega exited the console marketplace and became a software-only company, Sonic was indissolubly linked with Sega's consoles such as the MegaDrive. However, we also find that the allegiance to specific games may reflect hardware choices and may even inform them. For example, it is just as likely that we will find 'Sega' and 'Nintendo', or latterly, PlayStation and Xbox fans, extolling the virtue of the platform-exclusive *Sonic* and *Mario* or *Gran Turismo* and *Halo* titles respectively, as it is to find supporters of the individual games defending the hardware or platform manufacturer or their own purchase of a given console. The distribution of fan forums highlights the diversity with some forums dedicated to specific games or series (e.g. 'Metroid Guide' or 'Nintendojo'). Incidentally, the comparison of consoles is usually configured in terms of published technical specifications, which are at best misleading and not especially revealing in terms of actual performance or gameplay opportunity (see Norman 1988, on 'liquid features' in computer marketing), or are concerned with the exclusivity of forthcoming titles.

Indeed, there is no need for exclusivity in forum membership and it is likely that a gamer will belong to a number of communities and forums that reflect the full range of their interests, productive and play practices. What is important to note is that, regardless of the scope of the community, the collective intelligence necessarily extends beyond the experiences of play to technical details of the gaming technologies that enable the experiences and, most crucially of all, to an understanding of the contemporary videogames' business, publishing and development processes, and the existence and importance of exclusivity and platform-specificity. To recuperate and fill in the gaps left in the canon, to identify those that are genuine inconsistencies in the authorially authentic narrative and those that are the products of poor or insensitive translation, then, is to protect the game and validate the collective activity of the virtual community and is a personal act of identity management within the group and a chance to superimpose oneself onto the text by joining the hallowed ranks of the canonical authors. The canon is absolutely key to the activity of fanfic writers as it solidifies the suite of resources that are legitimate fodder and sets the limits of invention and creation. It is unsurprising that discussion and debate over its boundaries and margins occupy so much forum space and it is interesting to note the dual role that participants find themselves in as they defend and repair, play with and police the canon. For many videogame series where titles are still developed and released, the canon is a mutable entity and so the work of defining it is an ongoing process. Elsewhere, as we will see in the following section, the canon is not such an important issue, either because the productive work centres on a single game or because it is deliberately playful and concerned more with confounding the expectations of the fanfic and gamer communities than with 'authenticity'.

Writing playfully (about play)

Most studies of fanfic whether concerned with videogames (e.g. Burn 2006b) or other media (e.g. Hellekson and Busse 2006) tend to focus on the serious work undertaken by writers. The result of such studies is that, perhaps unintentionally, the output of these writers can appear a little dour even if imaginative, intertextual and intensely creative. However, it is important to note that much fanfic is exceptionally playful and a good deal is deliberately comic. In this section, we will centre on some of the more unexpected videogame fanfiction writing projects.

Fanfic is inspired by a richly diverse collection of games. *Ecco the Dolphin*, *Final Fantasy VII*, and *Championship Manager* each belong to different genres and engage their players in different ways offering a variety of pleasures (see Crawford 2006, on *Championship Manager*). *Final Fantasy VII* is a hugely complex RPG with rich characters and an epic narrative, *Ecco the Dolphin* is an action/puzzle game centring on the attempts of the eponymous cetacean hero to rejoin his pod, while *Championship Manager* is a football management simulator that reduces its audiovisual presentation to the absolute barest and concocts a world of statistics, overseas training programmes and transfer markets in what appears to the non-acolyte to be little more than an Excel spreadsheet in team colours. For all their many differences, these games have some things in common. Each is ripe with narrative potential. In the case of *Final Fantasy VII* and *Ecco the Dolphin*, there is an already rich and complex narrative to play through, extend and develop. In the case of *Championship Manager*, the course of the management campaign clearly facilitates the building of a personalised journey towards success or continued languishing in lower leagues. It is worth briefly considering *Championship Manager* as the fanfic that surrounds it has some interesting characteristics of its own. 'Champman' as it is know among its many fans (who are known collectively as 'the scene'), inspires a good deal of writing. Much of it describes formations, tactics and strategies or imaginary scenarios such as Korrekt's episodic (2005–2007) 'While the cat's away . . .' in which Chelsea, Arsenal and Manchester United are swapped with Oxford United, Rushden & Diamonds and Northampton Town. Perhaps the most interesting form of *Champman* writing, however, is the impassioned, emotional and often deeply personal fictional narratives based on game and gamers' reminiscences of their childhood memories of football, family and friendship. Jimmy Floyd's (2005) 'The Boy Who Would Be El Rey' weighs in at over 50,000 words and deals with complicated issues of friendship, personal and professional challenges against the backdrop of a managerial coming-of-age.

In addition to these games, we have also obliquely come into contact with an altogether different kind of fanfiction. *Tetris* is perhaps not the most obvious choice of games to inspire narrative fiction and it is surely for this reason that writers are drawn to it. Utterly devoid of the narrative potential or even the most basic of narrative framing that we might presume is essential for the fanfic writer, *Tetris* is the archetypal 'abstract game' (see Juul 2001). Intrepid fanfic writers have responded to the challenge in a variety of ways. What unites them is an inventiveness that is at once sensitive to the game and must be read as tongue-in-cheek, ironic playfulness that explores the boundaries of fanfiction itself. We will focus here on two approaches to *Tetris* fanfic.

The first seeks to capture the experience of play replete with its many frustrations and speaking of the compelling, 'just one more go' nature of the game. Written as a haiku, the form of LateNiteSlacker's piece echoes the bare simplicity and economy of the game while Simon Silvertongue's poem conveys something of the inevitability of failure. *Tetris* is based on a game design common in early arcade games of the 1970s and 1980s in which an 'infinite' structure that endlessly loops dooms the player to certain demise (see Newman 2004, for more on the infinite game structure). There is no ultimate goal or objective as with many linear game designs. The nature of *Tetris*, as with *Space Invaders*, *Asteroids* and other games of this type, is to delay the end for as long as possible:[2]

> Aishiteru
> Slow, but gradual,
> They fall provocatively,
> Blocks profane, I lose.
> ('LateNiteSlacker' 2004)

> A game
> I begin.
> I play.
> I lose.
> Therefore, I play again.
> ('Simon Silvertongue' 2004)

The second approach is perhaps a little more ambitious in that it seeks to build a narrative around the game. One particularly interesting example draws upon the development history of the game that began its life at the Academy of Sciences in Moscow where it was designed by Alexey Pajitnov (see Sheff 1993; and the 2004 documentary 'Tetris: From Russia with Love', for more on the game's history). In 'Shinan's' 'The Commune', *Tetris* is reframed as an allegory in which the endless march of the 'iron curtain' of blocks, the relentlessness of the game system, and the processes of collective, communal action assume new meanings. Moreover, there is an attempt to capture the mechanics and frustrations of play here also. The 'tall one' refers to the 'I' block which is required to complete a 'Tetris' and eradicate four lines simultaneously thereby achieving the highest score. Having built a suitable structure, the gamer will frequently find themselves frustratedly waiting for such a block to appear in the sequence often having to cut one's losses and pass over the chance for a Tetris in order to keep the system working:

> A long time ago someone said to me that the system should never fail. Together we can bring down the greatest of piles and fill up all holes. There is hope in the collective.
>
> There are those that are not as co-operative. The tall one comes and goes as he pleases when all of us rest are working hard to keep the system intact the tall one decides to leave. When the colours were yellow and green the tall one did not appear where he would have fitted perfectly. We built and built and waited for the release that the tall one would give us but he never came . . . With collaboration and hard work the system survived. It did not fail. We keep on but we will not forget the betrayal of the tall one.
>
> ('Shinan' 2007)

The playfulness of these *Tetris* fanfics, along with the forum and review commentary, speaks of the ways in which gamers seek out and enjoy challenges. To fictionalise an entirely non-narrative, abstract game certainly confounds most of our expectations of fanfic both as readers and theorists. However, in the pleasure of tackling such obstacles we perhaps note echoes of the motivations and pleasures of videogame play itself in which puzzles, conundrums and apparently insurmountable challenges are the stock-in-trade. Buoyed by the virtual community of appreciative, critical but supportive writers and readers, the fanfic writer's journey is one that is facilitated in a similar way to the videogame player's.

Chapter 4

Things to make and do
Fanart, music and cosplay

Videogames and art

The videogames industry has a rather uneasy relationship with art and the artworld. Clarke and Mitchell's (2007) collection *Videogames and Art* speaks eloquently of the issue. In some senses, the book may be seen as a celebration of artistic practice and the uses to which some artists have put videogames both in order to reflect upon them and to utilise them as tools and environments for expression and experimentation (see Clarke 2007; Winet 2007; Hunger 2007, for example). However, as Schleiner (2007) notes, we should temper our enthusiasm remembering that, 'Many artists, art critics, new media critics and theoreticians have expressed a disdain for games and game style interactivity, in fact, to describe an interactive computer art piece as "too game-like" is a common pejorative' (Schleiner 2007: 81).

Elsewhere in the book, we find figures from the videogame industry posing the hopeful and apparently aspirational question 'will computer games ever be a legitimate art form?' (Adams 2007). Given the vehemence and prevalence of the criticism noted by Schleiner above and evident in Roger Ebert's (2007) dismissal of videogames, for example, it is hardly surprising that the games industry might feel a little sheepish. The question seems to centre on the perceived legitimacy of videogames and highlights an uncertainty as to the value of games and fun. In this way, it is a similar endeavour to the attempts to align videogames with film or literature through the designation of 'interactive movies' or 'interactive fiction'. It is not my intention in this book to continue this debate, not least because it tends to focus on a narrowly defined sense of what games *should* become (i.e. more than just 'fun' as Adams 2007: 263 suggests) rather than understanding, celebrating and criticising what they are and typically dissolves into an endlessly recursive attempt to define 'art'. Rather, here I wish to draw attention to a few of the ways in which videogames have begun to make their presence felt in the art establishment. Perhaps more particularly, however, I am interested in considering how the activity of the legion of fanartists who produce works inspired by videogames not only enriches the cultures and communities of gaming but also provides mechanisms for gamers to heighten and reframe their relationship with their favoured games whilst developing their technical and creative skills in a public and supportive environment.

Following Schott and Burn's (2007) lead (in the same edited collection), we might view the practices of creating art inspired by and responding to videogames as

> [an] opportunity to understand art as something meaningful that symbolises an important part of their everyday practices. The value of 'production' and 'making' contributes toward an aesthetically evolved and culturally aware population, fostering a positive and informed attitude towards art.
>
> (Schott and Burn 2007: 253)

The art of videogames

In addition to the arguments played out in professional and academic literature concerning the status of videogames as art (see Adams 2007; Barker 2007; Denerstein 2007; Martin 2007), it is useful to note that there has been a small but steady flow of published work that aims to celebrate, investigate and record the visual artistry in videogames. As such, even though there might be disagreement on the status of 'the videogame' as an artform, critics are more comfortable in disentangling some of the creative and artistic processes and highlighting the resultant 'assets' that comprise the form.

Publications include Faber's (1998) collection of in-game graphics, layouts and backgrounds that present freeze-frames for considered analysis and contemplation or collages of multiple screenshots reassembled to map out worlds usually only visible in screen-sized portions; Choquet's (2002) edited collection *1000 Game Heroes* that focuses on the visual design and development of game characters; and more general, thematic discussions such as Morris and Hartas' (2003) *Game Art: The Graphic Art of Computer Games* that deals with the history of in-game representations, visualisation across a range of genres and a variety of possible futures. Books addressing specific games have also become commonplace and are frequently launched alongside key titles (e.g. Trautman's (2004) *The Art of Halo: Creating a Virtual World*, Kent's (2004) *The Making of DOOM 3*; Valve's (2004) *Half-Life 2: Raising the Bar*; and Capcom's (2006) *Resident Evil Archives*). What is notable about these publications is that they foreground the static, visual image. Volumes such as Faber's serve to recontextualise screenshots extracted from games encouraging viewers to read them in a more critical and attentive manner, while others such as Choquet's and the *Resident Evil Archives* combine in-game representations with character designs presented in publicity and marketing materials alongside boxart, packaging, flyers and posters to give a sense of the transmediality and range of representational forms that game characters take.

What is particularly interesting, however, is the 'behind the scenes' access that titles such as Trautman, Kent, Valve and Capcom's game-specific publications give gamers. Importantly, these collections offer considerable insight into the production processes of previsualisation – the design stage in which characters are imagined, refined and modified. Interestingly, even though its final incarnation will be as pixels on screen, much of this early work is performed with comparatively low-tech tools like pencil and paper. This appeal to the customs and traditions of artistic endeavour are surely an important function of these publications and they serve to inculcate a sense of continuity and tradition. Moreover, the character and layout sketches allow readers a glimpse into the ways in which videogames are made as well as the artistic techniques and processes involved. As we will see later in this chapter, this 'before the screen' material adds to the visual lexicon from which gamers can draw, thereby enriching the range of forms and expanding the aesthetic opportunities available to them in their own productions.

In a similar vein, 'Into the Pixel' seeks to 'take art from the game to the gallery'. 'Into the Pixel' is a touring exhibition and competition that showcases and judges the work of videogame designers. Like the game-specific art books we have noted above, it is not solely focused on the finished graphical product as it appears in the game, but rather gives public access to concept art, preproduction drawings and character sketches. It is impossible to account for the degree to which 'Into the Pixel' or any particular print publication influences the production of fanart, but it is important to note that, cumulatively, they work to reveal a sense of *process* that directs the reader or exhibition patron's attentions away from what Schott and Burn (2007: 247) call the 'surface aesthetic of the digital medium' and offers both an extended palette and also routes 'into' the game through accessible modes of production.

Fanart: practice, production and community

Before we proceed with the discussion here, it is useful to clarify the definition of 'fanart' as it is used in this book. The term is often taken to refer to the production of (static) images. I use the term here to cover a range of productive activity and output including music, craft and costume, though we might also include Machinima and walkthroughs as Dovey and Kennedy (2006) do. I have chosen to deal with these last two areas separately as they involve intimate engagement with the performance-related aspects of the videogame. Rather than being a form of production that is inspired by the videogame, Machinima, for instance, takes place within the gameworld which is rendered as a creative environment while walkthroughs are intrinsically bound up with performance and the transgression of rule systems and structures through often radical play.

Turning our attentions first to the production of visual imagery, it is helpful to consider Burn's (2006b) discussion of Yaoi *Final Fantasy* artwork. Yaoi is a Japanese genre of production that is broadly equivalent to 'Slash' (see Jenkins 1992). The genre centres on male–male relationships with the emphasis on sex rather than emotional character development. Burn's discussion of the pairing of Cloud and Sephiroth, enemies in the game and recast in an erotic tryst, is interesting for a number of reasons. We will return to the idea of Yaoi/Slash later in this chapter, but here we will focus on the point of view of the art compared with the game. For Burn, this change in perspective is one of the significant transformations that is undergone in producing fanart. The videogame is characterised by its ability to create a first-person perspective that allows the player to step into the shoes of the lead character, Cloud. Fanart, by contrast, cannot achieve this.

> The adoption of the protagonist's point of view inherent in the game and easily available in language through the first-person pronoun is not available in the visual image. This then becomes an objectified view of both Cloud and Sephiroth . . .
>
> (Burn 2006b: 98)

There are two issues of significance here. First, Burn perhaps overstates the degree to which *Final Fantasy VII* operates in this first-person mode. In fact, though the game offers the opportunity to perform as Cloud in certain sequences, this is not a singular mode of engagement throughout the game nor is it accompanied visually by a first-person viewpoint. Indeed, as Burn goes on to note, a good deal of the material presented in *Final Fantasy VII* is communicated through cutscenes that offer the player no 'personal agency' through control and it is from these sequences, which differ aesthetically from the 'interactive' sections, that the majority of fanart representations are drawn. As such, the objectification we note in fanart is perhaps not so representationally removed from the experience of the game that effectively teaches players to shift between perspectives. Second, as we will see, the adoption of this point of view does not necessarily imply distance and fanart often serves as a means by which gamers may explore characters and games in more detail, bringing them into a closer, more personalised relationship. Nonetheless, the shift in viewpoint is an important one and certainly provides a means of distinguishing the production of fanart from the 'I' of fanfic.

Where fanart production is similar to fanfic, however, is in its location within the social context of a community. Indeed, many of the fansites we have noted in earlier chapters host both fiction and art, along with other creative output, and we note some instances of collaborations and cross-disciplinary pooling of writing and visual design skills in the production of comics, for instance, such as the vibrant communities creating still poses and comics in *Half-Life 2* using Garry's Mod (see HLcomic; PHWonline). Examining the fanart surrounding the *Oddworld* series, Schott and Burn (2007) term the online repositories 'interactive galleries' highlighting the very public sharing, commentary and feedback that characterise the sites. 'Here exhibitors are receiving direct and immediate reinforcement from an audience that is deeply entrenched in the visual design of the game' (Schott 2006: 145).

And just as in the fanfic communities, there is a strong imperative not only to collaborate and share outputs but also to support the collective development of skills and technique. What is particularly interesting here, though, is the reverence for the artistry, design and visual style of the game's artists. With fanfic communities, we have seen how contributions are rated in terms of their compatibility with the canon and valued as pieces of creative writing but rarely are works criticised in terms of their similarity with the original writing styles or narrative structures. In fact, in the fanfic and commentary surveyed in this research project, no mention is explicitly made of matching or even scrutinising the styles of the original canonical texts. Indeed, we have noted some grammatical and stylistic leniency at play in competitions, for instance, in order that the story be privileged. This is perhaps partly attributable to the fact that many of the texts are encountered in translation (either official or 'fanslations', see Chapter 7) and thereby lose some of their nuance (particularly if gamers' claims to a certain insensitivity in official translations are to be believed). Regardless, the reverence of the canonical artists is certainly an important feature of the fanart community and leads Schott (2006: 144, see also Schott and Burn 2007: 246) to liken the situation to the apprenticeship practices of the Italian Renaissance studio where the master-practitioners were both admired and endlessly copied. While this situation may seem to create an impressive pedagogical environment, particularly when we consider the openness and supportiveness of commentary and critique, it has a curiously limiting effect also. By holding the visual style and artistic skill of the official texts and their producers in such high regard, they have become the virtual benchmark for contributions whose creators aspire to 'industry standards' of production. It is perhaps for this reason that we note a plethora of 'tribute' contributions that seek to reproduce existing production art (see Dovey and Kennedy 2006). These submissions, which are often reworked and refined in the light of community feedback and criticisms, may encourage us to view these interactive galleries as public forums for the development and refinement of technical skills and tool use.

In some cases, however, the admiration of the studio master and industry standard practice does leads to some interesting aesthetic opportunities. The availability of the kinds of videogame artbooks that we noted at the beginning of this chapter has both given videogame fanartists considerable insight into the processes of production and opened up a range of aesthetic avenues that are more available to them. *The Art of Halo*, *Half-Life 2: Raising the Bar* and countless other game-specific titles gain much of their currency from the pre-production materials they present and their pages overflow with character designs often shown in sequences that graphically illustrate their development and mutation through the creative process. As many of these designs, mockups and sketches are rendered with pencil, pen or brush rather than in CG, they are placed within the grasp of a good many aspiring game artists. As Schott and Burn note of the *Oddworld* fanartists:

> Far from aspiring to emulate the surface aesthetic of the digital medium, the actual look of *Oddworld* fanart such as the concept drawing . . . uses a medium that proclaims several kinds of social intention simultaneously: a serious interest in the craft of the artist, a desire to penetrate the surface of the game and reach into the early stages of its production and a desire to make an original contribution to the game world.
>
> (Schott and Burn 2007: 247)

What we see here, then, is very similar to the activities of the fan writers recuperating and repairing the canon with theories and narratives that fill gaps and bridge holes. In the case of the fanartist, the endeavour is to work backwards from the final text by imaginatively creating the pre-visualisation scene or character design in the appropriate idiom and aesthetic. While the activities are different in execution, for both artist and writer the desire is to imprint oneself onto the game through these creative endeavours, insinuating oneself if only virtually, into the genesis of the development process. The focus on pre-visualisation has another effect that works in concert with the community reviewing and commentary. The revision and reworking that are an inherent part of videogame development and that are made visible and manifest in both the evolving concept drawing and the successive refinement of technique under group advice and guidance encourage the gamer to see their creative endeavours as works in progress rather than completed products.

Drawing with a purpose

It would be wrong to create the impression that videogame fanart exclusively comprises rich, playful work that is executed with consummate technical skill. Much videogame fanart, just as much fanart inspired by other media forms, is derivative and lacking in imagination. For every contribution brimming with

originality and effortless technique, there are hastily traced reproductions of publicity materials, boxart and magazine covers. This may be in part attributable
to the admiration of the master-artists and the endless recycling of their work
or may simply speak of the uneven distribution of talent throughout the community. While Schott and Burn (2007) rightly note that there is much of the
Baconian technique of reconstruction and reproduction and little risk taking
in much fanart, their assessment that there is little transgression beyond the
adoration of digital game artists over the traditional, mainstream fine art elite
is perhaps a little harsh. The production and consumption of Yaoi and slash fanart
are perhaps the most immediately obvious example of the transgressive pleasures that accompany the reframing and relocation of characters and while this
is absent from many videogame fanart sites (just as slash writing is from fanfic
sites) in accordance with their (self-imposed) ratings systems,[1] it is prevalent
among webrings and dedicated fansites. It is interesting to note that much of
the political and radical power of the slash artist or fanfic author is derived from
the heteronormativity of specific videogames. Whether dealing with issues of
gender or sexuality, fan textual production is fuelled by the possibility of transgressive readings that emerge from its own situation on the periphery:

> Take for example Kratos, protagonist of God of War 1/2. At every level
> the text works to reinforce the heterosexuality of its hero, resorting to the
> well known sex minigames to represent that. The core mechanic of the
> game, its bloody violence, and its back story similarly structure the domin-
> ant mode of playing/viewing within the terms of normative difference.
> The recuperation of Kratos as a male pin-up for queer eyes nonetheless
> persists against the grain of the games rhetoric. The pleasure comes from
> the abrasive crunch of 'reading' in opposition, and most importantly par-
> laying those readings to others so as to socialise and reinforce the pleasure
> of countercultural consumption . . . Creating games for gays impacts greatly
> on the radical potential of gaymers, since it resolves the peripheral counter
> position of the community by making it its own centre.
>
> (Surman 2007 [online])

Videogame fanart communities provide a discursive space within which issues
of personal or group significance can be worked through. As Cassell and Jenkins
(1998) among others have noted, the representation of women in videogames
has caused consternation among many gamers, commentators and critics alike
(e.g. Adams 1998; Schott and Horrel 2000; Graner-Ray 2004; Bryce *et al.* 2006).
While some produce scholarly books and articles in response and others create videogames, gamers are not often in such privileged positions. However,
as I have noted elsewhere (e.g. Newman 2004, 2005), videogame fanartists have

turned their attentions to the issue and harnessed their creative skills to address matters. In their re-imagining of Princess Peach, the perpetually-captured, archetypical damsel in distress of the Super Mario universe, fanartists draw upon an intertextual web of references and connotations (Barthes 1973). In two of the pieces of fanart submitted to the 'NintendoLand' fansite, Peach mutates first into a strong, dominant character flexing her muscles as she clenches her fist and looks mischievously into the distance, and later into an amalgam of her former self and Xena Warrior Princess. In the comments that typically accompany uploaded fanart, the artist behind 'Peach, Warrior Princess' explains her intentions and demonstrates both a clear awareness with the circulating discourses and collective intelligence and a desire to engage with and change them:

> This is a funny picture I created in response to the complaint that the Princess is a push-over. I beg to differ! The Princess was always my favorite character, and I believe she can hold her own in a fight . . . so here's the proof! Princess Peach Toadstool stands triumphant, holding Smithy's sword high above her head, as she shows she's not some helpless bimbo!!!
>
> (Owston (n.d.) [online])

It is useful to consider briefly the issue of gender in relation to gamers' textual production. Jenkins (1992) has noted that certain types of fan text are the almost exclusive preserve of women. He notes that fanfiction, in particular, is dominated by women with Slash fiction counting few if any male writers or readers among its followers. More recently (e.g. Jenkins 2007), however, Jenkins notes that the once clear divisions in gendered textual production practices are blurring somewhat. Throughout the course of this research into videogame cultures, the kinds of strict delineations observed by Jenkins and others (e.g. Brooker 2002) have not been noted with fiction, art and indeed the walkthroughs, Game Guides and FAQs that we will encounter in the following chapter, produced by both men and women alike. Just as men produce lengthy fictional treatises on *Championship Manager*, so too do women investigate the innermost workings of *Pokémon* in the most thorough and intimate manner. One area of production, however, that does remain largely a female arena is cosplay. The remit of this research has not permitted space or time to interrogate possible links between gender and genre, for instance, and it is interesting to postulate that certain areas of production traditionally noted in fan theory as female-dominated, such as fanfic authorship, have become 'acceptable' avenues for male expression in the context of specific male-dominated game fandoms like that surrounding *Championship Manager* where the overarching cultural associations are masculine and within which fic writing might be legitimised and rendered safe. However, while we await further research into these issues, it is interesting to note two

points. First, the broad observation that the kinds of art and literary production that are the subject of this chapter are not so rigidly gendered presents
game culture in a somewhat different light to other media fandoms (cf. Bacon-
Smith 1992; Jenkins 1992). Second, as we noted earlier, the degree of male and
female participation in the textual production of gaming and game-related texts
provides yet another challenge to the taken-for-granted assumption that videogames are a male-dominated cultural space.

Even where fanart does not explicitly engage with such issues in its content,
it can be politicised through its use. As a home for *Mother/Earthbound* fans eager
to find a way to urge the developers to reinstate the cancelled *Mother 64/Mother 3*
project and Nintendo to provide English language translations of the titles that
are officially available only in Japanese, Starmen.net has amassed nearly 4000 pieces
of fanart as of June 2007 (see Chapter 7 for more Starmen.net's campaign for
translation). What is fascinating about this body of work is not only that it is
created in response to games that have had troubled development histories that
have seen considerable delays to release schedules and hiatuses of many years
between titles, but that the work has been utilised as part of the project to
convince the publishers and developers to release and translate the missing games.

> The EarthBound Fans' Last Stand:
> Nintendo has ignored EarthBound fans for over a decade. It's time for us
> to make our final stand, and not with a petition. Each of us is personally
> communicating with Nintendo – sending letters, drawing artwork, and talk-
> ing with them in person, on the phone. Will they finally recognize us, or
> is this the end of the line? You, the person reading this, will help deter-
> mine the fate of MOTHER 3. You will determine whether EarthBound and
> MOTHER ever see the light of day in America (and beyond) ever again.
> (EB Siege (n.d.) [online])

The 'EB Siege' moves on from the 30,000 signature petition already delivered
to Nintendo of America to a strategy that harnesses the collective power of
gamers in innovative ways. Postcards and envelopes of various designs have been
made from both official and fanart images and are available for download from
the Starmen.net site. They are to be printed, written and sent to various Nintendo
staff whose addresses are given on the site. An automated email form will send
a message to the game's creator Shigesato Itoi. The form even includes guidance
on writing style given that Mr. Itoi is not a native English-speaker. The lavish,
limited edition 'EB Anthology' (Starmen.Net Staff 2007), a 268-page collection
of 750 pieces of fanart and discussion, is designed to demonstrate the size of
the potential audience and has been sent to a number of game journalism sites
as well as Nintendo.

In this way, the videogame fans make their political point through the weight of their numbers and by demonstrating the degree of their interest in and passion for the game. This action comes as part of a range of activities that gamers are encouraged to partake of, including downloading the first title from Nintendo Virtual Console (VC) system when it becomes available.

> So, basically, we fans have become EarthBound's last-chance marketing team. The EB Siege has been focused (and timed) precisely for two goals – to let Nintendo know that we're still alive and kicking, and to get the word out about EarthBound so that the VC downloads will be off the charts. We are already making headway on the first goal, and I think we can make the second goal happen, but only if you guys continue to support us.
>
> When EarthBound is released on the VC, download it – even if you've got a dozen copies already – and get every one of your friends to download it! It's only going to be $8, and each download will be like a vote for MOTHER 3. Start Facebook groups, send messages to people on MySpace, talk about it on your favorite gaming forum – the goal is to pique people's interest in EarthBound.

While these gamers are clearly operating from a marginalised position and the ultimate decision as to whether to reinstate development of a new Mother game and translate previous titles remains one outside their direct control, the harnessing of fan-produced resources in this way is evidence of the creativity of the community. While it may be that some of the fanart lacks the 'aura' of the unique work (Benjamin 1935), in these cases, it is its intention, use and its existence as part of a coherent body of collective creativity that lend it its power.

The sound of gaming

There is a tendency to consider videogames as a predominantly visual medium both in academic (see Aarseth 2004) and popular literature. The emphasis on the visual that we see in magazine culture where reviews and covers foreground the spectacularity of graphics is echoed in the marketing discourse especially in the current era of 'high-definition' consoles such as PlayStation 3 and Xbox 360 and serves to drown out the sound of music and effects in much discussion. Articles on videogame music are scarce and usually focus on technical issues (Clark 2001a, 2001b, 2001c) or popular histories ('Ear Candy', *360 magazine* 2006). However, just as with videogame artwork, delving into the gamer communities reveals a rich seam of scholarship. As we will learn, for many, game music is not only an artform in its own right that may be enjoyed, collected and shared with others, but is also a malleable material to play with, to remix and perform.

It is only relatively recently that a market for videogame soundtrack albums has emerged outside Japan with the release of titles such as Amon Tobin's *Splinter Cell: Chaos Theory* and Nobuo Uematsu's music from the *Final Fantasy* series (both are available through the UK iTunes Store, for instance). Scouring the catalogues of European retailers, however, yields access to only a handful of titles which typically accompany major videogame releases like those above. Some online retailers specialising in videogames, such as Play-Asia.com, go some way to remedying the situation offering a fuller range of titles from a variety of games and series. Some fansites often flout issues of copyright and make available mp3 files ripped from soundtrack CDs or sometimes directly from game. Similarly, filesharing and BitTorrent networks provide rich pickings for those less concerned about intellectual property.

More interesting, though, are projects like the 'High Voltage SID Collection' (HVSC) which is dedicated to collecting and celebrating not specific games or series, or even particular composers, but rather the sound chip of a gaming platform. The 'Sound Interface Device' or 'SID chip' as it was colloquially known, was developed in 1982 for the Commodore 64 home computer. A fairly rudimentary device, especially by today's standards, it was capable of generating only three simultaneous synthesised notes (though in some circumstances a fourth voice was available for sample playback). Despite this, SID had a reasonably complex and powerful synthesis architecture with various modulation possibilities and highly musical filters. From the mid-1980s, when musicians increasingly took over composition duties from programmers who had limited themselves to bleeps and sound effects, videogame music quickly became an important component of the overall package. During the mid to late 1980s, composers such as Rob Hubbard and Martin Galway attained a degree of celebrity and were interviewed along with game designers in magazines such as *Zzap! 64*. The passage of time has seen a move away from chip-based music as CD and DVD replaced cartridges and tapes. These formats marked a significant change in the way videogame music was handled, with an increasing reliance on licensing the music of existing artists. This is only partly a product of technical convergence, however, and also reflects the rise of companies such as Sony whose industrial integration has seen the leveraging of the music of artists signed to Sony Music for PlayStation games, for example. However, while the C64 is no longer a mainstream gaming platform, SID music lives on in the HVSC which allows Windows, Mac, Linux and other modern computer owners to (re)play C64 game music via a specialised player that interprets the original code:

The HVSC Project is an attempt to accurately archive the most popular C64 SIDs into one complete collection. The project was started in May 1996 when a few ambitious people decided to merge the many SIDs collections available on the Internet into one masterpiece. The previous SID collections contained many bugged SIDs, repeats, and inaccurate credits not to mention being highly disorganised. Thus this task was not a simple 'copy & paste' unfortunately.

('HVSC Administration' 2007 [online])

The HVSC is notable in that, like most fansites encountered in this research and as Tushnet (2007) and Burn (2006b) suggest, it is scrupulous in its assertion of copyright and ownership. Indeed, one of the most impressive facets of the HVSC is the level of care that is lavished upon it and the extraordinary attention to detail:

As we merged the collections we began to realize that many famous SIDs were missing. This led to the HVSC Crew and many others to begin searching various C64 software archives for more SIDs to rip. Due to this effort the collection began to grow at an enormous rate. As we progressed, we then noticed that many inconsistencies and questions started to surface. For example, we would find a music credited to a famous composer yet the style of the music was completely different than his normal style. One sure way of solving these mysteries was to contact the original composers. Over time we gradually tracked several of them down and received a tremendous amount of information. As you may have figured out, we are SID archeologists patiently piecing together SID history with only fragments of information.

('HVSC Administration' 2007 [online])

It is important to note that the archive is not simply a repository of music. Where possible, additional contextual material is provided, including composer photographs, details of inspirations for the pieces or trivia about their composition. This information is carefully researched and derives from interviews both old and new and magazine features, for example. The care and sensitivity of the HVSC project team and the legion of contributors who upload SIDs or information about them, are more than evident and speak of considerable dedication and seriousness. Part of the imperative appears consistent with the desire to accumulate and collect that Fiske (1992) identifies as central to fan communities. Moreover, there is a strongly nostalgic undercurrent in the discussion of the HVSC:

You may be asking yourself, "Why go through so much effort for SID music?" Only a person who never owned a C64 would ask such a question. Many people long to hear these old, classic tunes that they enjoyed in their youth.

You don't believe us? Look at the amount of Television sites that recall many a program that as a child you treasured and how much memories you get from that.

('HVSC Administration' 2007 [online])

However, the consequence of the collection is rather more complex than this. Certainly, there is a nostalgic pleasure in listening to the music, but the collection serves also as a focus around which a community can coalesce. As such, one function of the HVSC is to raise the visibility (or perhaps audibility) of C64 music, game music in general, and the work of specific composers such as Hubbard, Galway, the Follin brothers and Daglish. The result is a broader videogame music culture that incorporates a variety of activities and events that spring out of, reproduce and rework videogame music.

The 'Play! A Video Game Symphony' works in much the same way as the 'Into the Pixel' art exhibition in that it takes the products of popular culture and places them in a traditionally high culture setting. 'Play! Symphony' sees music and themes from a variety of games such as *Final Fantasy* scored for full orchestra and choir. Given the already orchestral nature and, in some cases scoring, of Nobuo Uematsu's *Final Fantasy* videogame compositions, the transformation here is more in physical than musical setting. In much the same way that Schott and Burn (2007) observe in relation to fanart, the transgressive pleasures here are partly in revering the videogame composer and placing them alongside the mainstream of contemporary elite classical music. Perhaps even more interesting, however, are the reinterpretations of the chip-based music of the C64. The original aesthetic of this music is so far removed from all but the most extreme forms of contemporary electronica or glitch-hop, and the technical limitations of the original SID chip are so severe that the transformation into live performance is a far greater creative undertaking.

In addition to 'Play! Symphony', live events such as the C64-themed 'Back In Time, Live!' concerts combine performances by original composers such as Rob Hubbard and reworkings by covers bands such as the rock outfit 'Press Play On Tape' breathing life into these 20-year-old pieces of music, resetting them in a new aesthetic and temporal frame, and manifestly adding the figure of the composer-performer into the mix. The performance scene surrounding and supporting Commodore 64 music has become a rich and varied place with much material recorded and available for posterity at 'C64Audio.com'. Given the electronic, hand-coded nature of C64 music, Hubbard, who was simultaneously composer and coder crafting melodies, harmonies and pitch bend drivers, is transformed during the live work which centres on piano arrangements. The live performance simultaneously showcases his virtuosity as a musician, rendering him the master craftsman to be admired within the community of followers and musicians alike, and imbues the tunes with a timelessness and permanence that lifts them out of their location within the specific genre of videogame music or products of the 1980s. Similarly, Richard Jacques' live solo piano performance of a number of his more recent works for various Sega games at Nottingham's 'GameCity' festival in 2006 involved not only rearrangement but also a significant improvisational element that lent the works a fluidity that allowed them to move out of the videogame and into another context.

Remixing and replaying

A number of videogame music projects exist precisely to engage in the kind of reworking and reinterpretation that is hinted at in the live performances we have noted above. 'OverClocked ReMix' is an online community that exists to collate and help support the creation of 'ReMixes' of videogame themes:

> These arrangements are more than just updated versions of the original tracks, but are reinterpretations, often in an entirely different musical genre than the source material. What sets OverClocked ReMix apart from other video game music sites is the breadth of its content. We offer music from almost any style imaginable. Hillbilly, techno, rap, orchestral—you name it—we accept ReMixes from virtually any console or computer game soundtrack. Anything from Shinobi to Katamari Damacy is fair game.
>
> ('OverClocked ReMix FAQ' 2007 [online])

The mission of the project, which was established in 1999 and is the brainchild of David Lloyd (aka 'djpretzel') recalls the archival intentions of the HVSC but combines it with a desire to promote videogame music as an artform and stimulate the production of creativity among the community:

Appreciate and honor video game composers and their music
Encourage artistic expression and development through fan arrangements
Preserve and promote video game music of the past and present
Provide resources and connections for the game composers of tomorrow
Distribute great, free music to the world

('OverClocked ReMix Mission' 2007 [online])

In part, OverClocked ReMix was created in response to the popular discourse that denigrates videogames as ephemera and the music as disposable ('Z' 2006). What it has become is a home for the creative endeavours of fan-musicians who 'ReMix' game themes. ReMix is rather misleading as it conveys little of the radical nature of the majority of the transformations and arrangements. The sheer range of genres into which game themes are repositioned reveals the play-fulness that the community revels in: bluegrass, jazz, orchestral are among the many. Like other creative communities we have seen in this book, the level of support and collaboration is striking in its range and tenderness (see Schott 2006). The forums bristle with questions and guidance on technique, song structure and musical theory. In addition, the site hosts information on the mixing and sequencing software and the use of real and virtual instruments as well as a series of comprehensive tutorials created by the community (See 'OverClocked ReMix Tutorials' 2006) that cater for experienced and new ReMixers alike. The tutorials direct would-be arrangers to sources of inspiration, as well as offer-ing tips on studiocraft and recording technique. Information, like the ReMixes themselves, is shared in the most open fashion. Similarly, the emergent 'code of practice' noted by Durack (2000) is observed here:

> I try to highlight specific things I think a ReMixer did right, and will some-times mention a particular element that I think could be improved, but the point is to give listeners a general picture of the song, some of the highlights, and some (hopefully) amusing & insightful commentary.
>
> ('OverClocked ReMix FAQ' 2007 [online])

Ultimately, OverClocked ReMix provides a means for the community to further appreciate the videogame music that its members so revere. By better under-standing the structure, instrumentation and arrangement, the music comes under the control of the ReMixer who utilises the craft and skills they have acquired and honed within the community to rework them in their own image and for the pleasure of the group. And as the knowledge is freely shared, so is the music.

Walking in Mario's shoes? Videogame costume play

'Cosplay' is among the most esoteric of fan practices, and certainly one of the least interrogated in game studies literatures, and yet is one of the most imme-diately recognisable indicators of fandom and is frequently called upon as a marker of the fan as dangerous obsessive (see Jenkins 1992). A contraction of 'costume' and 'roleplay', cosplay describes the act of dressing up as characters from popular animation, film and videogames. Moreover, while it is not an essential part of the process, and not every cosplayer possesses the requisite skill or inclination, the manufacture of original costumes is an integral part of the culture. Cosplay, then, is partly concerned with exhibition and display and partly with the craft and invention of couture. For Shen (2007: 33), the cosplayer is the epitome of the postmodern subject, 'unlike the punk youth using their body as a political claim of their uniqueness, otaku cosplay makes their body into pure signifiers of playfulness, refuting a unified identity', while Konzack (2006) draws on Jenkins (1992) and Cahill (2003) in noting that cosplay is a 'geek culture' dominated by women. We might instinctively think that cosplay offers the most undiluted means of embodying game characters, literally stepping into their shoes and taking control of them in a way that fanart, with its perspectival transformations (see Burn 2006b), renders problematic if not impossible.

Cosplay is closely linked with Japan where it remains extremely popular. It is not a static form, however, and the traditional sources of inspiration such as anime, Manga and videogames have been joined by texts such as *Lord of the Rings* and *Harry Potter*. Interestingly, as Fron *et al.* (2007: 10) note, far from being a marginal and marginalised practice, in Japan, cosplay is both popular and socially acceptable. However, as they go on to note, although cosplay is some way from achieving these levels of popularity or prevalence, it has become increasingly popular outside Japan. In the West, however, rather than being an end in itself, cosplay is more specifically located within other cultures such as science fiction fandom, for instance, and contained with their institutions (see Brooker 2002), in an often ironic and parodic manner (Richards 1997; Duchesne 2007). It is notable, for example, that Japanese cosplay is frequently consumed in public with specific places such as Tokyo's Harajuku Station or themed cosplay restaurants serving as arenas for display. European and US cosplay, however, is predominantly confined to the fan convention circuit and online forums with public display usually restricted to publicity events such as film premieres where costuming groups such as the *Star Wars*-inspired '501st' are often booked to make appearances (see 'Vader's First 501st Legion').

In relation to videogames, cosplay has some interesting parallels. Not only are videogames frequently a source of inspiration, but as Fron *et al.* (2007) note, certain gaming activities play heavily on costuming. Offline, we might explore the Live Action Role Playing (LARP) game, for example. According to the creators of the Dreamscape LARP game,

> A LARP (Live Action RolePlaying game) is a game in which players adopt the persona of a make-believe character and act out the actions of that character in a make-believe environment provided by the staff of the game.
>
> (Dreamscape (n.d.) [online])

The LARP, like English and US Civil War battle re-enactments or the living history of Historic Jamestown, provides a specific context in which costuming is acceptable and contained and places it within a playful framework of rules with winning and losing states. The costume here is not the goal though it may be admired and displayed, and may add to the atmosphere and experience of participation and performance. In a sense, the LARP game costume is a means of accessing the game; a condition for play. In addition to the 'analog dress-up' of LARP gaming, Fron *et al.* note the increasing prevalence of forms of 'digital dress-up' in online videogames:

> In the digital sphere, while massively multiplayer games tend to focus on team-based combat, players pay equal attention to clothing and fashion (often masked by the more masculine terminology of 'gear'). The design and acquisition of virtual fashion is among the most popular activities in metaverse-type social worlds, such as Second Life and There.com.
>
> (Fron *et al.* 2007: 1)

As Pearce (2006) notes, Massively Multiplayer Online Games (MMOs) such as *World of Warcraft* that allow gamers to adopt the role of tailors and armourers facilitate and even encourage the creation of in-game costume through 'productive play'. *Second Life* is yet more flexible in offering its players a far freer hand in fashioning creations for their avatars. As Fron *et al.* (2007) note, while much has been made of MMO economies centred around virtual real estate, there is a significant virtual rag trade at work dealing in accoutrements and accessories for avatars (see Chung 2005). Interestingly, drawing on Miller's (1998) work examining gendered rationalisations of cosplay, Fron *et al.* suggest that the costuming in MMOs has the potential to affect the gendering of both gameplay and cosplay:

> These findings suggest an interesting implication for digital dress up: Perhaps the conflation of the 'masculine' space of the computer, combined with the notion of 'gear' (armor and weapons) actually regenders costume play in [a] more masculine direction. What this suggests is that while costume play on computers may be creating more female-friendly play opportunities, conversely, it may also be opening up more avenues of dress-up for men.
>
> (Fron *et al.* 2007: 13)

Additionally, as Taylor (2003) has outlined, costuming is woven into the very fabric of many games. Examining the mechanics of MMOs such as *EverQuest*, Taylor draws attention to the way in which the complexity and even amount of costume are used as a marker of success and competence. As they progress through the game, the new levels of achievement and character development are visually reinforced by the acquisition of new armour, for instance. Here then, game and costume are inexorably stitched together. Interestingly, despite this close-knit relationship between performance, game system and costume that might encourage us to at least partly understand MMOs as exercises in (virtual) cosplay, what is particularly interesting about videogame cosplay offline ('analog cosplay') is that it is typically decoupled from the gaming imperative. In this way, despite the interactivity and playfulness of the originating medium, videogame cosplay closely resembles that which surrounds anime and Manga, for example.

Websites such as 'Cosplay.com' and 'Cosplay UK' clearly illustrate the ways in which videogame cosplay is seamless located within the wider cultures of anime and Manga costuming and conventions and events typically bring together cosplayers from across the spectrum. Importantly, while sci-fi and anime conventions remain an important locus for cosplayers and are well documented online in Flickr albums and galleries, cosplay websites like those above are more than information portals and have become a vital part of the exhibition and performance in themselves.

Like the fanart and fanfic hubs we have seen earlier, cosplay sites frequently become the homes of virtual communities whose collective intelligence is developed through forums, tutorials and support. Advice ranges from craft technique through to assessments of facial and bodily similarity to ascertain fruitful cosplay opportunities. Interestingly, a number of forum posts to 'Cosplay UK' centre on body shape. The accentuated limb lengths of certain game characters drawn in the anime style and the potential indecency of their costumes raise theoretical and practical questions around cultural differences in attitudes to body image and the representations of gender, for example. Cosplayers seek reassurance from the community about the appropriateness of their modifications demonstrating the existence and importance of a shared sense of authenticity that arises through collaboration and discussion. The authentic is formed in the dialogue between the externally verifiable character design (with many sites posting screenshots to help costume-makers) and the community's agreed practices (e.g. 'Would it look okay if I lengthened FFVIII Selphie's dress?' 'Kazephyr' 2007). For those unable to create their own costumes, it is possible to commission others to create pieces. 'Commissioners' as they are known, often specialise in specific aspects of the process such as weaponry or armour as well as more traditional tailoring crafts. In a manner similar to that noted by Fron *et al.* (2007) in MMOs, there is a considerable trade in the cosplay community. This is partly a consequence of the closeness of the community and its foundation on collaboration and partly because, as a number of posters on the Cosplay.com forums suggest, complications surrounding licensing and copyright arrangements mean that commercially available costumes are a rarity. The presentation of sample costumes and paraphernalia makes for fascinating viewing and draws attention to the two worlds that cosplay straddles. Amethyst-Angel's exquisite recreation of Link's tunic from *The Legend of Zelda: Twilight Princess* videogame is clearly the product of an immense amount of work, created with tireless attention to detail and scrutiny of reference shots. It is photographed on a mannequin in a resolutely domestic setting far removed from Hyrule, however, and beneath the former Hero of Time's battle-ready garb, on a tea-tray, sit the cat's water and food bowls.

In fact, in speaking of the tension between the real and the virtual, the online and offline, this image of Link's tunic highlights one of the more interesting aspects of videogame cosplay. Mitchell and Clarke (2003: 341), see the problem arising from

> [the] two opposing notions of 'realness' at play in these works. The cosplay artist tries to look as similar as they can to the original character, but this is impossible when the original is a character from a cartoon or a videogame: the more real their costume looks, the more the realness of the person in the costume stands out as the jarring element.
>
> (Mitchell and Clarke 2003: 341)

Nowhere is this clearer than in the digital montages that cosplayers create to demonstrate their indistinguishability from the original game characters upon which they model themselves. By using digital image manipulation software, collages combine carefully posed cosplay displays with in-game screengrabs of the characters. The montages are usually created by graphics experts from within the community and serve to exhibit the cosplay artist's work within the group and beyond. To some extent, they fulfil some of the role of a convention allowing the work to be seen. However, they also bring the presentation of the costume more tightly under the control of the cosplayer as poses may be chosen and assembled as part of the decisive image. At CosplayLab.com, the digital montages are also rated in competitions (see 'CosplayLab Look-alike Contest Winners'). Yet, while the intention of the imagery is clearly to render the game and gamer, the character and the cosplayer, indissoluble, they perhaps serve to highlight the insurmountable gulf between them.

However, not all cosplaying centres on direct comparison with the virtual original and the distinction between the 'realness' of the person and costume is not necessarily jarring. Indeed, we might view Amethyst-Angel's photography of work-in-progress, the reportage from conventions that sees the intermingling of cosplayers of different games (and not only games), or the cast of *Katamari Damacy* kicking back in a chic boutique hotel lobby (see the front cover of the paperback edition of this book) as an opportunity to further explore these characters outside of the familiarity of their game settings thereby breathing more life into them. We get only the briefest glimpse of Link's house in *The Legend of Zelda* series which instead centres largely on the extremity and excitement of swordplay and world-saving quests, yet he must have a another, more domestic side. Even a hero must hang up their tunic and feed the cat from time to time. Similarly, while the Prince of All Cosmos is only seen hard at work attempting to roll up junk to make stars in Keita Takahashi's cult gameworld, it is reassuring to learn that he is allowed some time off to relax about town. These cosplay scenes remind us not only of the comparatively limited presentation of game characters but also of the rounded lives of the players that embody them. In this vein, we might contrast the digital montages that invite direct, side-by-side comparison of the real and virtual with Mandy Nader's cosplaying of Link from *The Legend of Zelda* series which locates the 'realness' of the costume in a carefully selected and equally real environment emulating the virtual landscape of the *Zelda* gameworld (see the back cover of the paperback edition of this book). By taking control of the way in which the performance is recorded as well fusing character and location into a more comprehensive simulation, Nader's vignette moves beyond replication. Far from inviting direct comparison, Nader's liminal *The Legend of Zelda* scenes deliberately play with the boundaries of the real and the virtual and while attention to detail is still clearly prized in the costume creation process, the imperative to directly compare and contrast is not paramount. Rather, these scenes speak of the desire for ownership of these characters and the embeddedness of virtual personae in the real lives of (cos)players.

What is particularly interesting about cosplay is that, despite the inference in its name, it does not typically involve role-playing. Unlike the LARP gamer, the cosplayer does not usually seek to perform the extravagant in-game actions of the character. To some extent, as Fuller and Jenkins (1995), Newman (2002a; 2004) and Aarseth (2004) have noted, by presenting a complex suite of capacities and capabilities, the videogame character as 'gameplay cursor' already offers the gamer an opportunity for spectacular performance. Indeed, we might be initially tempted to think that because it apparently concentrates on the visible surfaces and contours of game characters and disconnects them from the actions and capabilities that are the defining qualities of gameplay, cosplay disallows the embodying or deep exploration of videogame characters. However, much cosplay seems better understood as being enmeshed within a process of recontextualisation that derives pleasure and makes meaning from the interplay between the different types of 'realness' that Mitchell and Clarke (2003) note. Importantly, the practice of cosplay is entertaining and meaningful both for the cosplayers engaged in the manufacture and performance of costume and vignettes and for their audiences who are treated to displays of inventiveness and ingenuity. Above all, as the images on the cover of this book illustrate, cosplay's playful fusing, synthesis or even juxtaposition of the real and the virtual present a rich site within which the extraordinary characters of videogames may be lived and seen in the most ordinary of places and situations.

In the next section of this book, we will move from responses to the videogame as a representational system and consider the ways in which the configurative performances of gameplay are, themselves, rendered malleable materials to be played with.

Part 2

Videogames as configurative performances

Chapter 5

Game Guides, walkthroughs and FAQs

Frequently Asked Questions about walkthroughs

Within the gamer and development communities, 'walkthroughs' are among the most contentious of all gaming texts. This might seem peculiar as there is nothing in these innocuous looking books or the myriad text files distributed online to match the deliberate transgression or overtly political motivations of Yaoi or slash art and fiction, for instance (see Burn 2006b). Similarly, walkthroughs do not encourage or inform gamers how to perpetrate illegal acts of copyright infringement or Intellectual Property theft. In fact, for Mia Consalvo (2003a), walkthroughs may be thought of as 'virtual tour guides' that help gamers towards success. Although they are actually a good deal more complex and varied in their aspirations and intentions, at the simplest possible level, walkthroughs may be understood as texts that offer advice and guidance on completing specific videogames. They provide accounts of the journeys through videogames, detailing their spaces, explaining the solutions to their puzzles and laying bare their intricacies. As I have noted elsewhere, walkthroughs offer narrativised, egocentric accounts of the ways of tackling the game. They present a relational space similar to a pirate's treasure map (take ten paces forward, you will come to a rock, take three paces left . . .) that indicate the ways in which, for example, secret areas may be uncovered (Newman 2005: 57).

In some senses, walkthroughs can be viewed as the formalisation of the water-cooler talk and sharing of hints, strategies and tactics that we observed in Chapter 2. Yet, walkthroughs polarise opinion and discussion of them, their use and even their existence strike to the very core of game design and the pleasures of gameplay. As we shall learn, for some gamers, walkthroughs are indicative of no less than inadequate games:

> [They] help you when the game design is poor such that you get stuck somewhere. I think in a perfectly designed game you would never even consider

looking at the FAQ [Frequently Asked Questions] or walkthrough because you'd never get stuck. It would find a way to subtly lead you where you need to be led such that you felt you were always making progress and you were the one figuring everything out.

(Tavares 2004: 265)

Game designers often design games to please 'hardcore gamers' or worse, reviewers – who are not generally considered 'the mass-market.' They are a select few who are able to complete any game, no matter how difficult and solve any puzzle, no matter how arcane. Most people, however, can play the first level or two . . . and then they get stuck . . . and risk losing patience with the game and putting it back in its box out of frustration. And it's for those people that walkthroughs and FAQ's are ideal. If it helps them along in the difficult spots a little so that they don't get so frustrated as to quit the game entirely, then that's a good thing. They might enjoy the next level or two, even if they can't (for instance) rescue the girl in ICO cos the monster keeps coming from the black hole in the ground and dragging her down into it.

(San 2004: 261)

Veteran videogame designer Noah Falstein (2004: 264) hints at a commercial imperative in noting that the publication of walkthroughs in 'Official Strategy Guides' has become part of the wider business of financially exploiting a game or franchise. Scott Rubin concurs:

As of late there has been a strategy among game developers that is becoming more and more obvious. In certain video games there will be secrets, bonuses, treasures or other things that are unknown to the player. No information regarding these things is placed inside the game. No amount of deductive logic and reasoning will result in the player discovering these things. The only possibilities are if the player tries every possible combination of inputs into the game in hopes of discovering something secret. I believe these arbitrary secrets are put into video games on purpose by developers. Finding these secrets is only a matter of knowing or not knowing. The easiest, and sometimes only way, to become someone who knows is to read the strategy guide.

(Rubin 2004: 260–261)

Yet others point the finger at the gamer whose impatience or lack of skill sends them running to the solution the moment the going gets tough. If the pleasure of videogame play is to be found in the search to find strategies to combat the complexities and ingenuity of the game's puzzles, then walkthroughs undermine the game structure. Moreover, they speak of gamers as misguided and self-deluding at best, fooling themselves that their progress has been earned (e.g. Livingstone 2004: 267), or worst of all, as cheats. Of course, this assertion rests on a particular, and quite partial, view of the pleasures of gameplay.

This chapter seeks to explore walkthroughs and the larger 'game guides' that usually contain them in relation to the configurative performances of play. These rich and multifaceted texts perform a variety of interrelated functions. They record playing styles, encourage the adoption of new styles of engagement, and perhaps even seek to regulate the way videogames are played. It follows, therefore, that the goals of this chapter are similarly varied. Part of my aim here is to illustrate the ways in which walkthroughs and game guides can help us shed light on the range of available pleasures that can be derived from videogames. For some gamers, at least part of the pleasure of the videogame is found in the transformation of their play into the walkthrough and the formalisation of their knowledge and expertise into a guide for other gamers. As such, the walkthrough and guide are interesting texts in and of themselves and deserve scrutiny. But there is more at stake here. Clearly, not all gamers produce walkthroughs or guides and so the pleasures of creating them are experienced by only a subset of gamers. Accordingly, it is essential to consider how walkthroughs and guides are used by gamers to support their particular interests and approaches to gameplay and how the variety of playing styles is recorded and codified within the game guide or walkthrough text itself. By studying these texts, it is my contention that we can reveal much about the mutability and openness of the videogame as a form and its capacity to support different, often radical, performances or 'playings'. Finally, perhaps more than any of the texts we have encountered so far in this book, walkthroughs and game guides are texts located within social contexts and it is important to understand both their production and consumption in these terms. Walkthroughs and game guides are squarely situated within the community of fellow walkthrough writers and a constituency of gamers whose love of and interest in these games motivate the production, sharing and development of the texts and the sustenance of titles superseded by the marketplace (see Chapter 1).

Given the prevalence of walkthroughs and game guides and their contentiousness among gamers and developers alike, it is a little surprising to note that there have been few extant scholarly studies of these texts (see Consalvo 2003a; Newman 2005; Burn 2006b). Moreover, as we shall see in the next section, there is considerable room for confusion as the terminology in gamer, developer and academic parlance is far from precise. Before commencing our discussion of the production and use of walkthroughs and game guides, it is useful to clarify some of the terms of reference.

Walkthroughs, cheats, FAQs, Strategy Guides, and Game Guides: the language of gameplay

As we have seen, the term 'walkthrough' is bound up in a diverse range of discussions ranging from cheating, game design and marketing to the videogames industry's exploitation of Intellectual Property. To compound matters, the term is used in a slippery and imprecise manner. 'Walkthrough' might refer to an 'Official Strategy Guide', a lavish, full-colour book released alongside the game, produced in close collaboration with the videogame developer and taking advantage of access to the game code, artwork and development team during the production process. Yet 'walkthrough' might equally refer to a text-only file uploaded to a videogame fansite by a gamer who has assembled copious details and insights from their sustained and dedicated play and replay.

In fact, in most cases both uses of the term are strictly inaccurate, or at least only partially accurate. As I have intimated already, the 'walkthrough' is usually just one part of a much larger text. The Official Strategy Guide noted above will doubtless include a walkthrough section, but will also contain a host of other materials as Consalvo (2003a) correctly notes. Official Strategy Guides are highly visual texts. Instructions are relayed through short textual descriptions that make extensive reference to image annotations and captions. In addition, many Strategy Guides further embellish the package by interspersing production art or even posters and postcards (e.g. Hodgson *et al.* (2002) *Super Mario Sunshine: Prima's Official Strategy Guide*). These extras make the Strategy Guide something of a memento or souvenir of the game much like the art books we noted in Chapter 4 (e.g. Trautman 2004; Valve 2004) and they are often sold in reduced-cost 'bundles' with the videogame at retail. Similarly, while the many thousands of gamer-produced texts hosted at GameFAQs.com might be colloquially termed 'walkthroughs' by authors and readers alike, most strictly fall into the categories of 'FAQ' or 'Game Guide'. Like the Official Strategy Guide, the Game Guide will inevitably include a walkthrough but this will usually constitute only a part of the total material on offer, while the FAQ serves a wholly different purpose and is structured and written quite differently as we shall see below. In order to paint a more nuanced picture, it is essential to disentangle these different texts and components and expose the variety of motivations and contexts for their production and consumption.

In this short section, we will begin to explore some of the distinctiveness of walkthroughs and the ways in which they differ from the 'cheats' and 'FAQs' they are often conflated with. Furthermore, we will note the importance of analysing walkthroughs as parts of larger texts as we note often contrasting imperatives on display where different materials rub against each other and suggest markedly different approaches to gameplay.

Within videogaming parlance, 'cheats' tend to refer to exploits that alter the fabric of the game mechanic or ruleset. This may involve entering codes, performing combination sequences of button presses, or even utilising external devices to modify the code of the game program. As such, cheats may be considered to fall into at least two categories. The first are 'authorised' by the game developers and are enabled from within the game though, as Consalvo (2007) notes, the notion of 'cheating' here is problematic given that the tools are provided within the game itself. Codes unlocking gameplay modes that bestow invincibility or the ability to see and walk through walls may be built into the game and are available to all who know the code. Codes are rarely deducible though there is some referentiality with cheat code combinations such as Konami's 'up, up, down, down, left, right, left, right, B, A, Start' sequence or the *Colossal Cave Adventure* 'xyzzy' reused and recycled. The use of devices such as the multiplatform 'Action Replay' or 'GameShark' cartridges give rise to other, often unintended options. These unauthorised cheats, that is those that have not been programmed into the game's mechanic, arise from manipulating data registers. While successful and useful codes are published, the use of these devices is often a matter of playful experimentation and the results are often unpredictable. Some videogame software has the facility to search for likely cheat modes by 'watching' certain data registers for predictable changes to ascertain life counters or energy meters that deplete when lives are lost or the character suffers an injury. These registers may then be modified and exploited to increase or maximise them. We will return to the subject of 'codemining' in Chapter 7. Here, though, it is useful to distinguish these material changes to the videogame's underlying code, whether sanctioned by the developer or not, from ascertaining and using solutions, hints and guidance which, by and large, do not require the rules of the game to be altered or circumvented. Even though some may consider the use of walkthroughs 'cheating', the videogame 'cheat' has a very specific meaning that differentiates it from learning techniques or the solutions to puzzles. Importantly, even when a solution is known, its performance and execution remain a challenge for the gamer. The use of a 'cheat', however, typically alters the fundamental terms of the engagement with the game in a more drastic manner rendering a puzzle meaningless because it is simply circumvented by the acquisition of infinite energy or invisibility, for instance (Newman 2005; see also Consalvo 2003a). In the case of *Animal Crossing*, items and objects that have to be earned through work and toil in the game, can be freely acquired and accessed by entering codes that are compiled and distributed on websites and in some game guides. The advent of downloadable 'game saves' adds a further opportunity to sidestep the performative demands of the game. By downloading the save state of another more able or proficient gamer, for instance, access to sequences, levels and characters that would be otherwise impossible is afforded.

Closely allied to walkthroughs, FAQs (Frequently Asked Questions) are a common feature of videogame community sites and seek to address the kinds of issues and, in some cases problems, that gamers are likely to encounter in their play. Written by well-versed gamers for the benefit of those less able, and often assembled as collaborative works that pool and codify the collective knowledge, FAQs often deal in factual information such as the location of specific objects or the relative skills and weaknesses of characters. 'Boss FAQs' are particularly common and detail the strategies and techniques required to tackle and defeat the end-of-level characters that are a stock-in-trade of videogames. By focusing on the Bosses alone, these FAQs omit any discussion of the remainder of the game, the sequences that lead up to and proceed from the discrete moments of these climactic encounters. As fits their disconnectedness and specificity, FAQs are typically structured as unordered lists of questions and answers that are not usually connected and certainly not narrativised. Where walkthroughs differ from FAQs, then, is in the breadth of their coverage and in their presentation of a narrativised account that leads the reader through each step of the game as a continuous journey rather than isolating specific moments of gameplay for scrutiny. As Consalvo rightly notes:

> Walkthroughs are detailed guides to how a player should play a game sequentially to find all of the hidden bonuses and surprises, how to avoid certain death, and how to advance past difficult puzzles or trouble spots to best play and win the game.
>
> (Consalvo 2003a: 327–328)

Ultimately, although it is possible to identify clear differences between 'walkthroughs', 'cheats' and 'FAQs', we can perhaps explain some of the confusion and slippage in the use of the terms by noting that, in fact, all of these materials may be contained within the Official Strategy Guide or gamer-produced Game Guide. As such, while walkthroughs are distinctive in presenting a 'virtual tour guide' (ibid.) or 'relational map' (Newman 2005), that seeks to ease the gamer's progress towards completion, they are typically encountered within the context of other materials written in different modes and that address and encourage different types of play. Importantly, these various types of play might be more concerned with digression than progression, for example and, as such, we must be careful to recognise the specificity of the 'walkthrough' as a particular type of writing that is most usually contained within larger texts comprising diverse writings that address and appeal to a wider range of gameplay and performance possibilities.

The focus of the remainder of this chapter is on the Game Guides produced by gamers which necessarily brings us into contact with walkthroughs among other writings concerned with describing, shaping and modifying the performances of play. We will leave aside Official Strategy Guides for a number of reasons. First, the intimacy of the relationship between the professional Strategy Guide writers and the development teams and videogame publishers means that the insights and materials contained in their glossy pages are arrived at not through play and replay but by reference to design documentation. As such, they do not replicate the deductive and experimental working patterns of gamers learning through experience and observation. Second, Official Strategy Guides do not tend to mine games with the same forensic levels of detail as gamers often do in their guides. This may well be a further consequence of the close relationship between official Strategy Guide publishers and the developers and publishers of the games. For example, while a range of materials encourage players to explore and replay the game many times over, the inclusion of a checklist that details all of the available 'Shine Sprites' in *Super Mario Sunshine*, Prima's Official Guide encourages the gamer to consider their ultimate acquisition as the conclusion of the game. The final tick brings closure, completion and thereby may be seen to speak the language of supersession by moving the focus from the present and onto the (purchase of the) next game. As we shall see, Game Guides frequently serve to lengthen the engagement with a given videogame far beyond the exhaustion of the 'official' modes of play and challenge the notion of 'completion'.

We will begin our discussion with an examination of the structure and coverage of Game Guides including an analysis of walkthroughs before considering what the production and consumption of guides can teach us about videogames, community and the pleasures of gameplay.

The anatomy of a Game Guide

In the following sections, we will explore some of the key features of Game Guides ranging from the evolutionary nature of their production through to the interplay between walkthroughs centring on completion and the discussion of sidequests, trading sequences and the designation of new challenges that privilege exploration and extend the game beyond the narrative conclusion.

Changelog: recursion, iteration and fine-tuning

Even a quick scan of the version history of a Game Guide ably illustrates the immense amount of effort, time and care that is lavished upon these creations. As Consalvo notes:

> Most of these walkthroughs are dozens of pages in length, with minute levels of detail included. Gamers must play a game multiple times to find and record all of this information, and then must spend additional time writing and

organizing it for presentation on a web page. Although results can vary by fan, the level of work involved and the dedication to the activity, which is usually not paid, can be tremendous.

(Consalvo 2003a: 329)

It is clear that Game Guide authors take their work extremely seriously. MrShotgun offers the reader some thoughts on the task and responsibility of documenting *The Legend of Zelda: Twilight Princess*.

Author's Pledge
When Richard Taylor of New Zealand's Weta Workshop undertook the monumental task of the production design for the Lord of the Rings films, he gave this speech to his employees. Recognizing the significance of this speech, I have adopted it as my own pledge to the quality of my guides. God, I'm a nerd.

'If you can't rise to the highest level of enthusiasm, passion, and professionalism, and grasp this task as if it is the most important thing that you have ever taken on in your life, you aren't worthy of the task. We have been blessed with this opportunity.' – Richard Taylor, Weta Workshop.

('MrShotgun' 2007 [online])

Of course, not all Game Guides are alike. The overwhelming majority of Game Games, walkthroughs and FAQs are assembled by gamers passionate about the game. We need only glance at the 'Credits' section in most Guides to see the most heartfelt sincerity reserved for the developers of the game in question (see below). Mochan's *Evil Summoner*, on the other hand, guide draws attention to the myriad flaws and weaknesses in the game and the various ways of exploiting them. In contrast with the celebratory tone of most guides, *The Evil Summoner 'How to Be a Cheap Ass'* takes a rather more critical, if not downright scathing, tone:

Most people write FAQs for games they love and worship and adore above all else. However, being unlike everyone else, I have taken it upon myself to write this FAQ with the sole intention of utterly trashing Summoner because I totally hate the game. And therein is the answer: this FAQ is "evil" because it is based on hate, hate for the piece of trash called "Summoner!"

(Mochan 2001 [online])

Evil Summoner notwithstanding, Game Guides are usually the products of both passion and commitment. Darkfury3827's (2006) *The Legend of Zelda: Twilight Princess Full Walkthrough/In-Depth Guide* lists no fewer than thirteen updated versions, though this counts only those iterations uploaded to GameFAQs.com. The version numbering makes it clear that between the first and last posted version, many more minor fine tunings have been undertaken. Similarly, Apathetic Aardvark's (2007) *Final Fantasy VII: Complete Game Walkthrough* that was first posted 20 July 2003 is still being updated some four years later. That there are still substantive additions and updates to be made to these texts after this much time and attention has already been offered to them speaks of the depth and complexity of videogames such as *Twilight Princess* and *Final Fantasy VII*. However, it is also a clear indication of the extraordinary ambition of the authors of these Game Guides. There is a palpable desire to create the most complete Guide and the notes on updates list the minutiae of errors, corrections and newly unearthed facets of the game.

Just like 'betareading', the discussion of the version history alludes to software production practices. The carefully numbered versions in the changelog replete with descriptions of the key features of the update speak of the developmental nature of these writing projects that equates the practice with the creation of the game itself and draw explicit parallels between the recursivity of software development and the processes of documenting play. Moreover, unlike the Official Strategy Guides that are frequently created during development and released alongside the game they describe, the change history of a Game Guide reflects the acquisition of knowledge and understanding through play and replay. Without the privileged access to design documents, for the gamer, the principal means of interrogating the game, its system and demands, is observation and performance. Strategies are devised, tested and evaluated through play and findings are collated and evaluated. As we shall see later, it is common to find that the practices of gameplay observation and analysis are collaborative and draw upon the collective resource of a community of gamers experimenting with play.

Make it plain

As we have noted, the Game Guide typically comprises a range of materials and, while there is no accepted proforma or even a style guide for their production and implementation, a number of conventions and practices have emerged. First, Game Guides are produced in plain text. In an age of rich multimedia and given that the principal distribution channel for these Guides is the web where PDFs, jpegs and Flash movies are *de rigueur* among other gaming sites, hubs such as GameFAQs.com host many thousands of fixed-width, 80-column text files that, in format at least, belong to a different era. It is here we note another contradiction in Game Guides. While they describe and document some of the most inventive and imaginative uses of computing technology, they do so in a resolutely old-fashioned manner. Given that the principal delivery channel for these Guides is the web, it is natural to ponder why even basic markup functionality such as internal hyperlinks to facilitate navigation through the document, for instance, is not included. However, the use of plain text is a not simply affected retro chic. The use of .txt files and fixed-width typefaces serves a number of important purposes. Most obviously, plain text brings the broadest compatibility with web browsers and operating systems. However, this is the least significant reason. Plain text offers both functional and aesthetic advantages. The use of fixed-width typefaces such as courier enables non-textual representation by creating a virtual alignment grid within which alphanumeric and punctuation characters can be placed. 'ASCII art' makes it possible for authors and artists to illustrate their works in a highly efficient manner. Artwork may include game or series logos that typically precede the Guide and act as a title page or maps and dungeon plans that illustrate pathways or the locations of objects, for example:

```
                         The Blocks are arranged as per the diagram on the
      +-+-+              left with coloured blocks being the four chests and
      |E|F|              enclosed blocks with letters inside being the blocks.
    +++-+-+++            What you have to do is push block B down, then block
    +++   +++            F down, then block E left, then block D down, then
  +-+++-+ +++-+          block C left then block J down and then block I left.
  |B|C|D| |I|J|          This should set it up so you can now open every
 +++-+-+-+-+-+++         single chest to acquire 20 RUPEES, 20 RUPEES,
  +++      |G|H| +++     20 RUPEES and of course 20 RUPEES. Leave this
 +-+++     +-+-+ +++-+   house and make your way down to the middle area where
 |A|               |K|   you will find a man sitting on the ground beside some
 +-+               +-+   pots, he'll offer to sell you an MAGIC BOTTLE for the…
```
(AIex 2007 [online])

Additionally, the use of plain text allows Guides to be easily searched. While walk-throughs and Guides are rigorously well structured, they remain potentially unwieldy texts by virtue of their scope and extent. Indeed, to assist their readers, many authors include advice on how to effectively search for particular details in what are very often documents of many tens of thousands of words. Variations abound that differ in their syntax, but Dark Angel's system is typical:

```
HOW TO USE QUICK FIND
Each section has a quick find in the []'s. Press Control and F and
type in the letters in the []'s and press Enter to find that certain
section. This is so you don't have scroll through the entire
document looking for the right section.

CONTENTS
1. History
2. Character Bios [CHB]
3. Limit Breaks [LIB]
4. Walkthrough [WLK]

DISC 1 [DSC1]
- 1.1 Mako Power Plant [PP1]
- 1.2 Midgar City [MDG1]
```

(Dark Angel 2003 [online])

With twenty-two sections in total and some with as many as twenty-seven sub-sections, both the size of the Guide and the need for a means of accessing its secrets are clear. As we shall see later in the chapter, the Guide is usually completed with a Credits section that offers thanks and acknowledgement to the various contributors whose collective knowledge and intelligence helped compile the Guide. We will return to this clear signalling of the location of the Guide in its social context later. What is essential to note here, however, is that the bare aesthetic and uncompromisingly antiquated format of the Game Guide is one of its most striking features and certainly sets it apart from the visually resplendent Official Strategy Guides. Without doubt, the use of plain text has an aesthetic function to play also. While Game Guides are extensive, even exhaustive, documents, the absence of extraneous embellishment speaks of their, and their authors', seriousness, focus and unerring commitment to documenting the game. More than this, however, we might equate the austerity and economy of this mode of presentation with the bare, stripped-down approach to the game that typifies the majority of writing in Game Guides.

It is worth noting here that recently, we have begun to note the availability of full video walkthroughs that audiovisually capture a successful performance that can be reviewed for tips on strategy and technique. Still a comparative rarity, sites such as stuckgamer.com host a growing number of audiovisual guides, some of which show a playthrough of the entire game, while others focus on key moments such as Bosses. What is notable about these videos is that because they generally comprise raw footage from the PC or console with little or no critical commentary, context or explanation they make for interesting and entertaining viewing but their ability to communicate the nuanced advice and guidance that we see in text-based Game Guides, or to explain the consequences of actions or the path *not* chosen, is considerably limited.

The walkthrough: writing as 'reverse engineering'

In one of the few scholarly studies of videogame walkthroughs, Andrew Burn (2006b) discusses the work of Kao Megura (2000) whose two-part *Final Fantasy VII* 'complete walkthrough' is a lengthy and extraordinarily thorough account of Squaresoft's seminal PlayStation RPG. Burn draws our attentions to a number of features of the work but here, we will focus on two in particular: the mode of address and voice in which the piece is written, and the exclusive focus on the demand system of the game.

If we recall our earlier discussion of the production of videogame art, we noted there the presence of a transformation that shifted the first-person viewpoint of the gameplay to the third-person of the artist-observer. Similarly, we commented on the impossibility of cosplay to provide a means of accessing anything but the surface contours of the game character. The walkthrough text, however, is a rather different proposition. The voice and point of view of the writing unequivocally position the gamer/reader and their character as one and the same. Examining Megura's work, Burn notes the exclusive use of the second person which places the reader at the heart of the action:

> Once you leave the train, check the body of the closest guard twice to get two Potions. Then head north. You'll be attacked by some guards. Take them out with your sword (you may win a Potion for killing them) and then move left to go outside.
>
> (Megura 2000, cited in Burn 2006b: 90)

Consalvo (2003a) notes a similar process at work though in her study of *The Legend of Zelda* walkthroughs she observes a slippage between the second and third person. However, as she notes, this interchangeability actually serves to draw 'you' and 'Link' closer together confirming the identification felt during gameplay and reproducing the gaming relationship between gamer and character in the text. Like many contemporary 3D games, *Zelda* makes use of a shifting point-of-view that moves between first, second and third person perspectives. In this way, the walkthrough mimics the dynamism of the game's representation and subject positions.

However, there is more to this assimilation of character and gamer into the synonymy of 'you' than a replication of the experience of play. As Burn suggests, the incessant second person address (or even shifting second/third person of Consalvo's walkthroughs) creates a text that operates in the 'imperative mood'. As we can see from the brief extract above, Megura's text does not suggest but rather orders the gamer to follow the instructions. There is no latitude offered here. Indeed, as Carr *et al.* (2006) have noted, there is a cautionary tone present in most walkthrough writing. The walkthrough author urges the gamer to exercise vigilance and to be aware of the full extent and range of the attacks and surprises they may be subjected to. Carr *et al.* explain the presence of this monitory mode in terms of the prevalence of ambushes in videogames. With the surprise such a common trope in game design, the walkthrough author's task is at least partly concerned with forewarning the unsuspecting gamer of the danger that lurks in every shadow and around every corner so that guns may be loaded in readiness. There is a palpable voracity and non-negotiability of the imperatives offered in the walkthrough. Megura does not guide or benignly assist but rather adopts what Burn terms the 'regulatory mode' described by Halliday (1970). As such, the walkthrough may be read as a vehicle through which the author implicitly seeks to take control of and normalise the gameplay of the reader/gamer. We shall return to the idea of regulation later in this chapter and consider the ways in which other aspects of the Game Guide might contrast with this attempt at containment.

Here, however, it is useful to note that Megura's text reveals another important facet of the walkthrough. *Final Fantasy VII* is notable and lauded for the complexity of its narrative, the maturity of its characterisations and richness of its character development. However, none of this is evident in the walkthrough. Indeed, there is no discussion of the representational system at all, no analysis of the importance or contribution of music and sound effects, no consideration of dialogue, no comment on the visual shifts into cutscenes, for example. According to Burn's reading, the walkthrough strips away all of this in favour of a single-minded focus on the game system and its procedural demands. Where fanfiction, fanart and cosplay principally concern themselves with the surfaces and textures of videogames as representational systems, the walkthrough disregards this in favour of an almost myopic focus on the demands and requirements, the mechanics and systems of the game as simulation. The resultant text, according to Burn, is 'a technical, dispassionate text' (2006b: 91) that comprises a 'stripped down, efficient sequence of commands that gets the player through the game' (ibid.: 92). It is important to note, however, that while the text itself may appear bare, its creation stands as a testament to the passion of its author(s) as we have noted above.

Importantly, the use of fixed-width, plain-text ASCII files may be seen to have an additional resonance here. The austerity of walkthrough presentation underlines the clarity of intention and creates a document with a clear and unambiguous aesthetic that eschews discussion of audiovisual representation just as it tolerates only the most basic of visual embellishments and illustrations in its pages. The allusions to computer programming that we noted in the version history of the changelog combine with this mimicry of computer printouts, console terminals and the procedures of debugging to create a text in which emotional response is suppressed and subsumed by the machine-like sequence of commands that, if successfully executed, will bring success. In a sense, we can view the walkthrough as a program in itself, or perhaps more accurately a decompiled account of the game program. Each instruction in the walkthrough engages with and responds to an element in the game's simulation. Translating from the assembly code or high level language of the machine into a form intelligible by gamers, the walkthrough author is essentially a reverse engineer. Working without official documentation of the program code (unlike the authors of Official Strategy Guides) and trying to understand the videogame's functions and functionality through play, replay, observation and analysis, the walkthrough author's findings are documented in these evolving works that chart their explorations and successes. To finally beat the game here is to understand and expose its innermost workings. Whether the bits and bytes align to form an emotionally heart-rending experience on the screen is quite inconsequential as the simulation is irreducible. Regardless of the manner of their audiovisual representation, puzzles, decisions and narrative branches may be quite adequately captured as matters of logic, inputs and outputs and causation, while places and people are readily reduced to symbolic ASCII characters, machine-readable and easily searchable.[1] Walkthroughs then are concerned with process and progress. They are living documentation of the author's ability to decode the game and are sequential accounts that lead the reader step by step from start to finish, collapsing the narrative and representation system of the game into a series of events, episodes and moments that make demands on the gamer. It is important to remember, however, that even though they may be armed with the knowledge to respond to game system's demands, the gamer is still required to perform and enact the strategies so as to edge nearer their goal.

Sidequests, trading sequences and exploration: the many ways to complete a videogame

One of the overarching features of the walkthroughs we have encountered above is the centrality of 'completion'. As Consalvo (2003a: 328) reminds us, 'Walkthroughs . . . are detailed descriptions of where to go and what to do – in sequential order – to get through a game successfully.' To complete the game here means to traverse its narrative structure, for instance, to reach the dramatic climax and end credits. One natural consequence of this view of completion is that walkthrough authors treat the game as a linear sequence. The insistence of the imperative mood drives the gamer forward along the path mapped out in the walkthrough with little or no opportunity for variation. Indeed, many authors produce 'Speed Walkthroughs' that reduce the game to its barest essentials and guide the gamer only to those elements in the sequence that are absolutely essential to progress towards completion. For instance, AC Kid's (2006) advice for *Metal Gear Solid Portable Ops* suggests that 'you'll have to remember to skip all the cutscenes and Radio conversations. You must quickly and often place Surveyor Spies on maps to regularly receive reports to proceed in the game.' Cutting out the extraneous cutscenes and accelerating the narrative progression by sidestepping sections, levels and sequences are common themes. In the *Pokémon Fire Red/Leaf Green Speed Walkthrough*, strawhat (2006) explains that

> My goal in writing this FAQ is to get you through the game as fast as possible. Some people have a goal in playing games quickly, and I'm here to help . . . Completing the game means ONLY beating the Elite 4. This speed walkthrough will not cover this islands and such.

Before you start . . . Go to the options menu and change the text speed from medium to fast and the battle scene to off. Also, set the battle style to set to eliminate some extra text.

('strawhat' 2006 [online])

Although these are extreme cases, they illustrate the fundamental importance of 'getting through the game' in walkthroughs. As we note in these examples, for some players, this may involve ascertaining the speediest possible routes from start to finish. In the next chapter, we will see that the honing and competitive public performance of these minimal walkthroughs as 'speedruns' are a rich and vibrant part of videogame culture in itself. Before we move to that discussion, here it is useful to note that the speed walkthrough highlights an important quality of videogames. That one can strip away sequences entirely and concentrate solely on certain aspects of the game (the 'Elite 4' battle at the expense of the islands in *Pokémon*, for instance) should immediately alert us to the fact that not all gameplay opportunity is centred around progressing towards 'completion'. In fact, if we consider the structure of videogames such as the *Final Fantasy*, *Metal Gear Solid* and *Pokémon* titles, among many others, we note that 'completion' is an extremely problematic term as a considerable amount of gameplay is bound up in activities that do not seem to move the narrative forward but that offer considerable pleasure and performative potential. Moreover, where the walkthrough might encourage us to see the game as a linear sequence even if that sequence becomes so fragmented in the search for speed that it loses its narrative coherence, there are a multitude of other pleasures to be derived from digressing from this structure and engaging in detours. While these pleasures are, to some extent, incompatible as they make different temporal demands, gamers may oscillate between them in play and replay depending on their mood and motivation. It is useful to recall Marsha Kinder's (1991) discussion of gameplay as the interplay between the simultaneously felt desires to progress to 'the end' and to prolong the pleasurable engagement.

If we examine the structures of the videogames we have encountered in this chapter so far, we note that they support both types of gameplay. To read just the walkthrough for the *Twilight Princess*, we might be forgiven for thinking that the game consisted of a single narrative thread that charted the journey of the heroic Link to restore light to the world. However, while the imperative tone of the walkthrough would not encourage us to think so, this narrative can be ruptured in at least two ways. First, the gamer may engage in self-motivated, playful paidea (see Caillois 2001; Frasca 2003). This may involve the gamer's deliberate transgression and cessation of the game's narrative imperative in favour of diversionary play. Ignoring the demand system of the game in order to ride Epona around Hyrule Field, jumping fences and shooting Poes would be an obvious example. The gamer may even impose their own *ludus* upon the play and create their own bespoke minigame that may even be shared with other gamers as we will note below.

Second, the gamer may engage in the many 'sidequests' that the game offers. In *The Legend of Zelda* series, for instance, these might range from the relatively simply structured such as collecting all of the 'Poe Souls', 'Golden Bugs' or 'Pieces of Heart' in the *Twilight Princess*, to more complex trading sequences such as that in the *Ocarina of Time*. These 'sidequests' are often implied but undeclared in the game and it is often unclear whether there will be any significant reward beyond the intrinsic pleasures of diversion and performance. As is the case with collecting 'missions', there is frequently no plotline at work and the activity stands beyond the game's primary narrative and, therefore, beyond the scope of the walkthrough. That these non-essential elements should even be included within the game design is interesting as a good many players will not even be aware of their presence, let alone engage in them to their fullest extent. For Richard Hockey, the Game Guide's discussion of sidequests and the potentials beyond the primary narrative sequences open up the possibility of a different kind of completion that is not centred on progression towards the 'end' of the narrative, but rather that involves exploration of the game space and maximises the encounters with characters and collection of objects, skills and techniques, for example:

> Many so-called hardcore gamers may play certain games such as those in the Final Fantasy or Pokemon series and have a desire to fully finish them, unlocking every item and/or viewing every cut-scene, here a guide may well be required to find out about the often immensely obscure bonuses available.
>
> (Hockey 2004: 268)

As we have noted, for Scott Rubin (2004), this practice is a potentially scurrilous one on the part of developers and publishers colluding in the creation of a parallel market for Official Strategy Guides alongside games in which secrets and the totality of their interactive potentialities cannot be deduced but must be learned from the expert author. However, we can also see that the very structure of games such as *Final Fantasy* and *The Legend of Zelda* is a call to arms to the Game Guide author. Their task is to experiment, play and *play with* the game to explore and expose its limits and potential. As such, Game Guides for *The Legend of Zelda* and *Final Fantasy* titles give over much of their space to explorations of 'sidequests' with Apathetic Aardvark (2007) dedicating more to 'optional' quests than to the walkthrough. Discussions abound of the interrelationships and relative merits of different kinds of magic and spells. Bestiaries and character lists encourage gamers to explore every last pixel of the gameworld so as to experience the full range of opportunities and mine every aspect of the back-story by ensuring every branch of the non-playable character's dialogue is encountered. Game Guides for the *Animal Crossing* series are illustrative. As an open-ended 'sandbox' game, *Animal Crossing* is similar to *The Sims* in that it has no clear narrative trajectory, no winning or losing state other than in those *ludus* defined and superimposed by the gamer (Church 2000; Frasca 2001). Game Guides provide extraordinary detail on the workings of the game's simulation model. The bugs and fish that can be collected and caught in the game appear at different times of day and during different seasons according to the game's real-time calendar. By playing, replaying, taking notes and evaluating and collating the collective intelligence of the group of *Animal Crossing* gamers, it is possible to build up thorough lists that outline the behaviour and habitat of the many in-game creatures (as 'Pikachu 4 President' (2003) does). Moreover, Guides draw attention to the complex interplay of non-playable characters and thereby encourage gamers to explore the fullest extent of the interactive potential of the gameworld by conversing with every character many times and in different circumstances so as to expose the range of their responses and the richness of their histories. In the 'Animal Crossing: Wild World Guide', LethalLink99 notes that:

> A few of the miscellaneous characters listed in this section experience episodes. These are special dialogue sequences in which they reveal information about their lives. In order to trigger subsequent episodes, you must witness the first episode. However, if you miss the day of the first episode, you can still hear it on the next day ocassionally. Four days separate the first and second episodes. Three days separate the subsequent episodes. The below table summarizes the dates of the episodes, who experiences them, and the number of episodes there are for that character.
>
> ('LethalLink99' 2007 [online])

It is important to remember that the intimate knowledge demonstrated in the discussion and analysis of character episodes is arrived at through experimentation and the critical observation of play and replay. Gamers such as LethalLink99 demonstrate the remarkable insight of gamers and their ability to engage with the simulation models that underpin and drive these games. As Burn (2006b) observes in relation to the production of linear sequences in the walkthrough, the gamer apprehends the game at the level of a system, a procedural model that behaves according to, albeit often complex, chaotic or perhaps even random or pseudo-random, rules and principles. This recalls Friedman's (1995, 1999) discussion of 'thinking like the machine' (see also Newman 2002a, 2004). Through the act of play, these systems and rules are laid bare and potentially come under the control of the gamer through their subsequent, informed performances. As with the walkthrough, even though the rules, systems and mathematical models that are decoded and decompiled here might play out as emotionally rich systems of representation, narrative and character in the game (Able and Mabel Sable's episodes that recount the history of their mother are truly heart-rending), the discussion of them in the Game Guide is generally bereft of any sentiment and is motivated by the desire to thoroughly document, analyse and describe. The Game Guide provides information about the extent of the possibilities and the means by which the gamer might access them through play but it does not discuss their content. The pleasures of embarking on the treasure hunts or engaging in conversations with Non-Playable Characters (NPCs) are reserved for gameplay. In this way, we might argue that the Game Guide exists to assist gamers in extracting the fullest possible range of pleasures through play and is not a substitute for that play or an extension or adjunct to it in the way that fanart or fiction writing might be.

What we learn here is that while these pleasures may be ignored in walk-throughs whose imperative is to deliver the gamer through the game in as efficient a manner as possible, many videogames and RPGs in particular, offer copious opportunity to stray from the path of the primary narrative, thereby delaying its culmination (see Brooks 1982). In this way, the videogame opens itself to a variety of play styles centring around progression and digression, for example, and presents a further opportunity for the Game Guide author to marshal and organise these quests, activities and collecting missions. The treatment and coverage of sidequests vary greatly between Game Guides. Some offer maps that indicate the position of objects for collection and leave the journeying and route-planning to the gamer. Others provide great detail and reduce these sequences to walkthroughs. What is important, however, is that regardless of their approach, these are activities and parts of the game that followers of the 'walkthrough' alone would not, need not, and perhaps even *should* not, encounter as they exist outside or beyond the primary narrative. Crucially, they are almost always dealt with as separate projects or gameplay activities and are never woven into the 'walkthrough' which remains concerned with the completion of the principal narrative-driven sequence. 'Completion' in the context of sidequests involves the thorough scouring and exploration of the gameworld, uncovering and unearthing its nuances regardless of whether they bring the game's storyline closer to its resolution.

As such, although 'walkthrough' is often synonymous with or used in place of 'Game Guide', it is vital to recognise that the walkthrough describes and codifies a specific set of pleasures that are oriented around moving along the primary narrative and completing the sequence (or a subset thereof). Even where the discussion of sidequests and trading sequences follows the style and address of walkthrough writing, the activities described fall outside the usual remit of the 'walkthrough' section of a Guide.

Writing new games: challenging the community

It is almost a natural progression from documenting the collectible items in a videogame and forming missions around their acquisition to creating wholly new and original modes of play. The setting of 'challenges' not only further demonstrates the plasticity and mutability of the videogame in its support of multiple 'playings' but also speaks of the desire to keep alive the videogame long after the industry has superseded it with sequels, new franchises and platforms. Where we noted the tendency of the walkthrough writer to compel their reader into specific action thereby seeking to regulate, contain and normalise their gameplay activity (see Burn 2006b), with the setting of challenges in Game Guides we see an altogether more open attitude that encourages experimentation and new approaches to the game and gameplay. Similarly, we also note a shift from the second person to a more inclusive address that situates the gamer within a wider community who share the challenge.

Game Guides for Nintendo's *Pikmin* illustrate the point. The standard game mode as inscribed in the instruction manual takes place over thirty in-game days and charges the gamer as Captain Olimar to recover the scattered parts of their crashed spaceship within the time limit in order that they might blast off home. Various additions and superimpositions exist that seek to add replay value and longevity to the gameplay experience. These include limiting the use of certain objects and capabilities in the game (for example, tackling the game without one of the three varieties of eponymous helpers) or focusing on attainment of high scores (rendering linear 'completion' along the game's narrative structure either insignificant or merely a given). Most interesting of all is the formalised '9-Day Challenge':

> First off, this is not a normal Pikmin Walkthrough. If you're looking for a guide to beat the game normally, go somewhere else. This walkthrough is to help you beat the Pikmin 9 Day Challenge, a task originally devised by SnapDragon. The task is simple; collect all 30 of Captain Olimar's rocket ship parts in a mere 9 days. Sounds impossible? Then read on . . . but remember, even with a strat, this is quite a task, so don't attempt it unless you've beaten the game at least once.
>
> ('Dragorn' 2002 [online])

A number of features are noteworthy here. First, there is a clear sense of dialogue as gamers originate and refine the challenges. In these circumstances, the 9-Day Challenge is positioned as much as a competition with the game system as it is with the originators of the challenge. Second, we note again that while the walkthrough discussion may provide exhaustive description of the actions required to beat the game or this superimposed ruleset, the gamer is still required to enact and perform the solutions. The setting and description of the challenge again foreground and privilege the pleasures of performance and being in the world, the kinaesthetic pleasures of movement through space and the flow of control. However, there is another dimension to these challenges. As Dragorn explains, 'even with a strat, this is quite a task'. While we may read this as a cautionary note, it is better understood as an indicator of the required levels of skill and proficiency demanded by this challenge. What we see then is the 9-Day Challenge as a means of demonstrating gaming prowess. As Perron (2003: 253) notes, walkthroughs are frequently posted to demonstrate the gamer's 'gameplay tricks' and skill level. Prowess is most obviously demonstrated by Dragorn and SnapDragon and the many other authors who contribute to the discussion and creation of the challenge. The authority of their Game Guides indicates their mastery of *Pikmin* and their creation of a yet more difficult challenge speaks clearly of their desire to find a new, more fitting test of their abilities. There are echoes of the desire to prolong the experience (Kinder 1991) but with the narrative and available detours, sidequests and explorations exhausted, gamers invent and superimpose their own systems and formalise them in the ludus of the challenge.

For Consalvo:

> [T]he guides (I'm talking about unofficial ones) are for the people that wrote them – they demonstrate their knowledge of the game, and they are a way to establish yourself as an 'expert' on that particular game – it can be a status marker, especially on a site like gamefaqs.com, if your walkthrough is highly rated.
>
> (Consalvo 2004: 273)

The challenge is perhaps the ultimate expression of the search for expert status as gamers manage their identities within the wider community. However, we should also consider the impact of the challenge beyond its authors. By engaging with this new game mode, gamers are invited into the worlds of the experts and offered the opportunity to measure their prowess against the experts. In addition, by following the walkthrough and Guide suggestions, readers are given the chance to learn directly from the experts. We can see this principle at work elsewhere. *Championship Manager* gamers frequently share 'tactics' files that may be applied to the game to make available the honed techniques and gameplay styles among the wider community.

The 'Pikmin 9-Day Challenge' is by no means unique and countless examples abound of the imposition and formalisation of new ludus such as tackling the game without any additional weaponry or health upgrades as in HappyPuppet's *The Legend of Zelda: Twilight Princess* 'Cave of Ordeals Minimalist Challenge Walkthrough'.

Indeed, we might see the speed walkthrough as an example of a new game mode established by and for the community of gamers. As I have noted previously (Newman 2004), games such as *DOOM* and *Metroid Prime* encourage and even goad players by revealing the percentage of the challenge and secrets remaining to be uncovered thereby drawing attention to the expansiveness of the gameworld, the need to progress and continue and perhaps, by implication, the value-for-money of the game. Low-percent challenges demand an altogether different approach. Here, mastery of the game comes from tackling the various puzzles and challenges and completing the game with as few additional 'pick-ups' as possible. For example, it is quite commonplace to acquire upgraded firepower or entirely new attack and defence capabilities as a game progresses and the foes increase in complexity and number. The advocate of the low-percent game eschews such assistance and attempts to tackle the game with as close to the initial set of capabilities and capacities as possible:

> Welcome. This is a guide for the 1% challenge. What's the 1% challenge, you ask? Well, here goes . . .
>
> If you think that the game was not fulfilling enough for you, or it wasn't challenging enough for you, then this challenge is for you. Basically, you play the game again, but there is a twist. You are not allowed to collect any missile tanks, bomb tanks, and energy tanks throughout the whole time you play the game. Every tank you pick up will increase your ending percentage by 1%.
>
> The only exception is 1 missile tank that is unavoidable, and thus the 1%. So, your mission is basically to beat the game with 15 missiles, 10 power bombs, and only 99 points of energy. Sounds impossible, doesn't it?
>
> Not exactly, that's what this guide is for. My advice is that, if you're going to try the challenge, don't start reading the guide until you are sure you are stuck beyond reasoning. It is a challenge, and I don't expect anybody to complete it, but if you do, you earned bragging rights.
>
> ('Super Saiyan Zero' 2003 [online])

Extra credit

The clear address to a wider community of gamers in these challenges reminds us of the context within which Game Guides and walkthroughs must be understood. Not only are they products for the community but also are products of it:

> After many hours of working on this guide, the major problems are finally being fixed, the walkthrough is done, and the only side quests I have yet

to list are the heart piece and Poe locations. Thanks for everyone's support so far in what has been a massive undertaking; this guide's success is partly due to all the help I've gotten so far.

('Darkfury3827' 2006 [online])

The credit and acknowledgements section is a staple of the Game Guide and provides persuasive evidence of the embeddedness of the texts within gaming cultures. Guides, walkthroughs and FAQs are utilised by a wide constituency of gamers to aid and in some cases measure their performance and ability. Moreover, authors go to great lengths to accurately and fairly attribute the contributions as well as the rights of intellectual property and copyright holders. Pikachu 4 President's *Animal Crossing* Guide credits almost 100 contributors by name and says:

> Thank you to all the members of the Animal Crossing Message Board. You have inspired me, helped me, and become my "extended villagers." I wish you all the best in your AC lives. Thank you for being so kind to me.
>
> ('Pikachu 4 President' 2003 [online])

In concert with the version history, the lengthy credits section and legal disclaimers again speak of the software documentation imperative as well as a professionalism and seriousness of purpose that confirms Tushnet's (2007) and Burn's (2006b) assertion that gamers are well aware of the legality of fan production. However, we should note more than a desire to adequately acknowledge existing contributions or respect rightsholders. There is a clear sense that the Guides are products of collective intelligence. Indeed, contributions are actively sought and graciously accepted and acknowledged. As Jenkins (2006: 154) observes, the copyright regimes of mass culture are applied to the production of folk culture. This means that not only are rights observed but transgressions are publicly punished. After a lengthy discussion of his attribution policy and an offer to correct any missing or incorrect attributions, Megura (2000) offers a list of 'idiots' who he claims have plagiarised his work and posted sections of it to other websites without acknowledging the original authorship. 'This list is supposed to discourage people from doing this kind of thing. It's not so they can see their names in someone's FAQ!'

In keeping with many of the productive processes we have seen throughout this book, Game Guides, walkthroughs, and challenges negotiate a complex path between individual and group authorship and ownership. As well as being intended for public consumption from the outset, these works build on the efforts of different authors and gamers while details on the systems, simulations and processes of the game are discussed and refined through revision, evaluation, comment and iteration. I have noted elsewhere (Newman 2005: 58) that complex processes of collaboration and collective authorship are at the heart of the Game Guide. While they clearly represent labours of love for their principal authors or editors, Guides are usually replete with genuine requests for contributions from readers. As such, the creation of Guides provides a vivid example of the productivity of videogaming and the complex sociality of the discussion board and webring.

Glitching: playing with imperfection

In addition to the recognition of the contributions of gamers, public displays of appreciation directed at the developers, designers and producers of games are a common feature of the credits and 'thank yous' sections of Game Guides. Thanks, for instance, are offered to

> Eiji Aonuma, Shigeru Miyamoto, Koji Kondo, and all Zelda staff for their devotion to this franchise, and their continued desire to impress us.
>
> ('CyricZ' 2007 [online])

> Nintendo for creating this fantastic game and programming the Dynalfos AI as they did; I'd like to believe the enemy designers used their sense of humor there.
>
> ('HappyPuppet' 2007 [online])

In citing the contributions of game designers and music composers, the breadth of these credits demonstrates a knowledge of the production processes and personnel involved in game development. Moreover, in the wording of these acknowledgements we may detect a sense in which the Game Guide writers seek to communicate and consolidate their closeness to the game and its creators. In CyricZ's credit, Miyamoto *et al.* are drawn into an intimate relationship with the 'us' of gamers whom they try to impress, while in demonstrating intimate and esoteric knowledge HappyPuppet positions the expert gamer and developer in a knowing bond. This assertion goes some way to validating the forensic interrogation and analysis in the Game Guide. The somewhat bizarre behaviour of an enemy's AI (artificial intelligence) in one specific part of the game is treated here as an 'Easter Egg' for the gamer dedicated enough to hunt it down.

The idea that what might be seen as shortcomings in the game's system might be read as a morsel to be found and savoured by the expert gamer is an interesting one. We could treat this as an over-compensatory, even self-deluding, attempt to prove the perfection of the game and sanctify its developers. However, far from trying to draw attention away from inconsistencies or flaws, the practice of glitch-hunting demonstrates a willingness to expose such limitations.

A glitch, or 'bug' as it is sometimes known, is a generic term for the result of a programming error. Glitches vary significantly in their scale and severity and range from graphical artefacts or anomalies that do not dramatically affect or alter gameplay to those that can crash the game, and even the system on which it is running, or corrupt save data, thereby eliminating a gamer's recorded progress. Although not all are so predictable, many glitches are repeatable and, as such, may be deliberately replicated by gamers. The repeatability and demonstrability of these game glitches make them interesting facets of the game and Game Guides often list their existence and the conditions under which they can be called into being with as much rigour and detail as they list the qualities of spells, the traits of a roster of characters or the dialogue routines of NPCs. The presence of glitch lists in Game Guides and even as dedicated FAQs speaks of the degree to which they are considered valuable elements of the game, even when they have no intrinsic gameplay value or do not advance the narrative (perhaps even bringing the narrative to an untimely cessation in their severest forms). Such is their currency and prevalence that a number of projects are entirely oriented around glitches. 'David Wonn's Unique Video Game Glitches' and the 'Center for Glitch Studies' are but two, while many fansites dedicate sections to glitches and bugs. Certainly the willingness to document these flaws is one of the most obvious ways in which gamer-produced Game Guides may be differentiated from the products of commercial publishing, particularly those created in direct partnership with the game developers and publishers. This is partly because glitches are essentially remnants of a demonstrably, if understandably, imperfect quality assurance process and partly because glitches often only come to light after a game's commercial release and once the collective gameplaying and gametesting forces of the community of gamers has been set into motion testing their tactics and strategies and stress testing the game to destruction.

Interestingly, the tone of the glitch-hunters is not an indignant or dissatisfied one. They do not, on the whole, seek to criticise the game developers or undermine the value of the game. What is curious here is that something one might instinctively think of as being wholly undesirable is collected and curated with the same care and precision and is afforded the same desirability as the fragments of knowledge pertaining to strategy or the locations of objects in the gameworld. As we shall see, Game Guide writers search out and refine their descriptions and analyses of glitches in the same manner as they tackle other materials and, while they are generally listed under a separate heading in the Guide (just like the 'walkthrough' is separated from the 'controls' or 'preface'), they are not obviously differentiated from other gameplay features.

Among the more innocuous and well-known glitches is the *Super Mario Bros.* 'Minus World'. The structure of *Super Mario Bros.* is such that it appears to offer a finite number of levels (eight levels in each of eight worlds) and mastery of them all, as we shall see in the following chapter, is a continuing matter of precision jumping and timing. That the game so explicitly delimits itself in terms of its level structure automatically makes desirable even the possibility that additional levels or spaces to explore and conquer might exist. In fact, despite the rumour and speculation that surrounds it, and the number of tips and strategy books that hint at its presence as a 'lost level' or bonus, the consensus among gamers is that the Minus World is actually nothing more than a debugging area used to test the character control and play mechanic during game development. Such areas are extremely common and are often even left in the final game code where gamers with considerable technical skills and the necessary tools may later recover them, as we shall see in Chapter 7. What is unusual and unusually desirable about the Minus World is not only that it remained in the game code, but that it was inadvertently left accessible through play. However, as we note below, the means of accessing it is by no means a trivial affair.

The "Minus World" is not actually World Negative One, but is actually world "space", level 1. The "space" character actually represents a higher number (World 36 to be exact), but most people mistakenly refer to it as World Minus One.

OK, for those of you who aren't familiar with the "Minus World", here is how you reach World 36: In World 1-2, get to the end of the level and find the pipe that takes you to the exit. Mario must be big for this to work. Instead of exiting through the pipe, jump on top of it and stand on the leftmost portion of the pipe. Break some of the bricks above, but DO NOT break the rightmost brick. Now here's the tricky part. You will need to jump up and lean your jump to the right, so that Mario's head goes through the rightmost brick. This may take several attempts before you get it right. If everything goes well, Mario will then go through the rest of the bricks! Now you will appear where the three warp pipes are that ordinarily take you to Worlds 2, 3, and 4. As long as you don't scroll the screen too far, this trick will work. Go down the 1st (or 3rd) pipe and you're off to the "Minus World"! It's really World 36-1, but the programmers didn't make enough room for more than one digit in the level, which shows up as a space. The level is virtually identical to World 2-2 with one critical difference: THERE IS NO WAY OUT! The trick isn't very useful unless you plan on brushing up on your swimming skills :)

(Wonn (n.d.) [online])

The value of the Minus World is complex and ambiguous in that it has no intrinsic gameplay merit. As Wonn notes, it is a cul-de-sac, an endlessly scrolling level that offers little or no variety for the gamer and certainly nothing novel as it is made up of elements present in other sequences. Given that the *Super Mario* series is lauded for its inventiveness of game design and variety of experiential opportunity, the Minus World surely ranks as a low-point. Moreover, the means of accessing it is tortuously complicated. Prima facie, the benefits do not seem to justify the amount of work required by the gamer. However, this is to miss the point. While there are clear pleasures to be gained from divining the means of accessing or stumbling across the entry point, there is considerable personal satisfaction and public kudos in having played in the Minus World. As a part of the gameworld, one that is created by the game designers and, albeit in a complicated way, accessed from within the game, the Minus World pushes at the boundary of the canon. If, as we have seen above in our discussion of sidequests, for instance, some gamers desire to explore every last pixel and opportunity the gameworld can offer, then the Minus World must surely be a part of their journey.

So widely known is the Minus World that it has passed into the folklore of the Mario universe. 'Doubtless you've heard this one before – this was THE trick found in many tip books of the 1980's,' notes the 'Super Mario Bros. Glitches and Tricks' page (Team Rocket's Rockin' (n.d.) [online]). The existence of the Minus World has prompted considerable additional theorising as to the existence of further bonus levels within the game such as a chocolate factory. These have not materialised and we can safely speculate that they are fabrications spurred by an awareness of Easter Eggs, the knowledge that remnants such as the Minus World may exist within the game code waiting to be discovered, and the desire of the gaming community to consume such material.

The degree to which glitches may become part of the fabric of gaming folklore is merely hinted at by the Minus World, however. Perhaps the richest and most creative example of the appropriation and use of glitches in gaming culture is found in the world of *Pokémon*. The original *Pokémon Blue* and *Red* titles include many glitches that are well-documented in the Game Guides and Glitch FAQs hosted at GameFAQs and other fansites. Some of the glitches corrupt the game data or crash the game in progress while others are less serious graphical aberrations. There are much more intriguing situations, however. Keen *Pokémon* trainers will be well aware of the roster of 151 available monsters and the game's slogan 'Gotta Catch 'Em All'. Not all will be conversant with the additional critters that are available – if a trainer knows where to look.

Wild MISSINGNO appeared!

Missingno has been a long-time favorite of Glitch Hunters everywhere. However, despite the fact that it has been highly popular for several years, it seems to be very difficult to find solid and detailed information on the phenomenon. For that reason, I began researching and collecting data on my own. Somewhere along the way, I seem to have become an authority on the subject. If Jolt135 is the leading expert on how this game works, I seem to be the leading expert on how it doesn't. Regardless of whether this title is deserved, I've put together this guide documenting my findings and theories. I've done this partly out of obligation, but also to issue a WARNING. There is a great deal of false information floating around regarding the risk of using this glitch. Some say that Missingno is harmless so long as you don't capture it; this is not true. Some say that saving after an encounter will prevent damage to your save file; this is also not true. It is my intent to clear up these myths once and for all.

(Raddatz 2005 [online])

The brute fact is that both MISSINGNO and 'M are the products of glitches. They manifest themselves as real Pokémon though in fact their names and graphical representations reveal their status as errors (MISSINGNO or 'missing number' refers to a data call in the program that searches for a non-existent Pokémon from the checklist while 'M is represented on screen as a garbled mass of pixels, roughly in the shape of an inverted L and looking not dissimilar to a *Tetris* block. Neither glitch is serious in that they do not crash the game (though some reports do suggest conditions under which game data may become corrupted), but they are anomalies that arise from coding errors that arise under a specific set of repeatable conditions that are comprehensively documented in Game Guides such as Raddatz's (2005) and even on Nintendo's own corporate website:

MissingNO is a programming quirk, and not a real part of the game. When you get this, your game can perform strangely, and the graphics will often become scrambled. The MissingNO Pokémon is most often found after you perform the Fight Safari Zone Pokémon trick.

To fix the scrambled graphics, try releasing the MissingNo Pokémon. If the problem persists, the only solution is to re-start your game. This means erasing your current game and starting a brand new one.

('Game Boy Game Pak Troubleshooting' [online])

A number of things are revealed by MISSINGNO and 'M. The processes by which they come to be revealed are, like the Minus World, extremely complicated and convoluted. Moreover, gamers go to great investigative and analytical lengths to try to explain what they are encountering (e.g. Raddatz 2005 and the discussion at 'Tales from the Glitch 4: MissingNo Mystery Solved' (n.d.) for instance). They note and examine their evidence and question the operation of the game in the most insightful manner. Importantly, they do not do this alone. Sites make express calls for accounts of individual 'sightings' so that evidence may be collected and analysed. Team Rocket's 'Tales From the Glitch: MissingNo Visitor Accounts' are manifest examples of the collective intelligence of gaming communities with participants trading experience and offering respectful critique and assessment of each other's positions.

The desirability of two additional Pokémon should not shock us greatly. If you 'Gotta catch em all' then surely there can be no better endorsement of the prowess and skill of the Pokémon trainer than to capture monsters that even the developers were not sure existed within the gameworld. What is surprising, however, is the way in which the gaming communities around Pokémon have made these 'glitch Pokémon' real. Giving them a category of their own to sit alongside the Fire, Water and Leaf monsters is just the beginning of the assimilation. Fanart and fiction abounds. Rita Buuk (n.d.) and Mandy Nader (2004), for example, have both written narratives that attempt to detail the backstories of MISSINGNO and 'M while hand-drawn sketches, computer-generated artwork and even cookies inspired by the likeness of 'M bestow upon the characters a reality and position within the canon of the game regardless of Nintendo's official protestations to the contrary.

Furthermore, inspired by the presence of these new Pokémon lurking inside the gameworld, gamers create and share their own imaginary glitch Pokémon designs and descriptions (see 'Team Rocket's Rockin fanart' [online]). Just as with the Minus World, the revelation that glitches might uncover parts of the game that could be considered canonical or Easter Eggs or at the very least inspire creativity and continued interest in the game, spurs on the glitch-hunters:

> What Now?
> But there's much more to learn about these "mistake" Pokemon. For example, why are these Pokemon in the game at all? Obviously MissingNo looks like a REAL Pokemon. Was it originally a character that got cut from the game? Is this some sick programmer's idea of a joke? Did the developers think that 150 (151) Pokemon were enough? Why didn't it show up in Gold and Silver as one of the 100 NEW Pokemon? CAN you catch MissingNo? Since there are weird glitch Pokemon, accessed only through a bizarre sequence of events, might other strange events (talking to people in a specific order, etc) trigger the appearance of OTHER glitch/high-level Pokemon?

Rumors abound regarding these glitches. For example, one source claims that catching a MissingNo and feeding it a Rare Candy will produce a Kangaskhan. These are also the sources that claim buying a Magikarp for 500 Poke-bucks and sending it off to Daycare will produce a Mew, so I'm not putting too much stock in these stories. But IS there anything cool you can do with a MissingNo or an 'M?

. . . Join me next time for Pokemon Mysteries Revealed. Or better yet, why not send me an account of YOUR experiences with MissingNo and 'M. And let me know which high-level Pokemon lurks within YOUR game! And has it caused any glitches in your Hall of Fame data?

(Nader, M. (n.d.) [online])

What is most interesting about glitch-hunters is that they do not seek to hide the imperfections of games but rather celebrate and publicise them. To some extent, the motivations of glitch-hunters might be seen to be similar to those of the fiction writers and theorists we saw earlier who aim to address the inconsistencies and contradictions in canonical texts or between series episodes by narrativising them away. We noted in that case that there was an evident desire to imprint oneself onto the text by implicating one's own work and practices into the canonical textual production process and we certainly see this at work in the case of MISSINGNO and 'M above. However, this is an unusual case and, for the most part, there is no equivalent attempt to ameliorate the situation through explanatory or compensatory textual production. More typically, the pleasures of glitch-hunting are somewhat similar to those derived from scouring the gameworld for obscure, collectible objects or from the mapping exercises that seek to chart every corner of the videogame space. However, they also reveal something altogether more interesting about the boundaries of the game and the limits of gameplay. We have seen already that the focus on the game system means that walkthrough writing largely eschews discussion of the videogame as a representational system and instead treats it as a simulation model with inputs and outputs and as a series of complex mathematical models, logical systems and programming loops that govern the behaviour of the world and its content and that may be exploited through the act of informed play. What glitch-hunting suggests is that the reduction of the videogame to the operation of a simulation model does not distinguish between the 'intended' and 'unexpected' outcomes of the game code.

As such, the identification of the properties of the different kinds of Materia in *Final Fantasy VII* involves the same processes of investigation and the information is equally interesting as the identification of a graphical anomaly or game-crashing bug in the game's program. For gamers wishing to fully appreciate the game in its entirety, each facet is an equally legitimate part of the simulation even if it were wholly unintended by the developers. As we learn from designers such as Raph Koster (2005), part of the job of the videogame developer is to create an environment in which gamers can play and *be* and in which gameplay can emerge. In one sense, then, we can see playful engagements with glitches and their adoption and adaptation within the community of gamers as a form of emergent gameplay. As we shall see in the next chapter, this emergent gameplay very often makes use of glitches and tricks that enable gamers to operate in ways not only un-envisioned by developers but also unsanctioned by the rules and systems they (attempted to) put into place. By exploiting these glitches and anomalies and by pushing and even exceeding the limits of the simulation, gamers are able to expand their performative repertoire and tackle games in new and innovative ways. Importantly, in the strictest sense, this is done within the rules. Playing with the videogame relies on the fact that the rules are imperfectly designed and imperfectly operated within the code.

The search for and revelation of glitches illustrate that for the avid fan the videogame is not simply a static text to be read or decoded, nor is it merely an experience to be had, a world to be and exist in, or a journey to travel. Through conversation, analysis and discussion, the game is refigured as a living, dynamic, malleable entity revealing new secrets as it is continually probed, investigated and played, and it is capable of being probed, investigated and played in new ways as it is placed in new critical and ludic contexts. Moreover, fans interrogating these glitches gain significant insights into the game development process and knowledge of the technical principles that underpin the game as they apprehend the game as a simulation and, in Ted Friedman's (1995, 1999) terms, 'think like the computer'.

Game Guides, walkthroughs and cheating

It is clear that only a small number of gamers produce Game Guides and it would be tempting to overlook them for their marginality. However, the uses to which they are put and their readers and users are far more widespread. As we have seen, Game Guides are diverse texts that document and codify modes of play and even provide a virtual forum where new ways of playing, often radical and subversive, are devised and shared. Ultimately, Game Guides speak eloquently of the variety of pleasures that may be derived from playing videogames. For Juul (2004), Guides, walkthroughs and FAQs are so much a part of the culture and landscape of videogaming that we should understand them as playing a central role for many gamers:

> It allows players to choose the level of difficulty as they wish. Walkthroughs and FAQs are an integral part of the game experience by now – you know

that you can find a FAQ/walkthrough if you want, so it's simply an option available in all games.

(Juul 2004: 242)

However, as we noted at the beginning of this chapter, Game Guides, walkthroughs and FAQs are very often considered to constitute cheating by gamers and developers even though they do not interfere with the game's program or code and still require that solutions are performed on the usual terms with the game (not taking advantage of the many 'cheats' that are built into the very fabric of many games' options screens). In the face of this degree of legitimised 'cheating' where 'cheats' are indistinguishable from gameplay modes, it seems curious that Game Guides would be considered so problematic. Interestingly, Game Guides themselves provide a compelling explanation for this situation. Game Guides demonstrate the variety of ways in which videogames may be tackled and the range of pleasures that may be derived from playing them in different ways. Where the walkthrough privileges the completion of the narrative, sometimes in record times, sidequests may encourage more thorough if not leisurely detours and explorations of the gameworld while challenges reframe the gameplay superimposing additional rules, restrictions and conditions on play. The very act of consulting a walkthrough, FAQ or Guide may seem to those players who privilege puzzling and problem solving to defeat the very object of the game. As such, the activity may be construed as pointless, if not cheating. However, it is important to note, as Kentner does, that even though the puzzle structure might be undermined, there still remain the pleasures of performance and execution:

Walkthroughs and FAQ's are for people who enjoy the experience of the game, who enjoy the story of the game, but who do not have the time to completely immerse themselves in the world. I myself do not have the time to write down the stats for every weapon and part in an RPG. Walkthrough's and FAQ's mean you still have to do the things the programmers designed. You still have to make the jump, or fight the battle, or score the goal. Now you just know where to jump, how to fight the battle, or the move to make to score the goal.

(Kentner 2004: 265)

For gamers who seek and privilege such pleasures of performance or perhaps even dislike puzzling, Game Guides support their gameplay choices just as they assist those who are stuck and unable to progress or those who wish to conquer the game, collecting each and every one of its secrets thereby bringing them under their control. To extend Juul's assertion above then, Game Guides not only allow gamers to select their difficulty level but even support them in tailoring the type of gameplay they experience by allowing them to focus on some aspects rather than others. In the next chapter we will turn our attention to the ways in which Game Guides and walkthroughs are enacted through the performances of play and 'superplay'.

Chapter 6

Superplay, sequence breaking and speedrunning

Superplay, high scores and performance

> JERRY: Hey, look at the high score – 'G.L.C.' George Louis Costanza.
> That's not you, is it?
> GEORGE: Yes! 860,000. I can't believe it's still standing. No one has
> beaten me in like 10 years.
> JERRY: I remember that night.
> GEORGE: The perfect combination of Mountain Dew and mozzarella
> . . . just the right amount of grease on the joystick . . .
>
> ('The Frogger', *Seinfeld*, Episode 174, 1998)

Though they may not be familiar with the term, most people with more than
a passing interest in and knowledge of videogames will be aware of 'superplay'.
Superplay is a generic term that describes a range of gaming practices that differ significantly in their execution and implementation but that are bound together
by a common desire to demonstrate mastery of the game through performance.
As we shall see throughout this chapter, superplay may be oriented around completing games in the fastest possible time, or by tackling the challenge in a 'pacifist'
mode dispatching only those enemies that actually bar progress and cannot be
avoided. It may seek to use as few additional capabilities or weapons as possible,
and it may involve exploring as much or, indeed, as little of the gameworld as
possible by engaging in 'complete' or 'low percent' runs to completion. Moreover,
some forms of superplay may even centre on pushing gameplay beyond the limits
of human performance by harnessing technical tools to enact the theoretically
perfect performance. All of these practices require great skill and commitment
and involve meticulous planning and the utilisation of the Game Guides and
walkthroughs we saw in the previous chapters as reference works that document
the extent and scope of the game as well as other documents and collaborative strategies that are devised and refined by gamers reviewing and discussing

each other's work. What we note in the practices of superplay is the use of the knowledge and techniques uncovered and laid out in Game Guides, the exploitation of the structures, (non-) linearity and limitations of videogames as designs as well as the harnessing of glitches in game code. All of these are combined by superplayers and used to gain gameplaying advantage. This point recalls Dovey and Kennedy's commentary on Eskelinen's (2001) and Moulthrop's (2004) conceptualisations of gameplay as configurative practice in which they note a tendency towards an 'incipient humanism' (2006: 105) that privileges the player as principal or even sole agent. As we shall note, both player as performer and game system should be considered agents in the processes of gameplay. Krzywinska (2002) makes a similar point in drawing our attention to the 'textual' and 'performative' aspects of videogames and the ways in which the game system restricts and limits the gameplay potential of the player. However, we should be mindful that this system of rules and boundaries is not fixed but rather is permeable and in a state of flux as it is interrogated, operated on and played with. Moreover, the system may behave in an unpredictable manner unintended by the game designers due to imperfections in the code or unanticipated emergent contingencies.

As we shall see, superplay need only be obliquely concerned with the ostensible 'aim' of the videogame and frequently superimposes an additional ruleset. In this way, superplay is closely related to the 'challenges' that we saw circulating in Game Guides in the previous chapter. Superplay is essentially the performance or enactment of gamer-designed and imposed challenges. Completion, in terms of moving along a narrative or through the branching structure of levels or sequences towards an 'ending' is not always the primary concern of superplayers and again the various activities, challenges and practices highlight the complexity and fluidity of the idea of videogame 'completion'. The task of the superplayer may involve reaching the 'final' sequence in a game, though if the challenge is to move from 'start' to 'finish' as speedily as possible, the journey may involve devising and implementing strategies to allow the sidestepping of huge portions of the intervening narrative or a large number of levels along the way thereby making for a stripped down, discontiguous and potentially incomprehensible narrative experience. The superplayer in search of a high score, on the other hand, does not necessarily want to move through the game's structure at speed and may rather explore each detour in some depth so as to maximise the point scoring potential, unless of course the game's rule system awards points for speedy traversal of the levels and assuming the game is even one that has a finite structure.

As the extract from *Seinfeld* above illustrates, probably the most culturally visible form of superplay is the attainment of high scores. Perhaps surprisingly, the high score has not always been a part of the videogame and it was not until

1979's *Asteroids* that gamers were afforded the opportunity to tag their achievements with their initials and both broadcast and evaluate their performance. While the entries in the Coin-Op cabinet's high score table were retained, they were not permanent and would be reset if the machine was powered down (the events of the *Seinfeld* episode see George buying and attempting to move the *Frogger* cabinet with his still resplendent high score atop the table, rigging up a temporary battery so to preserve his initials for posterity). The very existence of a scoring system that operates as the means of assessing progress and a table of the highest scoring gamers goes some way to embedding superplay into the reward structure of the game. In *Asteroids*, with its infinite structure (see Newman 2004) that theoretically allows the game to continue *ad infinitum* (see also Brzustowski's (1992) work on *Tetris*), the score is the primary means of comparing and evaluating progress but it is interesting to note the presence of scoring systems in games where other, sometimes more obviously dominant, reward systems are in place. Games such as *Super Mario World* and *StarFox* that proudly advertise the number of levels they offer the gamer and where progress through the gameworld is communicated via movement across the overview map towards an ultimate confrontation, also include scoring systems, while *Rez* offers a 'ScoreAttack' mode that foregrounds the challenge of accumulating as high a score as possible.

In these games, then, we see the presence of an at least two-tiered system of rewards where gamers can concentrate either on the movement across the map towards the final encounter or on the acquisition of points through a thorough investigation of the space and the collection of items and objects, or perhaps they may try to combine both. In fact, the titles in the *Super Mario* series, like *Sonic the Hedgehog* and many other titles, also include countdown timers that further add to the array of measures of performance. Regardless of the way the game presents itself, the ways gamers play, what they privilege, what they ignore, is partly a matter of personal choice and preference and may well alter through time as the game is played and replayed. What is important to note, is that the game itself suggests and even hardwires the evaluative mechanisms for a number of different game types and play styles encouraging gamers to personalise their experience and challenge themselves in new manners. Often, of course, these modes of play and their contours are suggested by other agencies.

High score challenges are among the most venerable in videogaming culture. As we noted in Chapter 2, magazines have long run competitions and challenges that, among other things, have the effect of locating the gamer in the wider context of a community of gamers. We noted also that in the 1980s in particular, magazines sought evidence in the form of photographs of the gamer's final score card. In this regard at least, things have changed markedly. More recently, developments in networked gaming devices and services such as Xbox Live,

PlayStation Network as well as systems built into many PC-based MMORPGs have meant that gamers' achievements are frequently and automatically logged at an online high score table where success can be assessed and broadcast and where relative performance is located within a potentially global community of gamers. For those wishing to compete at the highest level, the formalisation of rankings and ratings has, in fact, been carefully monitored and controlled for nearly a quarter of a century. Twin Galaxies describes itself as,

> the world authority on player rankings, gaming statistics and championship tournaments, with pinball statistics dating from the 1930s and video game statistics from the early 1970s. As the electronic gaming industry's premiere statistician, Twin Galaxies preserves the history of gaming in a historical database, which documents the historical milestones of the electronic gaming hobby as it evolves into a professional sport.
>
> ('Our Unique History' 2004 [online])

Gamers dedicated to achieving world record scores indulge in marathon sessions in search of their goal. Jeremy Mack's (2006) documentary *High Score* follows Bill Carlton's attempt to claim the *Missile Command* title:

> HIGH SCORE follows Bill as he attempts to take down the Atari classic Missile Command and its twenty-year-old record. To get the 80 million points he'll have to play the game on one quarter for over two days straight. There is no pause button. There will be no sleep. There can be only one victor in this classic story of Man versus Missile Command.
>
> ('About the film' (n.d.) [online])

Unfortunately for Carlton, the technology is simply no match for his ambition, let alone his skill and each Missile Command cabinet resets or freezes as its antiquated components prove incapable of operating for such prolonged periods. Curiously, again, we note here the manifest fallibility of videogames, and the ways their glitches and inconsistencies impact on play. In this case, the unpredictable imperfection of the game technology has a devastating effect. Later in this chapter, however, we will note other ways in which similar aberrant behaviour may be brought under the control of the gamer and turned to their advantage.

While the fortitude and resolve of the gamer who is prepared to play for over fifty hours without pause in order to capture a high score must impress, it is important to note that the high score is a somewhat peculiar marker. The high score is a record of achievement but it says little about the actual performance itself. Certainly, a table-topping or even world-beating score implies mastery and technique, but it does not illustrate, showcase or share it. Indeed, while the policy of Twin Galaxies demands video verification of the performance, such materials are not made public so as to protect the strategies and tricks of the gamer. Similarly, online scoreboards tell nothing of the journey and focus only on the outcome of play. However, other superplay proponents engage in altogether more open and public displays of gameplay skill where the journey is foregrounded.

The gamers at Ikaruga.co.uk, a fansite dedicated to the vertical scrolling shooter that is the spiritual if not actual successor to the lauded *Radiant Silvergun*, are illustrative. The site hosts a scoreboard with some 126 entries but of more interest are the gameplay videos. *Ikaruga* presents a deceptively simple game mechanic that is centred around 'polarity'. Each enemy and the hail of bullets that they unleash exists in one of the two states (indicated by their rendering in either black or white). Importantly, the player's spaceship is capable of switching polarity. The switch is neither inconsequential nor merely cosmetic as in each state enemy fire of the same polarity does not damage the player's ship but boosts its energy while attacking enemies of the other polarity enhances the power of the onslaught. Additional points are awarded for chains of attacks making careful planning essential. Moreover, the severity of the incoming ordnance is such that polarity shifts must be carefully controlled to chart a route through the screenfuls of bullets. The novelty of this gameplay design has even given rise to strategies that eschew firing on enemy craft and focus instead on 'bullet eating' or changing polarity so as to move through the like-coloured fire. Opportunities for superplay in *Ikaruga* then revolve around acquiring points by destroying enemies, maximising chains of consecutive kills, charging weaponry through bullet eating, and dispatching end-of-level bosses with speed. For the gamers at Ikaruga.co.uk, mastery involves combining all of the techniques so as to come as close as possible to the perfect playthrough. Simple completion is implied and not even considered to be an issue for these expert gamers. The downloadable videos show the current crop of highest achievements. What is interesting about them is the commentary that accompanies them. The notes accompanying Chapter 1 'Ideal' at Normal level of difficulty are indicative.

Pilot: rjpageuk
Score Detail: 4,279,330
Chain: 134
Boss Time: 74 seconds
Comment: This is a full chaining of chapter 1. Putting together a complete run of ch1 is very difficult indeed because there are so many small mistakes which one can make easily.
The bullet eating on this run is nearly optimal – about 5–10k is missed throughout the level in bullets.

It is also possible to kill the boss faster too, 75 seconds is quite possible, and rjpageuk has recorded an example here for you to see.

('Ikaruga: Chapter 1' (n.d.) [online])

In addition to the recording of such masterful examples of play, it is the commentary and annotation that separate these videos from those hosted at StuckGamer that we noted in the previous chapter. The *Ikaruga* videos exist both to showcase the skill and expert status of the pilots thereby confirming their position within the community and providing a benchmark, and also to teach less able gamers of successful routes through the often seemingly impassable and impenetrable melee. Where Twin Galaxies protects gamers' strategies, these videos lay them bare where they may be scrutinised, aspired to, adopted, adapted and perhaps even improved upon. It is in the site's forums that we see the clearest evidence of this collaboration and the emergence of collective knowledge as performances and the relative merits of specific strategies are discussed and analysis of the theoretical possibilities for chains is played out and formalised. It is important to note that *Ikaruga* itself encourages this kind of perfectionism. In its console iterations, it includes a tutorial mode that takes the gamer though each level in slow motion allowing a more considered scrutiny of the arrangements and patterns. This comparatively unusual gameplay mode helps to cement the idea of the game as a perfectible entity as well as the act of play as the performance of a strategy.

The careful planning of routes through the bullets reveals another interesting facet of *Ikaruga*. Complex though it might be, unfathomably so to the non-literati, the patterns and waves of attacks are entirely scripted, non-random and therefore predictable. We are used to considering the videogame as a responsive, adaptive simulation where inputs and outputs are in delicate balance and where the game system reacts and changes in real time to the player's button presses (see Pearce 2002). Yet, it is the predictability and repeatability of *Ikaruga*, a quality that it shares with a great number of games, that makes it ideally suited to the practices of superplay. Nowhere is this clearer than in the practice of speedrunning where the scripting and illusory non-linearity of videogames are exploited by gamers wishing to push the game to its limits, and sometimes beyond, taking advantage not only of the intended qualities, structures and rulesets of the game system but also many that the developers had not intended but that emerge through gamers' collaborative investigations into the possibilities and potentialities of the simulation.

Speedrunning: play as public performance

The practice of speedrunning,[1] as its name implies, is concerned with completing videogames in as speedy a time as possible. Typically, the games that speedrunners tackle do not include time as a primary factor in the game design. Accordingly, driving games in which lap times are the principal measure of success and where finding the racing line and shaving off fractions of seconds by hitting the apex of every corner are the cornerstones of the gameplay are eschewed. Instead, speedrunning concerns itself with games such as First Person Shooters (FPS) and even Role Playing Games (RPG) that were not designed with speedy completion in mind. At least part of the reason for the choice of games such as these is that they offer more scope for variation in strategy. With the exception of the shortcuts available in titles such as *Super Mario Kart*, most racing games offer an extremely limited potential for individual or personalised strategies. This is not to say that there are not potential and highly personalisable pleasures such as driving backwards or spinning the car around along the back straight and, indeed, performances such as these are distributed via YouTube, Google Video and other game video sites.[2] However, for the speedrunner, there is insufficient latitude as barring discrepancies and anomalies in the simulation model (such as the *Gran Turismo* AI tricks that allow gamers to bounce off other cars around corners, see Newman 2004), the racing line is typically the most efficient route around the circuit and, importantly, is not difficult to discern. FPSs are favoured because of their apparent non-linearity and the scope they seem to afford gamers to invent and create their own routes and develop their own styles that move them through the gameworld. There can be little doubt also that the list of games at the 'Speed Demos Archive' includes games chosen precisely because they are unlikely candidates for this kind of activity. *Chrono Trigger* and *The Secret of Mana*, for instance, belong to a genre more usually associated with complex, twisting, branching narratives, rich characterisations and gameplay measured in tens or even hundreds of hours (we will return to the scope of RPGs in Chapter 7 in our examination of 'fanslations'). There is an almost perverse pleasure to be derived from reducing games of this scale and complexity to their barest and as we examine this playing practice in more depth we might argue that speedrunning represents the ultimate expression of gamers' mastery of the system and of playing with videogames.

In much the same way as the high scores we noted earlier and much of the activity we have seen in this book so far, speedrunning takes place in a competitive and yet supportive environment in which a community of gamers share strategy and learn from one another while seeking to better each other's virtuoso performances and conquer the game in their name.

> think.circle- did the first Half-Life run in April of 2004 and watching it, it blew me away. The shortcuts and inventive tricks he used were just off the wall, but I saw potential for improvement. Having played Half-Life mods since the game came out, I had the requisite movement skills, plus I saw

opportunity for improvement using grenade jumps and several other small areas. Also I simply loved the game, so it seemed like an ideal choice for my first speedrun. The next several months I spent looking for shortcuts, practicing, recording, and talking with other people who were stirred up by think.circle's run. During the whole process people were finding new shortcuts, some being small optimizations, some biting off whole minutes. In fact in the middle of recording, Dopefish came up with a run that cut the time down from 55 minutes to 50 minutes. However, with the help of some amazing shortcuts devised by Spider-Waffle, I was able to beat 50 minutes by a significant margin. Since new tricks were being discovered in the middle of recording, I would have to replace segments, being very careful to make sure my health and ammo stayed the same at the end, so it worked in seamlessly.

(Rickard 2006 [online])

We might think that the management of personal identity within the cultures and community of videogaming represents a key motivation for speedrunners. For Perron (2003), the demonstration of tricks and techniques speaks of the expert status and there can be little doubt that, like the initials on the high scoreboard, the attribution of speedruns and the visibility of speedrunners in forums and on discussion boards tie these acts of gameplay virtuosity to the performers. However, the situation is really rather more complex than this. There is a high degree of community participation and a manifest collective knowledge that underpins and supports speedrunners. We might be better advised to think of speedrun strategies and techniques, plans and exploits as being the products of group discussion and the speedrunner as a performer enacting the script. Whether or not speedruns are attempted by individuals or groups as we shall see in the following section when we examine the 'Quake done Quick' project, the gameplay performance is always situated within the context of the group. As Rickard's comments above demonstrate, there is a self-evident reflectivity that is acutely aware of the contributions of others in the group who have helped to shape and evolve the overall, emerging strategy. This namechecking is not simply a matter of copyright or IP respect. As Ali Campbell, one of the administrators of the Speed Demos Archive, explains, there is a clear sense in which the products and processes of speedrunning are owned by the community rather than any particular individual.

'It's nearly always a single individual that performs a particular run,' points out Campbell, 'but the end product usually "belongs" to the community as a whole in some way, because many people will have had input into it.'

('Speed Freaks' 2007 [online])

What we should note here is that while speedrunning appears to privilege the performance of play, it is in fact an activity in which planning and strategy are equally valued components. The originator of a particular technique makes a contribution that is valued alongside the performer who enacts on screen. Consequently, in addition to the cumulative, collective knowledge that builds upon and adopts the strategies of other runners in the community, what we note in Rickard's account is an extraordinary level of dedication and planning. Andrew Gardikis' *Super Mario Bros.* speedrun is similarly enlightening. The speedrun compresses the entire game into just 5:00 minutes. Yet, despite his obvious gameplay skill, Gardikis is keen to recognise the contributions of other speedrunners and locate his feat within the context of a continually unfolding and evolving collective intelligence.

Author's comments:

I believe that this may be a perfect time by Speeddemosarchive's timing of Super Mario Bros. 1.

First off, I'd like to thank my brother for helping me figure out a faster way of beating the game. If it weren't for him, a run like this probably wouldn't have been seen for a long while. I also want to thank those who encouraged me to keep trying to improve my run even after playing near perfect, including Scott, Trevor, Stanski, and many others.

Scott's run made me decide to push this game to its limits. After seeing his near perfect run, I wanted to completely perfect the game. I give a lot of credit to Scott for achieving a run played perfectly (within the second) without the use of alternate pipe glitches and the walljump. Same goes for Trevor.

I hope you all enjoy this run. I've worked hard to make this possible. Thanks to everyone at SDA who supported me. I'm sure you'll enjoy this one.

(Gardikis 2007 [online])

It is interesting to note that 2007's *Super Mario Galaxy* builds the practices of speedrunning and superplay into its game design with the inclusion of 'Daredevil Comets' that require the player to replay an already 'completed' level subject to an additional rule such as strict (and usually harsh) time limit, or by using only one life, for instance. The inclusion of these modes of play both speaks of the mainstreaming of superplay and speedrunning and is a direct reference to the work of speedrunners on the *Super Mario* series.

It is is clear that the task of speedrunning is an exceptionally demanding one that requires that gamers know their chosen game in intimate detail. Moreover, the search for perfection means that runs will be abandoned and restarted if they fall short of expectations. The implications of failure are particularly problematic for those undertaking 'single-segment' runs and who seek to complete the entire game in a single session with no breaks. By contrast, 'multi-segment' runs tackle each level or sequence as a separate entity. It follows that, freed from the pressures of completing the game in its entirety, multi-segment runs are typically faster. Regardless of whether they are tackled in a single session or as a series of discrete episodes, the intentions of speedrunners can be broken down into three main categories. According to the 'Speed Demos Archive':

> In general there are three types of runs you can do on a game. The first is the "pure speed" run, where you do whatever it takes to get to the end of the game as fast as possible. Next is the "100%" run where you get everything in the game. How to define 100% for any given game is usually a matter for debate. In general, any item that improves your character's abilities should be collected. Things that don't, such as maps, aren't necessary. This isn't true for all games however, it is only a general idea. The third type of run is the "low%", where you get the bare minimum number of items and upgrades and still try to go fast. A low% run does not restrict the usage of items you are forced to obtain. Almost always the low% run will be slower than the pure speed run, but sometimes it ends up that skipping everything possible is the fastest way. In this case the two categories are merged.
>
> ('Speed Demos Archive FAQ' (n.d.) [online])

As with 'Twin Galaxies', the rules and regulations that govern speedrunning activity are meticulously detailed and govern issues as diverse as the means of verification to specific guidance on timing runs of particular games. However, in order to appreciate the full significance of the practice, it is essential to understand that unlike online leaderboards or Coin-Op cabinet high scores that simply record the outcome of the achievement which disappears into the ether to be replaced only by three initials and the score, speedrunning does not only concern itself with the end result. The document of the journey is a vital element of the speedrunning endeavour. While the final time is of undoubted importance, and competitions abound, speedruns are captured on video and distributed in their entirety either on DVD or more usually as downloads or streaming video on the Web at sites such as the Speed Demos Archive. As such, where Twin Galaxies protects the strategies of its champions, the culture of speedrunning is oriented around the public exhibition of these performances in their entirety. Indeed, if we consider the origins of speedrunning, the centrality of this public exhibition is easily explained.

QdQ: 'Quake done Quick'

As Henry Lowood (2007) observes in his history of what he terms 'high-performance play', id's First Person Shooters *DOOM* and *Quake* have provided rich pickings for speedrunners. Along with the developer's earlier title *Wolfenstein*, the games practically gave rise to the FPS genre. I have noted elsewhere (Newman 2004) that *DOOM* is notable for drawing the gamer's attention to their success rate at the culmination of every level. This single, static screen that lists various statistics including secrets revealed, for instance, is a powerful device that urges reflection on the performance and encourages replay so that performance may be honed. Quite apart from the innovative gameplay, revolutionary graphics systems and peerless level design (see King and Borland 2003; Newman and Simons 2007), one of the interesting features included in both *DOOM* and its successor *Quake* was its 'demo recording'. The proprietary .DEM format files are not movies *per se* and cannot be viewed without the *DOOM* or *Quake* game. .DEMs are data files that record the gamer's inputs and the behaviour of the game system and can be used to effectively play back a recorded performance from within the *DOOM* or *Quake* game. The availability of .DEM files had a number of significant consequences. Most obviously, while both *DOOM* and *Quake* offered simultaneous multiplayer game modes, the single player game was transformed into something that could easily be shared with others. The comparatively small size of the .DEM files made transferring them easier in an era of dial-up Internet connections. As such, the demo files afford the public display of single-player prowess. Additionally, and perhaps more unexpected, the emergent community of *DOOM* and *Quake* demo makers joined forces to form teams dedicated to producing collaborative demos. The ease with which .DEM files could be exchanged eased the sharing of tips and strategies and simplified the process of portioning out duties. However, the sharing of demo files has a number of unexpected consequences.

While by no means the first, one of the most famous team projects is 'Quake done Quick'. QdQ is centred on producing an array of speedruns of *Quake* under various conditions, including 'pacifist' and '100%' challenges that involve minimal kills and the revelation of all secrets respectively. The project has been steadily refined and new runs shave off seconds and even minutes as new techniques are discovered and honed. Many of the speedruns operate at the highest levels of difficulty (e.g. level four 'Ultraviolence' and the highest, level 5 'Nightmare!'). The issue of difficulty is an interesting one for speedrunners. As putatively 'hardcore', 'extreme' gamers for whom completion is a mere formality and the grace and elegance of the execution are paramount, one would imagine that only the hardest difficulty levels would be acceptable. It comes as something of a surprise to find that some QdQ projects such as 'The Rabbit Run' and 'Quake done 100% Quick lite' stipulate the Easy setting.[3] However, a better understanding of the way difficulty levels operate sheds light on their inclusion in the criteria for play. First, although the implementations vary between titles, different difficulty levels often affect changes in the behaviour of the simulation. There might, for instance, be different numbers of locations of enemies and some random elements may be rendered wholly predictable (as in the case of *Metroid Prime*, a game we will examine in some depth in the following section). Each of these differences makes possible different routes through the gameworld as areas become more easily accessible while the simple fact that the difficulty is either increased or decreased allows for and encourages differing levels of risk-taking. The consequences of losing too much energy or, worse still, losing a life and rendering the entire run void, are so serious that speed is not always the central concern. If a route is too risky, it may be abandoned in favour of one more certain to succeed. This reveals an interesting tension. On the one hand, we might rightly think of speedrunners as maverick gamers developing and using edgy techniques and operating at the boundaries of the simulation. However, simultaneously, they often display an unexpected conservatism. Cody Miller is the current world record holder for completing *Halo 2* on the hardest level of difficulty ('Legendary'). His performance of 3 hours, 16 minutes, 28 seconds is the first speedrun to make the *Guinness Book of Records*. In his submission, he explains that:

> I approached each level thinking: 'What is the safest way to beat it?' Speed wasn't a concern, although often the fastest route is the safest. Even after finding the safest route through the game, it was still pretty damn hard.
>
> ('Speed Freaks' 2007 [online])

Among the most striking and intriguing features of the QdQ speedruns is the exploitation of the game system. As Rickard (2006) noted in relation to *Half-Life*, there is more to speedrunning than careful routeplanning. Part of the process of speedrunning involves exploring the very limits of the simulation model, pushing at the edges. In some cases, this means more than just mastering the controls or choosing the best character, weapon or attack/defence strategy for a given sequence or enemy. In some cases, this means taking advantage of the game's foibles. Glitches, inconsistencies and the undocumented features of the game are explored and exploited. Where the glitch-hunters we noted in the previous chapter were engaged in the process of exposing and documenting such programming errors as curios, speedrunners are in the business of application. Anomalies are sought out in order that they might be exploited and used to the advantage of the speedrunner. As such, speedruns are frequently comprised

of behaviour, play and performance that run contrary to the intentions of the
developers or, at the very least, were unintended:

> One of the things I do is investigate the physics of the universe of Quake,
> trying to understand more about how the engine underlying the game works
> so that we can turn its little nooks and crannies to our advantage. You
> could call it research if you liked, but basically it's just running around,
> having fun and blowing things up same as normal, except maybe with a
> few little numbers flashing up on the screen monitoring the engine's vital
> statistics. It's experimental physics in a whole new universe.
>
> (Bailey 1997 [online])

The QdQ project website hosts a number of extremely in-depth articles that
detail various ways of exploiting the vagaries of the game's engine. These mostly
involve the physics simulation and outline what are now staple techniques such
as 'Strafe Running' in *DOOM* or 'Zigzagging' in *Quake* which rely on the velocity
advantage the gamer is afforded if running forwards and diagonally simultaneously and 'Bunny-Hopping' which tries to avoid the in-game effects of friction
by spending as much time as possible in the air. Perhaps the most famous technique to emerge from *Quake*, however, is 'rocket jumping',

> the most obvious is the trick known to every Quaker – rocket-jumping.
> In fact, rocket-jumping is only one of several applications of a more gen-
> eral principle of Quake physics which can be briefly summarized by saying
> that when you are hurt, your velocity is changed. Once you've understood
> this principle, and have got to grips with the way explosives work in Quake,
> you can take advantage of some of the finer points of rocket-jumping.
>
> (Bailey 1997 [online])

That Bailey's insight into the game's mechanics and knowledge of the game engine
is earned through informed and well-observed play is more than evident here.
Moreover, it is clear that what is often termed 'emergent gameplay' in the game
development community (see also Smith 2001; Salen and Zimmerman 2004)
is at the very heart of speedrunning, even though much of this emergence is
centred on the exploitation of glitches rather than the use of an open set of
tools or resources. As such, it is difficult to define exactly where and whether
the emergence is intended by the developers or is a consequence of their inevitable
programming errors and anomalies and limitations of their modelling and design.
Where the walkthrough movies of StuckGamer take the player on a journey
through the 'ideal game' as envisaged by the developer, working strictly within
their rules and elucidating the most efficient and legitimate use of the tools,

speedrunning seemingly takes advantage of any exploit that assists in enhancing the run. In fact, it is not quite that simple and speedrunning communities like Speed Demos Archive and QdQ have a somewhat complicated attitude towards what they refer to as 'cheating'. The QdQ project team rightly draw attention to the extraordinary adaptability of *Quake*. Developers id ensured that *Quake* (like many other games subsequently) could be modified by gamers in an often dramatic fashion (as we shall learn in the next chapter). Perhaps as a consequence, the speedrunning community at QdQ has found it necessary to establish a baseline by determining a set of conditions that runs must conform to in order to qualify for inclusion in the collaboratively created portfolio: 'Here at QdQ, we attempt to draw a clear line between altering your Quake configurations to suit your style, and altering it to play a different game altogether' ('Allowable console changes' 1997 [online]).

Thus, while tampering with server-side variables is precluded, Zigzagging, Rocket Jumping and Bunny-Hopping are *de rigueur*. As we noted in the previous chapter, the latter are actions that are performed within the game and take advantage of glitches or programming anomalies. Given their existence within the fabric or mechanic of the game, these appear to be sanctioned as legitimate tools that fall into the arsenal of the gamer. They do not change the code but rather exploit the peculiarities of its construction and implementation. Thus, enabling a God Mode that bestows invincibility modifies the fundamental terms of engagement by altering the collision detection routines, for instance, and cannot be considered an example of emergent gameplay in the way that the exploitation of the physics engine with the rocket jump can. Rocket Jumping, Bunny Hopping and Zigzagging all take place within the confines of the unmodified simulation and take advantage of its vagaries, imperfections and undocumented behaviours. We might be tempted to see speedrunning as little different from the *ludus* rules superimposed by gamers onto the existing game's rulesystem (see Church 2000 on *The Sims*; Frasca 2001 on flight simulators, for instance). However, there is more complicated work here. The *ludus* that gamers impose frequently involve subverting, bending or stretching the existing rulesystems and disrupting the game's mechanics and 'normal' operation. Nowhere is this clearer than in the case of sequence breaking.

Sequence breaking: the (non-) linearity of videogames

Of all the emergent gameplay practices and playful explorations of the boundaries and limits of the game system, sequence breaking is perhaps the most intriguing. Not only does the practice offer yet more evidence of the creativity, imagination and invention of gamers but it sheds light on the structures of games and the often illusory nature of their non-linearity. Much has been written on the non-linearity of videogames and their hypertextuality or even 'ergodicity' (Aarseth 1997, see also Newman 2002b). The branching narrative structures of games like *Metal Gear Solid 2* or *Final Fantasy VII* certainly lead us to believe that these titles offer myriad possible outcomes and pathways depending on the choices gamers make or the competence of their performances. The question of interactive narrative has exercised many videogames scholars (see Murray 1997; Frasca 2003). While there is much truth in the assertion that gamer's choices may affect the course of games such as *MGS2* and *FFVII*, the structures of these texts are far less complex and extensive than we might ordinarily believe. In fact, there are a vast number of 'bottlenecks' at which all gamers will arrive (all those who progress that far into the game, at least). There are clear economic reasons for bottleneck structures as the cost of designing, implementing and quality testing material is sufficiently high that effort expended on material that many gamers may never experience is difficult to justify (see Newman 2004, for more on the relationship between development and publishing and game structures). Moreover, as Smith (2002) notes, the maintenance of a consistent, singular narrative demands bottlenecks, the restriction of choice and 'loaded dice'.

> *Final Fantasy VII* does not allow totally free choice in these 'interactive' dialogue situations. Often it offers two separate possible responses, only one of which is truly enticing or plausible. When given the choice of making sweet feminine Aeris a flower seller or the town drunk, only one choice maintains any kind of narrative consistency. Frequently we are given a choice between doing something that advances the plot or doing nothing ("No thanks," "I don't care"), providing the appearance of choice while allowing the game to continue its story arc.
>
> (Smith 2002 [online])

Many videogames that appear to present rich, branching, infinitely variable structures highly contingent on gamer performance and choice are, in fact, structured in such a way that the completion of specific sequences in a prescribed order is essential for progress to continue. Specific items need to be acquired before access is granted to parts of the gameworld. Skills and techniques need to be bestowed or earned before challenges can be undertaken. This model of progression has become a staple of game design and sees gamers commencing the game with limited capacities and capabilities that are expanded as the game develops and with which the player may tackle an ever more complex set of tasks. Nintendo's *Metroid* and *The Legend of Zelda* series are just two that follow the pattern. The craft of the videogame designer is often to conceal the bottlenecks and linearity of the progression path by guiding the gamer along the 'right' path as Smith observes.

Of course, designers and developers might try to guide gamers along particular paths by giving them loaded or even wholly inconsequential binary choices that in fact have no bearing on the trajectory of the narrative, or they may be more blunt and physically bar access to parts of the gameworld and portions of the narrative by literally locking doors and barring paths. The guards who stop Link leaving Kakariko village until he has undertaken the various tasks required of him are a typical reminder that there is a 'right way' to tackle the *Ocarina of Time*'s heroic quest. Recalling our discussion of sidequests in the previous chapter, it is useful to remember that games such as *FFVII*, *Ocarina* and *MGS2* offer many detours that contribute to the 'non-linearity' of the gaming experience as they divert gamers' attentions but which do not necessarily greatly impact on the central narrative thread that continues to play out linearly. However, for all the efforts and techniques of game developers and designers, there is no reason to suppose that gamers will necessarily oblige and follow the prescribed path. We have seen already that QdQ speedrunners are willing and more than able to find ways of exploiting code to their advantage. In these restrictive, linear progression paths that force sequential completion of levels, sequences and quests, they are faced with something altogether more injurious to their endeavours. Where glitch exploits such as Rocket-Jumping and Bunny-Hopping amplify the capabilities of the gamer, sequence breaking is concerned with subverting or circumventing systems and structures that have been put in place. To draw a parallel with athletics, if using Rocket-Jumping and Strafe-Running is equivalent to taking performance-enhancing drugs, then sequence breaking is like finding a shortcut and missing out half of the race. Of course, in speedrunning, neither tactic is outlawed and both are key weapons in the arsenal of the gamer determined to strip down the performance to its barest and arrive at the finish line as quickly as possible.

> Sequence Breaking is the act of obtaining items in the game out of order, or of skipping said items entirely.
>   Much like Sequence Breaking in Super Metroid, Sequence Breaking in Metroid Prime has been refined into an art. The goal of the Sequence Breakers is to push the game as far as they can, either by getting the lowest percent of item pickups, by beating the game as quickly as possible, or by beating the game as quickly as possible with all items (100% pickups).
>
> ('Sequence Breaking' 2002 [online])

Nintendo's *Metroid* series has offered particularly rich pickings for sequence breakers and the speedrunners of the 'Metroid 2002' community who have centred their attentions on *Metroid Prime* are among the most prominent and proficient practitioners of the art.

Metroid Prime follows a broadly similar conceit to other titles in the series that sees the gamer adopting the role of Samus. Bristling with weaponry, suited in armour and possessing a vast array of capabilities and powers, a catastrophic event robs Samus of all but the most basic skills. The remainder of the game is, in part at least, a journey to regain these lost abilities which are re-revealed in a sequential fashion. The linearity of the acquisition of weaponry and capability implicitly governs the route through the gameworld and narrative as certain missions can only be tackled once specific skills and capacities are possessed, for example. The ability to switch from human to 'morph ball' allows entry to otherwise inaccessible spaces in the gameworld. The consequence of Metroid 2002's extensive investigation and experimentation has been to uncover a vast array of sequence breaking exploits that is as impressive as it is surprising. Indeed, the exploits start at the very beginning of the game with the out-of-sequence acquisition of the Space Jump Boots item (the 'Space Jump First' sequence break). The technique is described in considerable detail, with variations in strategy noted depending on the specific version of the game as Japanese, European, Australian and North American 'Player's Choice' versions behave differently from the standard North American version. Moreover, annotated movies illustrate the operation of the technique offering a visual walkthrough of the emergent glitch exploit:

> Sequence Breaking means you do things in Metroid Prime the developers probably didn't intend, such as getting items out of order or going places you're not supposed to go yet.
> *Why Sequence Break?*
> If you've played through Metroid Prime a couple times, and you think you've seen all the game has to offer, think again. You can hone your skills and do things you probably never thought possible (while getting better and better completion times to boot).
>
> ('An Introduction to Sequence Breaking' 2002 [online])

As alluded to in Metroid 2002's definition of sequence breaking above, the many *Metroid Prime* techniques can be split into two (related) categories. Some are focused on skipping sections or sequences. These breaks are most obviously useful to the speedrunner as they allow large chunks of the game to be sidestepped entirely thereby reducing the amount of space to be traversed. Other techniques allow gamers to reach items and objects out of sequence as in the case of the 'Space Jump First' exploit. Equipping more powerful weaponry than the developers had intended the gamer to possess at a given point in the game may, for instance, render battles easier thereby potentially assisting the speedrunner. Additionally, toting advanced weaponry or armour, may also serve to minimise the risk to the gamer which, as we have seen, may give rise to more adventurous performances.

Ultimately, then, the practice of speedrunning shares many of the characteristics of glitch-hunting but with the express intention of applying the vagaries of the game model and utilising the emergent gameplay behaviours to the advantage of the speedrunner. Like glitch-hunting and the deployment of Zigzagging and Rocket-Jumping, sequence breaking is an inherently community-based activity with the collective knowledge codified in the series of sequence breaking techniques, tutorials and guidelines. Sequence breaking reveals much about the pleasures of gameplay as an exploratory activity that plays with the systems and rules and is oriented around replay and careful, attentive performance. Moreover, it reveals much about videogames themselves drawing attention to the often linearly structured progression pathways and the bottlenecks and loaded dice of narrative-driven games such as *Metroid Prime*.

Beyond human ability: tool-assisted speedruns

Thus far, our discussion has centred entirely on speedrunning as a configurative, transformative gameplay practice that pits gamers against the game, or perhaps more precisely, the game design and implementation. Though they might be exploiting tricks and tips not known to all gamers and maybe not even known to the game's developers, the speedruns we have examined in the first part of this chapter are essentially similar to non-superplay performances. There is, however, a branch of speedrunning that engages the gamer in a quite different relationship and which exploits the game in entirely different ways and for quite different purposes.

Tool-assisted speedruns (TAS) use the qualities and affordances of technical systems to eliminate the imperfections of real-time human performance and seek to create the theoretically perfect playing of a game. Ostensibly similar to 'normal' speedruns, TAS are video recordings of performances but with a crucial difference. Where the gamer in a normal speedrun performs in real-time, entering inputs like any other gamer and differing only in the techniques, strategies and tactics they deploy, the gamer in TAS does not play 'live'. Rather, videos of Tool-assisted speedruns are built up, in super slow motion and often frame-by-frame, in an almost unbelievably long-winded process. Curiously, then, while the intention is to create the perfect speedrun, the TAS gamer works remarkably slowly and with painstaking attention to detail.

As its name suggests, the practice of Tool-assisted speedrunning is made possible by a series of technical systems that allow fine-grained control over the inputs into the game system. Chief among the tools is the emulator. Where normal speedruns are performed on original hardware such as consoles or handheld devices, TAS make use of 'emulation' software that runs on general purpose PCs or Macs and that can mimic, often with great accuracy, the operation of a specific gaming device. These emulators offer many advantages over the original gaming device. Most obviously, they afford a greater degree of control over the input and output systems allowing gamers to slow down the operation of the game, to make play a less hurried experience. Additionally, where the game played under original conditions may have offered only a limited, or perhaps even no mechanism for saving progress, emulators allow the gamer to save their game at any moment. So, where the original game may have required the gamer to complete an entire level or a particular sequence before progress could be saved, with the game running under emulation saving can be undertaken at will. This is because the emulator software effectively pauses the program and saves the state of all variables and so the built-in save system of the game is essentially bypassed. The free availability of savestates is a critical affordance of the emulator as gamers can tackle the game in extremely small sections which can be returned to if a subsequent error is made. The emulator savestate is the equivalent of an 'Undo' feature on a word processor and effectively renders the performance non-committal as steps can be easily undone and the performance rewound. The availability of emulators with their slow motion and savestate affordances makes possible an entirely new way of playing videogames. In an interview with Kyle Orland, Tool-assisted speedrunner 'Bisqwit' explains the workflow and gives a sense of the amount of dedication that is required. Again, we note here the cumulative effort at work. TAS are based on observation and criticism of previous runs with strategies and techniques adopted and adapted.

> For a gameplay movie to be flawless, it must be as fast as possible, it must not miss a shot, have no wasted efforts, and so on. Creating a such movie involves planning and carefulness.
>
> The game is played at slow speed (the emulator slows the game down), doing small segments at time and optimizing then as well as possible, redoing until it goes well. The finished (and unfinished) product is reviewed many times, at full speed and at slow motion, to find things to improve and to invent new strategies and then played again.
>
> Creating such a movie is very timeconsuming. You can easily elapse 4 hours for a 10 minute sequence – and that's only for the first revision. For some games, planning can need lots of time. Creating a releasable movie can take anything from 4 hours to 6 months, depending on how much free time you have, how complex the game is, how careful you are and how skillful you are. Many improved movies are also based on observations from

previous movies, so it's actually difficult to estimate how much time goes into producing a good gameplay movie.

('Bisqwit interview' 2004 [online])

The idea of the flawless game performance is an intriguing one and clearly reflects the mission of TASVideos which states that the authors of these movies use an emulator as a tool to overcome human limitations of skill and reflex. Clearly, at least part of the intention in this practice is to deploy all of the glitches and tricks that a gamer operating at normal speed would be able to achieve but to push yet further to identify new exploits that are beyond the reflexes and reactions of even the most proficient gamer. Moreover, these tricks are to be executed each and every time with no missed opportunities. The level of discussion and analysis of videogame systems among TAS communities is staggeringly detailed and informed. Insights into the collision detections or the synchronising of inputs to frame rendering that allows techniques such as moving through solid objects, show a quite remarkable level of detective work as well as a deep knowledge of the technologies of gaming and the protocols of software programming and gaming hardware:

> In a similar fashion to the sequence breakers and glitch-hunters we have noted previously, TAS movie makers do not consider their use of emulators to constitute cheating as they do not tamper with the integrity of the game code. The use of tools only affects the ability to input and control the game and while they seek to attain a Godly level of performance, they do not implement the 'God' cheat modes available in games such as *Doom* that bestow invincibility, for instance.
>
> Perfection is not easy.
>
> Yes, using the tools makes *playing* easy – but we do not just play here.
>
> We attempt to perfect the games to a godly level of precision, which involves handling the game as if it were The Matrix – observing every slightest detail to gain control over it in ways that the makers never imagined. We search for perfection.
>
> To reach that goal, using the features provided by an emulator is irrelevant, as long as the "world" – the game – is unmodified.
>
> ('FractalFusion' 2007 [online])

It would be easy to consider the Tool-assisted speedrun as a cold, mechanical operation that rids the gameplay experience of humanity and replaces it with machine-like clinical perfection. However, this would be to misunderstand the intentions of the community. According to TASVideos, the twin aims of the Tool-assisted speedrunners are entertainment and art. For Bisqwit and other proponents of the practice, the ability to unearth and expose unexpectedly graceful and elegant performances is a key motivation. In this way, we might note the transformation of often antiquated games such as *Super Mario Bros.* by contemporary technologies. These transformations leave the original game code intact as the ROM that is run under emulation is a bit-for-bit carbon copy, but offer new ways of engaging with it by releasing the code from its original hardware. By allowing a different kind of input and facilitating the most minutely detailed interrogation of each frame of the rendered game, retracing steps where perfection is not reached, emulation may give rise to new forms of expression, and reveal new patterns and dimensions to these games. In the end, these are still human performances but they are impossible for any human to perform without the cyborg-like extensions offered by emulator. If normal superplay showcases the inventiveness and skill of the gamer as real-time performer, TAS ultimately showcases the potentialities of the game and game system, revealing new possibilities and highlighting the malleability of the game, its openness to different 'playings' and the sheer number of imperfections that go unnoticed during normal play.

In the final section of this chapter, we shall further examine the ways in which technological interventions have been developed and deployed by gamers in order to reimagine and re-present the game in new contexts and for different purposes.

Machinima: playing moviemaker

For all their differences in objectives and techniques, the superplay practices we have seen so far share one thing in common. Whether they are races to the finish that shortcircuit the narrative logic of the game by disrupting the intended flow of sequences, or are attempts to exploit the imperfections of the game and eradicate the imperfections of human reflex and reaction by manipulating the mode of engagement through technical means, each of these practices clearly takes place within a ludic framework. However subversive or radical these alternative 'playings' might be and regardless of the manner in which they interrupt the game with emergent gameplay strategies and techniques, they remain predominantly geared towards completion of specific game-related tasks. The ludic system is, in most cases, a combination of the intrinsic rules established, operated and policed by the game system and additional gamer-derived *ludus* rules that are superimposed on the gameplay and that stipulate the conditions of speedrunning or the acceptability of specific strategies, equipment or techniques (see Caillois 2001; also Frasca 2001, on player-imposed *ludus* in videogames). What these superplay practices ably demonstrate is the malleability and plasticity of the videogame and the transformativity of gameplay (Salen 2002). Importantly, we note also the inseparability of the two. The videogame is material which is given shape, form and meaning through the performance of the gamer. For Salen and Zimmerman (2004: 41), 'a *designer* creates a *context* to be encountered by a *participant*, from which *meaning* emerges'. What is particularly interesting about this situation is that there is no necessary reason why this performance has to be so clearly bounded by the ludic framework of the game. We might then impose a *ludus* rule that does not relate to the aim or goal of the game but is instead concerned with storytelling, for instance. Simply because *Quake* primarily deals with shooting does not mean gamers have to shoot. We have seen that 'low%' or 'pacifist' speedruns preclude this behaviour and centre on moving through the gameworld. But even here, the *ludus* of completion, of moving through the gameworld to accomplish some other goal or outcome, reassert *Quake* as a game albeit a radically different one now the FPS loses its 'S'. However, one interesting feature of the openness of videogames such as *Quake*, *Metroid Prime* and *Halo* and their susceptibility to different types of playing – the different meanings that may be made in their context – is that the ostensible objectives and outcomes of their game system, the shooting and puzzling, the competitive, combative play, the purposeful movement through the game space, the winning and losing states, may be suspended in favour of wholly different, perhaps even non-ludic, activity. Superplay, as Lowood (2005, 2007) notes, transforms the player into 'performer' but these remain performances of gameplay. Speedruns are video recordings of virtuosity, showcasing the prowess and inventiveness of gamers, or in the case of TAS, the theoretical limits of the gameplay. Machinima, on the other hand, typically dispenses with ludic intentions, and recasts the videogame as a creative environment for performances perhaps connected with and even commenting on, but importantly, not of play. Here, 'performer' takes on a rather different meaning.

Machinima (a contraction of 'machine animation' or 'machine cinema') is essentially filmmaking in videogame environments, using game characters and environments of games as cast and location for cinematic production. As Jones (2006) observes, Machinima has existed for over a decade yet it has only recently blipped onto the radar of mainstream media (e.g. Buchanan 2003; Thompson 2005; Bray 2004). According to the 'Academy of Machinima Arts and Sciences':

> Machinima . . . is filmmaking within a real-time, 3D virtual environment, often using 3D video-game technologies.
>
> In an expanded definition, it is the convergence of filmmaking, animation and game development. Machinima is real-world filmmaking techniques applied within an interactive virtual space where characters and events can be either controlled by humans, scripts or artificial intelligence.
>
> By combining the techniques of filmmaking, animation production and the technology of real-time 3D game engines, Machinima makes for a very

cost- and time-efficient way to produce films, with a large amount of creative control.

('The Machinima FAQ' 2005 [online])

By eschewing the narrative and gameplay demands of the game, Machinima makers embrace the game's potential for play and performance to serve their artistic ends. The performative repertoire of controllable characters, the variety of actions they can be coaxed into performing on-screen, the extent of their available animation, are wholly disconnected from gameplay imperatives and are repositioned as part the character's 'range'. Where the player-controlled character might be thought of algorithmically in terms of gameplay-affecting capacities, capabilities or properties during play or superplay (see Eskelinen 2001; Newman 2002, 2004), in Machinima, they are reframed as part of a representational system. Characters, backgrounds, objects and their manipulatable behaviours become part of a moviemaking toolkit. For Lowood, the act of moviemaking remains a playful engagement, but the transformation from the ludic imperative of the Deathmatch to the narrative production of moviemaking remains clear. 'Machinima can in part be understood as a replacement of one game structure with another, as the "free movement of play" alters the game from playing to win to playing to make a movie' (2005: 13).

In some senses, Machinima and the use of videogames as virtual animation sets populated with actors may be seen as providing little more than a low-cost 3D modelling environment and certainly the Academy of Machinima Arts and Sciences itself promotes the form in this regard while Marino (2004) and Wilonsky (2002) enthusiastically note that Spielberg used Machinima based on *Unreal Tournament 2004* as a preproduction testbed for blocking effects shots during the making of *AI*. However, the positioning of Machinima as a digital storyboarding tool sells it short. Treated as a means of creating finished pieces, this is a fundamentally different means of making cinema to the frame-by-frame rendering that gave life to *Luxo Jr.* and *Toy Story*. Though there may be postproduction, editing and voice-over work, Machinma is generally created in real time which means that pieces often rely on the carefully stage-managed and choreographed performances of multiple 'actors'. In this regard alone, Machinima marks a fascinating departure from traditional production methods.

In addition to their openness and malleability and the way in which the structures of games such as *Quake* and *Halo* with their myriad detours allow gamers to veer from the central narrative and gameplay threads and suspend the ludic imperatives, the disentangling of viewpoint and camera has proved essential in facilitating Machinima. Gamers familiar with *Quake* will, no doubt, be struck by the potential limitations of the game's mode of presentation. Even if we can sidestep the requirement for shooting, the First-Person Shooter (FPS) seems to inhibit the creative endeavours of the Machinima maker with the insistence of its viewpoint. Like *DOOM* before it and countless FPSs since, *Quake* presents its gameworld as though seen through the eyes of the gamer. Save for the POV shot, there is little scope for cinematographic expression. While more recent titles afford the gamer some degree of virtual camera control making the task somewhat easier, pioneers of videogame movie-making such as the QdQ speedrunning team took matters into their own hands and designed and implemented the requisite software add-ons. In their earliest incarnations, these 'recamming' tools that allowed the in-game camera to be disconnected from the gamer's POV and freely moved around the playing arena in postproduction, existed to enrich and enliven speedrun videos. While the speedrunner retained the first-person viewpoint that enables gameplay, recamming, and the 'editing' of the camera position once the run was complete and recorded, afforded the creation of a video that communicated a greater sense of context for an audience as well as potentially creating a more visually engaging and diverse piece. For Marino (2004), the development of recamming tools and the subsequent dissociation of camera and POV in postproduction, marks the 'defining moment' for Machinima. Projects have moved far beyond recammed speedruns and productions are ambitious in their intentions with many narrative and abstract pieces (see Cannon 2007, for more on the distinction) including Chris Brandt's extraordinarily skilful and humorous 'Dance, Voldo, Dance' (2005):

> The choreographed moves in this recording are all actual game play; no programming was done. "Soul Calibur" is a game in which two combatants battle to the death using their weapons of choice. It's common in this style of fighting game for each character to have multiple costumes, and this is why there are two equally freaky Voldos dancing with each other. Over a week's worth of full-time training and performance went into this production, which sparked more than one comment of "you need a job" (a phrase I'm not all that unused to hearing).
>
> (Brandt 2005 [online])

In this piece, we note not only the suspension of the gameplay imperative (a game in which 'two combatants battle to the death using their weapons of choice' but in which there is no fighting) but also its replacement with a parodic alternative. The sight of two armour-clad warriors brandishing a bewildering array of deadly weaponry dancing in perfect choreographed synchronicity to the strains of Nelly's 'Hot in Herre' is about as far as can be imagined from the bone-crunching combat that *Soul Calibur* gamers are used to.[4] Indeed, parody and humour are much in evidence in Machinima work (see Dovey and Kennedy 2006 on the Rangers Clan's 'Diary of a Camper'. Note also the *South Park* episode

'Make Love Not Warcraft' (2006, Season 10, Episode 147) which demonstrates both the visibility of Machinima in mainstream popular culture and its links with comedy and parody). The *Halo*-based 'Red vs Blue' series created by Rooster Teeth, for instance, is among the best-known and lauded works, and deals in part with videogames and game culture turning its attentions in on itself in a deliciously self-referential manner and to a considerable audience with 900,000 downloads per week, according to Allen (2004):

> The writing and novel production techniques have earned praise. And some say the sophomoric jokes bespeak something more profound. "The literary analog is absurdist drama," says Graham Leggat, director of communications at the Lincoln Center film society and a videogame critic. "It's truly as sophisticated as Samuel Beckett."
>
> (Delaney 2004 [online])

As Sotamaa (2003) suggests, Lionhead's *The Movies* is perhaps indicative of the mainstreaming of Machinima. Placing the gamer in the role of a Hollywood mogul, it affords the opportunity to create original movies by assembling and developing talent and amassing budget. While *The Movies* is interesting in offering a single environment in which movies can be made, its editing tools are less extensive than those of video editing software such as Apple's 'Final Cut' or even 'iMovie', for instance. Similarly, the scope of the movies is limited by the palette of the game in a way that would preclude some of the more avant-garde pieces we see in the Machinima scene. This recalls Consalvo's (2003b) critique of the limits that technical tools place on expression and resistance among online fan communities, though as Jones (2006: 273) observes, the transformativity and transgressiveness of superplay, hacking and cracking push further at the boundaries than the fan activities Consalvo documents. However, where *The Movies* is similar to 'traditional' Machinima is in the way it encourages gamers to share their creations. Movies are uploaded and hosted online and a considerable community has built up around the game and its outputs.

Ultimately, Machinima, like superplay, is concerned with the transformation of the player into performer and the creation of spectacular records of instances of gamers playing, or playing *with*, videogames. In the next part of this book, we will pick up the discussion of technological interventions that we have seen in relation to TAS and Machinima when we examine the phenomenon of modding. Where we have seen technical systems and tools used to modify the engagement with videogames through their interfaces in TAS and the re-presentation of gameplay as video through postproduction, editing and in some cases through the development of recamming tools, the practice of modding involves rather more dramatic and radical changes to the videogames. In this part of the book, we have focused mainly on the transformativity of play and performance by examining the ways in which the imposition of ludus rules through the establishing of speedrunning challenges, the exploitation of glitches and the disruption of narrative or spatial sequencing, and even the suspension of ludic, gameplay imperatives in favour of playful, narrative production, have shaped the meaning of the videogame in creative and often unexpected ways. We have seen gamers probing the effects and operation of the code that underlies the videogame, exploring, documenting, analysing and taking advantage of the patterns it creates in the simulation model. This often deep knowledge of simulation, program and algorithm acquired through deduction and attentive play is put to work through strategies and tactics, and performances that are dedicated to exploring, exploiting and extending the videogame. Gameplay performance, as we have seen, is not merely an interactive but an interrogatory and emergent practice that transforms the videogame which exists as malleable, plastic material or context shaped and given meaning in the interaction (see also Salen 2002; Salen and Zimmerman 2004).

In the final part of the book, we will examine the even more literal transformations of the videogame as we explore the way in which the code and audiovisual assets of the game come under the control of gamers with sufficient technical skill. Where performance and play may exploit, interrogate and deduce the operation of the code, modding facilitates its direct modification. Where Machinima affords opportunities for reframing characters by resetting their context in much the same manner as fanart or fanfiction, modding affords the ability to change the graphics, 3D models, sound effects and music of the game. In fact, as the tools have become more sophisticated and extensive, the distinction between modding and gamemaking has begun to blur. Importantly though, in modding we not only encounter a practice which may fundamentally alter the game system and even create wholly new gaming systems and experiences, but also find one that is sanctioned and encouraged by the videogame industry. The tools with which mod teams operate are freely distributed by developers who are keen to support the extension and enhancement of their games. As we shall learn, however, despite this arrangement, the position of the amateur producer remains a problematic one that is both inside and outside the commercial industry and that is subject to restrictive licensing agreements.

Part 3

Videogames as technology

Chapter 7

Codemining, modding and gamemaking

Playing with code

So far, we have explored a range of practices that repurpose videogames through the manipulation, extension and adaptation of their representational systems or reconfigure them through the transformativity of sometimes radical play. In Part 2, in particular, we noted that this configurative play frequently involves a close scrutiny and analysis of the operation of the game system that exposes a clear consideration of the videogame as algorithmic rather than representational, as malleable material for playing with rather than static text, and as a nonetheless bounded system that is exploitable due to the permeability and minute imperfection of the underlying program. The hunt for and use of glitches and the production of detailed Game Guides speak of an engagement with the game as code, its operation, rules and inconsistencies. The practices we have seen so far involve scrutiny of the manifest effects of the program, whether these outcomes are intended by the developers or not, assuming that it is even possible to discern the intended from the glitch. In Part 3, we will turn our attention to some of the ways in which gamers may modify the actual program itself. The authors of Game Guides and walkthroughs seek to understand, analyse and virtually decompile the code, interpreting and re-presenting the complexity of routines, subroutines, contingencies and loops as plain advice, guidelines and principles that can be understood by gamers and, most importantly, used in their gameplay. Practices such as 'modding', however, in which commercial games are literally modified or even remade using software tools, involve tinkering with and directly affecting the codebase of the program, altering its operation, creating different and sometimes wholly new playing experiences.

Clearly, there is a high degree of technical competence demanded here that places some of the practices we will examine in this chapter out of the reach of many gamers (see Dovey and Kennedy 2006, on 'technicity'). However, two things are noteworthy. First, and in common with a number of the creative and productive endeavours we have encountered throughout these pages, while the direct modification and manipulation of the code are practised by a minority, the outputs of this work exist within and even create wider cultures, communities and rich contexts for criticism, review and play. As such, even though the highly technical work of creating modifications is open to only a small subset of gamers, the availability of the products of these groups sustains and provides renewed opportunities for a far more extensive group using, discussing and offering critique of these products. These modding communities that might include the active programmers, level designers and artists as well as eager players and supporters of these individuals and teams are embedded within the processes of production and consumption as they offer feedback and non-technical input. Second, gamers operating in these highly technical areas of production do not necessarily operate in isolation. We have noted that the support of a community is commonplace within videogame and wider fan cultures, but it is important to note that while media fandoms often exist in a tenuous relationship with the mainstream of the commercial media industries, tolerated or ignored in the shadow economy of fandom (Fiske 1992) until they present problems or challenges (see Jenkins 1992, and note the issue of 'Foxing' below), in the case of videogame modding, gamers enjoy a quite different position. Indeed, as we shall see, the work of modders is not merely accepted but is positively encouraged with tools, support and means of distribution on offer. Of course, all is not unproblematically rosy, and mod teams work under often restrictive licensing agreements that severely curtail their ability to exploit their work and that appear to significantly advantage the commercial producers who benefit greatly form the work of these dedicated teams of gamers.

We will investigate the reconfiguration of the game and the creation of new levels and even new games through the use of bespoke modification tools supplied and supported by the game's developers in the second part of this chapter. Before that, however, it is useful to remind ourselves that resourceful and dedicated gamers do not need an official invitation from developers to probe and modify program code.

Codemining: looking inside the game

In Chapter 3, we noted the inventiveness of the community of gamers coalescing around *Sonic the Hedgehog*. We observed the depth of analytical skills and the breadth and rigour of research that extended far beyond the original canonical texts into magazine articles and interviews with the development team often read in translation as well as the authorship and attribution of the titles themselves. Moreover, we noted that the collective knowledge created in the online dialogical space of the forum displays a remarkably detailed understanding of the canonical and extended universe texts as well as the practices and processes of production that give rise to them. However, the knowledge of the production practices with which the Sonic community operates goes deeper still than an awareness of the authorship and a, perhaps misplaced or overstated, notion of the involvement of individuals such as Yuji Naka in development and design. While pre-release screenshots are scoured for indications of abandoned levels, characters or modifications of graphics, for more technically-savvy gamers, the code of games reveals many palimpsests that may be able to shed yet more light on these pre-release directions. Within the released and therefore publicly available code, it is often possible to find the remnants of graphic designs that were sidelined or superseded. These are not secrets designed to be found by avid players or acolytes of the game and cannot be accessed via the game itself. Rather, these are simply materials that remain unused in the game but undeleted from the code and that may only be revealed by probing the original code with PC-based editing and programming tools such as Hex editors, for example. As we will see later, the legality of these endeavours is at best a grey area.

For those gamers keen to glimpse into the production processes, access to pre-production or 'beta' code is the Holy Grail as it might contain underdeveloped ideas, unfinished levels, sequences, animations and even characters that are later abandoned and absent from the publicly released game:

> Welcome to S2B [Sonic 2 Beta]. This site is dedicated to the archival and research of prototype versions of SEGA's video game Sonic the Hedgehog 2 made for the Genesis/MegaDrive. Much like a movie, a video game undergoes heavy "editing" before shipping, and significant amount of data is stripped due to time or space constraints. In the case of Sonic 2, several zones were completely cut from the final version. For years, questions have been asked regarding the staggering discrepancies between Sonic 2 and old magazine preview screenshots. Gamers could only dream of being able to play the lost levels first-hand – until the binary image of Sonic 2 Beta surfaced on the Internet in late 1998 . . .
>
> ('The Sonic 2 Beta Page' (n.d.) [online])

The sources of pre-production code vary though it is common practice to send incomplete preview versions to magazines and television programmes or to demonstrate them at trade shows, for instance, whereupon the code may be intentionally leaked or even stolen. Speaking of the *Sonic 2 Beta* code that is the focus of much of the Sonic Secrets Scene's activity, Sonic Team lead developer Yuki Naka explains:

I guess I am pretty surprised at the level of dedication of fans on the Internet. But how do I say this . . . there is a bit of a problem. I mean, I am glad that people really, really like the games, but if it gets to the point where they are engaging in activities that can hurt us or Sega in some way, that's not good at all. Like, way back when we had a beta ROM of Sonic 2 that was stolen by someone. That one even had the Hidden Palace in it . . . You see, back in mid-1992, we had taken a demonstration cartridge to a toy show in New York. It wound up being stolen, and although we searched and searched all over, it was never found. So that's probably where the data comes from.

(Kemps 2005 [online])

For the members of the 'Sonic Secrets Scene', the *Sonic 2 Beta* code provides unheralded insight into the videogame production processes and unparalleled access to this evidently much-loved game's assets and resources that may be interrogated and celebrated. The continued research of gamers and their investigative efforts, revealing graphical fragments and theorising about reasons for the abandonment of levels and ideas, keeps *Sonic 2* alive long after its release fifteen years ago, and long after its original platform has been superseded and disappeared from retail.

What is Sonic 2 Beta?

Sonic 2 Beta is an unfinished, prototype version of Sonic 2. Sega sent these out to magazine companies for preview before the final version was out.

What's the big deal about an unfinished prototype version?

Some "lost" levels can be found in the beta version. Lost levels are zones that were originally planned to be included in the final release of Sonic 2, but were missing in the final version. The lost levels include a desert level, Wood Zone, Hidden Palace Zone and Genocide City Zone. Some existing zones have special features that are not available in the final version, such as the wooden balls in Oil Ocean Zone.

('Frequently Asked Questions about Sonic 2 Beta' (n.d.) [online])

The 'Sonic Secrets Scene' thrives on the investigation of the raw beta code and gamers have even developed their own software analysis tools and level editors to access the inner workings and extract the fullest possible level of detail and information from the incomplete program. Pages at 'The Sonic 2 Beta Page' meticulously document the changes in animation cycles between beta and release code as well as differences in level design and layout and even missing levels. What is important here is not only the level of technical expertise on display as sprites, backgrounds, music and levels are extracted from the original game code, but also the degree of triangulation. Magazine articles and TV previews of the in-production game are scrutinised for corroborative detail and suggest new directions for research ('staggering discrepancies between *Sonic 2* and old magazine preview screenshots'). As such, we note the way that the videogames press's focus on the imminent presents a rich resource for gamers who pore over screenshots and interviews not only to seek out clues of forthcoming games, but also refer back to this library of reference materials as they compare final games with their earlier incarnations and the claims of their developers.

Without doubt, the value of the *Sonic 2 Beta* code is found in the opportunities it offers for visible mastery of the series. It is an extension of the canonical texts that offers new pleasures for play and interesting juxtapositions as music, levels and animations familiar and unfamiliar are combined in unexpected ways. Available for this degree of scrutiny after the release of the final game, and consequently encountered outside its chronological position in the Sonic canon, it appears as a remix of the released title. However, there is more to the beta than this. The code provides glimpses into the production and pre-production processes and sheds light on the development cycle. In this way, even though it precedes it in development time, the beta is a means of better understanding and recontextualising the original, canonical game as a playable experience.

However, while the revelation of these palimpsests may represent a considerable technical achievement and is evidence of a dedication and interest in the very workings of the game, not to mention an awareness of the processes of production, they do not always simply give up their heritage or neatly provide answers to fans' questions. It may be considered that this is precisely compatible with the fans' desires. The revelation of ambiguous graphic designs, for example, encourages deliberation and analysis as to what they may have been, how they might have been deployed, why they were unused. This, in turn, gives rise to a separate strand of fan writing: the 'theory'. As we have seen, within the *Sonic the Hedgehog* community, fanwriting may be differentiated in terms of its compatibility with and closeness to the canon. Theories that attempt to posit explanations for apparent inconsistencies in the games' narrative continuity are thus differentiated from 'fanfics' that are more fanciful and imaginative in their scope. The extract below is taken from the 'Missing Sonic 2 Levels' community website:

Sonic 2 Time Travel Theory
So far, Sonic CD is the only Sonic game with a time travel feature. But as I recall, Sonic Team was going to put time travel into Sonic 2 too! So, they designed levels with TT in mind. Sources claim that each level was supposed to be set in a certain time period, however, that may be incorrect. I think I've found the proof Sonic 2 was going to feature a Sonic CD-type

time travel (without the Past). Take a look at first five levels in Sonic 2 Beta . . .

I may be going too far, but- listen to the music. 01 certanly sounds like a Good Future remix of 00. And 03 sounds like a Bad Future. As for Wood Zone, it uses the same music as the two Metropolis Zones, but that's okay, they would remix it in a later date.

Talking about Wood Zone- its design and idea are pretty pointless; a forest with conveyor belts and hollow trees? But when you look at it differently (what a factory looked like in the past) then it makes sense. And the hollow tree was going to be a warp tube from Metropolis- try jumping on it. You can't. You can't jump on warp pipes too! And speaking of Metropolis, why are there two Metropolis Zones? They are both Bad Future. One of them was supposed to be a Good Future, which is basicaly Bad Future with graphics changed. Wait . . . something ain't right here . . . I know. Wood Zone only has two acts, but Metropolis has three. This is the real proof. In Sonic CD, act three always goes on in the future. And, as far as I can think (not very far) 01 and 03 zones have act 3 too! So, depending on how you completed acts 1 and 2, act 3 was a good or bad future.

('Missing Sonic 2 Levels' (n.d.) [online])

The richness of this work, and the subsequent discussion and debate among the community, and the willingness to engage in critical recuperations and analyses of the canon in light of these new findings derived from inside the game code illustrate the technical savvy, inventiveness and rigorous research upon which these theories are often founded and the way in which the revelations from the beta codemining are worked into the more general analysis thereby becoming part of the community's collective knowledge.

Rewriting videogames: hacking *Mother*

In a media environment in which global corporations appear to dominate and gaming experiences are increasingly available both offline and online, it is useful to remind ourselves that not all videogames enjoy a release in all territories. We briefly noted at the beginning of Chapter 3 that the Japanese RPG is one genre in particular that has been denied a wider audience. The argument usually concerns the potentially marginal profitability of the titles given the high costs of translating and localisation. As we have seen, the copious quantities of text in RPGs make the translation alone a significant task. As such, a number of titles such as the *Fire Emblem*, *Final Fantasy* and *Seiken Densetsu* series (known in Europe and the US as the *Mana* series) assumed sizeable fanbases among Japanese gamers and garnered considerable respect among gaming aficionados but did not (initially at least) see releases outside Japan. However, the magazine culture that we noted in Chapter 2 brought glimpses of these exotic and elusive experiences to gamers outside Japan some of whom went beyond lusting over screenshots and took action to remedy the iniquity of the situation.

In common with fans of other media forms protesting the cancellation of television series, for instance (see Jenkins 1992; Tulloch and Jenkins 1995), gamers have engaged in letter writing campaigns that seek to urge publishers and developers to release titles or reinstate abandoned projects. Petitions amass signatures in the hope that the sheer number will convince the publisher or developer that a market exists and a translation is financially viable. Speaking to the UK Official Nintendo Magazine about the *Earthbound* series whose third instalment, *Mother 3*, has had a troubled development history that has seen the project cancelled and restarted but which has not been officially translated for English-speaking gamers, Nintendo's Shigeru Miyamoto notes:

> We had high hopes for Earthbound, the Super NES version, in the US, but it didn't do well. We even did a TV commercial, thinking, 'Hey . . . this thing could sell three million copies!' But it didn't. You might not know this, but there was a petition in the US, a 'Please make Mother 3' petition and it got about 30,000 signatures! After that, we thought 'Wow . . . Earthbound fans are really solid.'
>
> (Miyamoto 2003 [online])

Much of the work in co-ordinating the petition was undertaken by contributors to Starmen.Net who operate as an important fansite in the Earthbound community and continue to campaign for the release of the title by assembling fanart and fiction to illustrate the extent of the regard that is afforded the game (see 'Starmen.Net's Mother 3 Petition (n.d.) [online]) for further information on the petition and the creation of 'The Earthbound Anthology', a 268-page bound volume of fanart and discussion used to highlight the commitment of gamers to the series (see 'Starmen.Net Staff' 2007).

While organising petitions and assembling fanart and critical commentary on a videogame series are mightily impressive acts of dedication, even more radical strategies are available to the RPG community and a number of unofficial translation projects have been undertaken. The team at Starmen.net, for instance, have teamed up with other gamers to form a 'Mother 3 Fan Translation' team to work on an English language translation of the recently released Japanese GameBoy Advance title (see 'The (Unified) Mother 3 Fan Translation' (n.d.) [online]) while others have attempted work on titles such as *Final Fantasy V* and *Seiken Densetsu 3*, for example. 'Romhacking dot net' hosts information on a range of active and abandoned projects as well as tools, news and information for would-be translation hackers.

There are clear parallels between the practices of videogame 'fanslation' or translation hacking and the 'fansubbing' in which television or film texts are translated and subtitled by fans for distribution among a wider audience. Jenkins (2006: 158) cites an interview with Sean Leonard, president of the MIT Anime Club who explains, 'Fansubbing has been critical to the growth of anime fandom in the West. If it weren't for fans showing this stuff to others . . . there would be no interest in intelligent, "high-brow" Japanese animation like there is today.'

However, there are important differences between the practices of fansub-bing anime (or any televisual or film text, for that matter) and translation hack-ing videogames. Perhaps the most significant difference arises as a consequence of the sheer size of the videogame. RPGs are commonly marketed and described not only in terms of the richness of their narratives, settings and characters but also in terms of the number of hours of gameplay they offer. As an example, recent sleuthing in Japanese forums for information on the forthcoming *Crisis Core: Final Fantasy VII* for the Sony PSP has unearthed claims of 100+ hours of gameplay ('Oldschool' 2007). We should immediately get a sense of the scale of the translation project but the situation is further complicated if we consider the structure of the videogame. The RPG is not a linear text and, as we have seen, while we may be able to identify a main plot thread, the structure is actually comprised of multiple, overlapping sequences and scenes, detours and sidequests. Even if spoiler writers like those identified by Burn (2006b) can reduce the non-linear complexity of the branching structure to a single, coherent narrative thread, the translation hacker cannot. Each element of the game, whether or not it appears to advance the ostensible 'plot' *per se*, is a potentially valuable part of the experience that helps gamers better understand the motivations and histories of characters, contextualises events or just simply offers pleasurable opportunities for play. The prevalence of sidequests and detours, the poten-tially branching structure of the narrative and the sheer amount of materials (some of which may only be revealed under certain playing conditions demand-ing that the game system and mechanics are utterly known and appreciated) render the videogame translation a significant undertaking. One can begin to appreciate the reluctance of publishers to approve and fund localisation even with full knowledge of the extent of the game. For gamers, the game has to be learned to discern even what elements exist within it before translation can proceed. The structure of the videogame certainly makes the project of trans-lation quite different from that faced by fansubbers of anime which remains, in itself, an impressive demonstration of ingenuity.

Just as the fansubbers Leonard describes made use of technical systems such as time-synchronised VHS and S-VHS recorders for dubbing and rerecording with the newly fashioned subtitles, translation hackers rely on a series of software and hardware tools to gain access to the game code. Like Tool-Assisted Speedrunning, the practices we have seen in this chapter so far rely on the availability of emulation software that turns the general purpose PC into a virtual console machine, and ROMs which are 'dumps' of the original game code. As such, these are not remakes of games, but the original code extracted from the cartridge, disc or tape, and made investigable and playable.

In some cases, gamers go far beyond interrogating this code, theorising the development trajectories it appears to indicate, or even translating the text and exercising their game design skills creating variations of the original title by modifying graphics or level designs. Where the Mother translators are concerned with retaining the integrity of the original, revered canonical game, other hackers are concerned with modifying the game and creating new, derivative works. As such, for some games, including the *Sonic* and *Mario* series, technically-savvy gamers have created dedicated game editors. These software applications allow the assets of the game to be altered, replacing character designs or moving objects and pathways around to create new levels. In some cases, changes may even be as trivial as palette shifts where references to colour tables are edited and in-game graphics appear with new hues or may go beyond the aesthetic to include modifications of character attributes. As well as providing a public forum for the demonstration of high level technical skills, the creation of modified games performs at least two important functions. First, like the theorising and fiction writing we have noted earlier in this book, we note a clear desire to imprint oneself onto the canonical work. To fashion a new game from the assets of the original or placing one's own visual designs into the context of the original game is to meld one's own productive endeavours with those of the canonical authors. As we shall note in the following section, such activities move gamers beyond participation and the attentive position of readership *par excellence* into what Sue Morris has termed a 'co-creative' relationship where 'producer' and 'consumer' are both responsible for the ultimate experiences of gameplay. Second, there is more to the development of modified games than the creation and management of personal identity within the community. Indeed, this highly technical work is often motivated by a desire to extend and remake the original text to maintain its life by offering both new challenges within the context of the canonical game, and also new challenges that stretch the community of gamers. Modified games may be redesigned to be more difficult than the original thereby mirroring both the superplay imperative and the desire to share additional challenges that separate out the expert gamer. Many of the *Super Mario Bros.* 'hacks' hosted at 'Zophar's Domain' ('NES Hacks' (n.d.) [online]), for instance, revolve around increasing the difficulty level of the game thereby operating in a similar way to the community challenges that encouraged gamers to impose and respect new *ludus* to constrain and modify their gameplay. With these hacks, however, the code of the game is altered and the modified *ludus* are programmed into the new game system.[1]

All of this creativity, imagination and collaboration comes at a significant price, however. The practices described here are legally problematic as they frequently rely on the unauthorised acquisition and use of program code running under emulation. Emulators are software applications that enable one piece of hardware to manifest the operational and functional behaviours of another. Typically, this involves rendering a PC capable of running the original, unaltered code of a game system such as a MegaDrive, Super Nintendo or even PlayStation. While the creation of emulation software is not an illegal activity in itself, 'ripping' and distributing code from commercial videogames is highly problematic (see Conley *et al.* 2004, for more on the legality of videogame emulation). For Nintendo, the situation is clear:

> The introduction of emulators created to play illegally copied Nintendo software represents the greatest threat to date to the intellectual property rights of video game developers. As is the case with any business or industry, when its products become available for free, the revenue stream supporting that industry is threatened. Such emulators have the potential to significantly damage a worldwide entertainment software industry which generates over $15 billion annually, and tens of thousands of jobs.
>
> ('Legal Information (Copyrights, Emulators, ROMs, etc.)',
> Nintendo (n.d.) [online])

While this position is understandably intolerant of game copying and the distribution of emulators and ROM images as it harms sales and infringes copyright and IP, it is important to note that theft is not the only motivation of emulator users and the practices of TAS, codemining and translation hacking are significantly jeopardised. However, while some of these practices might operate in the murky world of illegally dumped and obtained code and stand in opposition to the mainstream videogame industry's commercial imperatives, other types of game modification are rather more legitimised and even encouraged within the mainstream.

Modding, hacking and cracking

Before proceeding, we should note that the term 'mod' is an ambiguous one with a variety of uses in videogame and wider computing cultures. The term can refer to physical, artistic modification of the 'semblance' of personal computing or console hardware (see Sotamaa 2003). 'Case modding' involves altering the external appearance of a PC tower often transforming it into something almost unrecognisable as a personal computer. The intricacy and inventiveness of mods such as 'Doom 3 Project Mars City' are more than evident in the detailed instructions and step-by-step annotated illustration of the creative process ('Crimson Sky' 2005 [online]). While this *DOOM*-inspired case is undoubtedly impressive and speaks of the visual and cultural power of the *DOOM* identity and aesthetic, it is a mod unlike those that we will turn our attention to as it is only obliquely concerned with modifying the experience of play and performance.

'Mod' is also frequently used in relation to efforts to 'crack' videogame systems. Where hacking may cover legitimate or illegitimate activity (see Lister *et al.* 2003), cracking is usually understood to describe illicit performances of technical skill. The attentions of crackers may be directed towards disabling security systems. In relation to videogames this can mean one of three related endeavours. First, crackers may seek to bypass region coding systems that prohibit the use of games distributed in one territory from running on hardware from another territory. As we have seen previously, region coding is utilised in the videogames industry to protect markets and releases are often staggered or even restricted to specific territories making some titles extremely desirable given their temporary or permanent scarcity. As such, the circumvention of region coding opens up the possibility of a grey market of imports that extends beyond the control of videogame publishers. The public debacle involving Sony Computer Entertainment and videogame importer Lik-Sang (see Chapter 2, note 4) speaks eloquently of the tension that exists between videogame publishers and retailers and gamers seeking to take advantage of the affordances of region free consoles. Second, videogame crackers may seek to bypass copy protection systems that are designed to restrict unauthorised duplication and distribution. This activity may involve developing software tools that enable discs or downloads to be duplicated using a personal computer or may centre on mechanisms for extracting or 'ripping' code from cartridges such as those presently used by Nintendo for the GameBoy and DS handheld consoles or the proprietary disc format used by Sony's PlayStation Portable (PSP). Once the code exists only in digital form and has been decoupled from the physical cartridge or disc, it may be distributed across networks, often using file sharing systems, and used by gamers whose consoles are suitably equipped with custom hardware and software that enables code to be run in this form. Third, in order to run copied or ripped code, consoles typically have to be modified to bypass the checks that run to prohibit the use of illegally obtained material. Accordingly, some crackers seek to modify videogames hardware to enable what is often referred to as 'unsigned' code to be run.

In fact, there is more to the attempts to run unauthorised code than piracy. The Sony PSP is illustrative. The PSP has come under a sustained attack from crackers keen to enable the system to run 'homebrew' software (that is, software that has not been officially sanctioned or 'signed' by Sony through the legitimate development process). Chief among the 'homebrew' applications are emulators that afford the ability to transform the PSP into a different virtual console. Crackers have sought to exploit software bugs in the PSP's operating system and have even produced their own customised firmware to run on the machine that facilitates the operation of these amateur software applications. The relationship between these hardware modders and the commercial videogames industry is an extremely uneasy one and each iteration and update of the official PSP firmware seeks to address the security vulnerabilities that afforded the cracker's exploits. It is unsurprising to note that these releases are met with feverish attempts from the cracking fraternity to find new ways to run unsigned applications (see the 'N00bz!' PSP homebrew site, for further information).

In a related use of the term, 'mod' may also refer to chips or other hardware devices that are fitted to videogame consoles and that circumvent the kinds of security systems that usually prohibit the use of games from different retail and distribution territories (thereby allowing Japanese titles to play on European systems, for instance, by bypassing the region checking routines). In many cases, these 'modchips' are used to enable copied rather than original games to be played on modded systems. As such, modchips have become indissolubly linked with software piracy.

In this chapter, following the work of Morris (2003) and Nieborg (2005) for instance, we will focus on yet another type of 'modding'. Here, modding centres on the modification of game code, assets and level designs and we see concerted efforts to alter the experiences, aesthetics and structures of games. As Sotamaa (2003) suggests, this activity is distinct from 'game hacks' that seek to unfairly alter the gamer's ability to perform in the game. This is especially pronounced in multiplayer games where game hacks may be used to gain an advantage over others.

> In contemporary gaming culture 'game hacks' seem to have a bit different resonance. Popular forms of game hacks range from skill hacks that boost the skills of the player character to map hacks that enable [the] player to control the game world more easily. An illustrative example of skill hack is aimbot, used especially in first-person-shooters, that significantly improves the accuracy of aiming. Then again, a programme called wallhack makes all dungeon walls transparent and thus help to locate enemies, monsters and bonuses. Usage of hacks is usually treated as cheating and cheaters normally gain little appreciation among other gamers. Gamers using cheats are often banned from multi-player servers and several anti-cheat websites and projects can be found in the net.
>
> (Sotamaa 2003: 4)

In fact, as Sue Morris (2003) points out, many of the automated anti-cheating systems that identify and restrict the use of 'aimbots' were originally developed by gamers and have been formally adopted by game developers and service providers thereby further demonstrating the embeddedness of the endeavours of the modding community within the mainstream, commercial videogames industry.

The practices of modding that we are concerned with here appear to bear much in common with the beta codemining and ROM hacking we encountered at the beginning of this chapter. There are some important differences, however. Unlike the ROM hacking we saw earlier and that gave rise to fanslations and even new versions of games based on the resources, assets and systems of originals, and unlike the hardware and software cracking above, this form of 'modding' is wholly legal and even endorsed, supported and enabled by the mainstream videogames industry. Indeed, where emulation, the ripping and distribution of ROMs, and the cracking of systems threaten the commercial videogames industry, modding has been adopted within the business practices of certain game developers. At one level, modding may be seen as an exercise in marketing and building brand loyalty through high levels of participation (Jones 2006). However, things are more complicated. According to Nieborg (2005: 4), the relationship between modders and the commercial industry is quite different to that between the producers of television series and fans. 'The latter is one more of mutual suspicion or even open conflict (Jenkins 1992), emotions which seem to be absent in the FPS mod community'.

However, as we shall learn, we may consider that the industry operates in an overly restrictive manner, exploiting the community and productivity of gamers to serve their corporate, commercial ends by locking modders into a commodity culture in which the terms are far from equal. In the remainder of this chapter, 'modding' is taken to refer to this authorised modification of game code using developer-supplied and supported tools.

Make it mine: modding, agency and co-creative media

Histories of videogame modding invariably begin with discussions of gamers making their own level designs or 'maps' in *DOOM*, or analyses of the emergence of 'skinning' in which in-game character graphics are altered and replaced with scans of figures from other games, other cultural texts, or images of gamers themselves (see Dovey and Kennedy 2006, for example). The lineage may, in fact, be traced back further still to games such as Electronic Arts' *Pinball Construction Set* (1983), *Adventure Construction Set* (1985), *Racing Destruction Set* (1985) or Sensible Software's 1987 title *Shoot Em Up Construction Kit*. As their names imply, these titles were not so much games as they were resources with which to make games.

The underlying code of the game was essentially fixed – hence the Adventure 'Set' differed from the Racing 'Set' as their programs were optimised to facilitate a specific style or genre of game and gameplay. However, the art and audio assets, the content of the adventure texts, the layout of the racing tracks, were placed under the command of the gamer whose task it was to create their own specific and individualised implementation. While the sophistication and scope of these early editing, game design and assembly tools are significantly limited when compared with those of current systems, we see the emergence of an interesting relationship in these 'Construction Sets' that foreshadows that between the contemporary modding community and commercial videogames industry, and between the gamer and the game.

We noted in the opening of this chapter that the detailed documentation of the effects of combinations of Materia in *Final Fantasy VII* or the systems that govern the dialogue loops, sequences and branches in *Animal Crossing* are indicative of an engagement with the game code, its operation, implementation, rules and inconsistencies. These practices involve highly attentive play and deep analysis of the manifest effects of the program and its operation as gamer and game system exercise agency, adapting and responding, in the creation of the rich gameplay experience (see Moulthrop 2004; cf. Eskelinen 2001). If we consider the literal opportunity that the *Construction Sets* offer gamers to collaborate in the creation and shaping of the levels, aesthetics and rule systems with and within which their configurative play with the adaptive and responsive system takes place, we see a further means by which their agency may be expressed and also a further blurring of the distinctive positions of author and consumer. This reminds us of du Gay *et al.*'s (1997) calls for consideration of the interrelations between production and consumption practices (see also Deacon 2003). For Nieborg, an analysis of modding encourages us to move beyond assertions about the agency of gamers being expressed through 'interaction' within textual and rule boundaries defined by the 'producer' (see Marshall 2002, for instance).

> By producing additional or replaceable game content, the agency of gamers goes beyond the mere interaction with the text itself. Gamers are able to change almost any aspect of gameplay of many FPS games and by doing so, taking their agency to another level, rivalling but also cooperating with the cultural industry.
>
> (Nieborg 2005: 4)

It is interesting to note that while the *Construction Sets* straddled a number of genres, modding has developed in a rather more specific and focused manner. Indeed, although modding tools and communities exist for Real Time Strategy games (see Morris and Hartas 2004b) as well as specific titles such as *The Sims* and MMORPGs such as *World of Warcraft*, the First Person Shooter (FPS) has become particularly closely associated with modding and modding culture. Importantly, this activity is largely restricted to the PC as a gaming platform as access to the code and the ease of installing and running additional applications to modify and work on the program are mostly prohibited in console gaming (though see the final section of this chapter for a glimpse of a shift towards console game modding). Among developers of PC-based FPS titles, modding is not merely tolerated but actively encouraged. Indeed, as we have suggested, the very tools that facilitate modding are created and distributed by the game's developers and made available with the game package in a wholly open and equitable manner. This stands in stark contrast to the tools deployed by ROM hackers to modify their games of choice which are not supplied with these resources and are not designed to be modified. Such is the currency and centrality of modding to the FPS genre that Henry Lowood (2007: 75) observes, 'When a computer game is released today, it is as much a set of design tools as a finished game design.' Lowood's comments are particularly useful in drawing our attention to the increasingly extensible and flexible sets of resources, systems, and software tools that are made available to gamers by the developers of FPS games such as *Quake* and *Unreal Tournament*. We should note, however, that mod tools are not quite as ubiquitous as this might suggest and certainly those tools that do exist are not always created by developers. *World of Warcraft* is blessed with an extremely vibrant modding community yet the tools are developed by third parties although Blizzard offers considerable support to these independent developers. In fact, mods may even transcend or transform the popularity of the original game. As Sotamaa (2003) has suggested, *Quake III Arena* has been revived and sustained by the vibrancy and productivity of the modding community that seized on its tools and created new modes of play after the original game was less than well received.

For Morris (2003: 9), the widespread nature of modding tools and the agency they offer gamers in directly shaping their gameplay environments and opportunities are sufficient for her to name contemporary FPSs 'co-creative media' as 'neither developers nor player-creators can be solely responsible for production of the final assemblage regarded as "the game", it requires the input of both.'

We would certainly want to argue that the contours of this 'dual input' should include the configurative play that we have seen in our analysis of practices of superplay, for instance, but Morris's point is that there are yet more direct means by which gamers engage in the process of transforming the game, some of which even precede the transformativity of play and performance, and directly impact upon the worlds, environments and systems to be played with. Moreover, the technological systems and tools that facilitate the modification, gameplay and even distribution of the FPS might seamlessly mesh tools, products and services created by gamers and professional developers alike. According to Morris, investigation of the modding culture of FPSs and the embedded nature of the outputs of the mod community in the systems deployed by the commercial industry demands that we move beyond conceptualisation based around the participatory cultures of media fans or the tactics of poaching:

> An FPS gamer playing online uses not only the game software and content as purchased on the CD, but also a variety of software, game content and services provided by mod makers and the wider gaming community. Some programs are originally developed in the mod scene, and then bought by game companies and released commercially.
>
> (Morris 2003: 9)

Even though we have seen that there are clear antecedents in the *Construction Sets* of the 1980s, the journey towards the mod culture and the development of freely available mod tools was not a clearly planned project. In fact, as Kushner (2003) recounts, it was an unofficial mod for id's *Wolfenstein* that set out the current course. In a marked shift in aesthetic, the *Wolfenstein* mod had replaced the WWII-themed music and imagery of the original with that drawn from children's television series Barney who assumed the role of Camp Commandant. The mod was created without support or official tools but id software were visionary enough to identify this as an important direction of travel for their games and adjusted their development patterns accordingly. For their follow-up title, *DOOM*, libraries and directories of files were reorganised so that media assets such as character graphics could be more easily accessed and edited. Lead programmer John Carmack also released the source code of the program online as a shareware project and very soon development tools and editors were being fashioned by the emergent community of modders. The success of the *DOOM* mod scene is well documented by Kushner (2003) and others and we have noted that it formed the basis for a variety of superplay and Machinima projects. Whether or not modding was the invention of the commercial videogames industry, as Sotamaa (2003) notes, it has become institutionalised as a key development and marketing strategy.

Since *DOOM*, the embedding of mod culture in the FPS genre has been anything but accidental or haphazard. As Lowood (2007) notes, developers and publishers provide easy access to level design tools and other suites of applications that facilitate the modification of game assets such as graphics, music, virtual cameras, object behaviours and even physics. With each iteration of an FPS series or major overhaul of the game engine, toolsets become increasingly complex and Dovey and Kennedy (2006) rightly point out that the high levels of technicity demanded place the practice of mod-making out of the reach of many gamers. Indeed, as we shall see in the following sections, mod tools such as those supplied with *Unreal Tournament 2004*, for instance, have mutated into little short of game development environments. Where the *Construction Sets* prescribed the genre of the gamer's productive efforts, the flexibility of modern mod tools gives rise to the possibility of developing games unrelated to the original, not just aesthetically, but deviating from the core gameplay and genre. However, it is useful to note that mod tools are frequently supported by developers who offer tutorials and guidance as well as technical documentation and incentives for community participation in mod-making. As Nieborg (2005: 6) observes, two features of the release of *Unreal Tournament 2004* are particularly revealing. First, the Special Edition DVD package includes a variety of materials designed especially for the modding community. The three disc set includes the game itself along with a variety of maps, graphics and other options to play with and the user-friendly GUI editor UnrealEd 3.0 to edit all Unreal related material, as well as other tools used by the original game developers. The final disc is particularly notable as it is primarily made up of educational and support materials and includes in excess of 150 hours of video tutorials that cover level design, the principles of weapon, character and vehicle making, and even the basics of producing Machinima. The package speaks of the high level of support that is offered to potential mod makers though it also indicates the complexity and scope of the tools which are a far cry from the accessibility and user-friendliness of the *Construction Sets*. Second, to further stimulate the *UT2004* modding culture, the game's publisher teamed up with graphics card manufacturer NVIDIA to launch the '$1,000,000 Make Something Unreal Contest'. In offering lavish prizes for the best mods, the competition adds a range of incentives while offering new possibilities for collaboration and channels for distribution.

Regardless of the degree of technical support, there is no doubt that the practice of mod-making necessarily remains one open to only the most technically-savvy in the community. Although, we should be mindful that as Ray Muzyka of Bioware notes, 'If only one percent of a million user base makes content, then you have a lot of module designers. And that's enough to make a game self-sustaining for a long time.' However, it is important to remember that, in common with a number of the productive endeavours we have encountered in this book, although the direct manipulation and modification of code and assets may be practised by the minority, the outputs of these endeavours exist within, and even help to create and sustain, the wider cultures, communities and rich contexts for criticism, review and gameplay. As such, the influence of the mod culture of FPS gaming extends far beyond those who create these transformed versions of the game to those countless millions who play with them and whose gameplay opportunities are irretrievably enmeshed within the co-creativity of commercial and amateur development. We should note also that Morris (2003: 5) suggests that some level of involvement in the mod scene is commonplace. In her email survey of *Quake II* gamers conducted in 1999, 83% 'had completed some sort of creative project related to the game, from creating webpages to model and level design.' Morris demonstrates the centrality of creative input in the culture of FPS gaming and observes that this productive activity 'allows players to see themselves as playing a recognised role in the games they enjoy and in the gaming culture'. Importantly, these 'creative projects' do not only include the physical manipulation of code and the direct use of mod tools. Immersion in the culture of FPS modding might range from the creation of graphics, music and sound effects, level designs, models or the design and maintenance of webpages hosting materials for community members.

Certainly, it would be a mistake to consider that high level programming, 3D modelling or advanced physics simulation skills were the only routes into modding. Level design and playtesting require deep knowledge of the operation game system, the pleasures of gameplay and considerable gameplay virtuosity without necessarily demanding any coding competence, for instance. Similarly, there is no reason why the programmer or physics modeller should be an especially good level designer. As a consequence of the variety of skillsets demanded in the production, it is quite usual for modders to work in teams. In this way, the working practices among amateur modders may be seen to broadly reflect changes in commercial videogames development (see Newman 2004).

There is considerable variety in the flavours of mods which range from comparatively simple alterations of graphics that serve to relocate the game in a different setting (transporting the action of *Quake* into the *Star Wars* universe, for example) through to complete transformations and overhauls. As we hinted at above, some of the transformations are so significant that they practically reinvent the game leaving it unrecognisable. Consequently, and further adding to the ambiguity of the term 'mod', it is important to make an additional distinction. For the most part, and perhaps truer to their name, mods leave the underlying game mechanisms largely or completely unaltered and change assets such as graphics, sound or, most often, redesign levels and 'maps' to create a new gaming experience that is clearly and unambiguously located within the locale and context of the original game. These 'Partial Mods' are differentiated, however, from 'Total Conversions' which utilise the increasing extensiveness and scope of contemporary mod tools to build what is often a wholly new game involving radically new gameplay and even belonging to a different genre than the original. In the following sections, we will examine some key case studies and explore the ways in which modding is simultaneously locked into the protocols of FPS development and the business of videogames publishing and marketing, and yet remains for the many gamers who partake in this amateur development, a marginalised and decoupled activity governed by often restrictive rules and agreements.

Total Conversions, partial mods and the challenge of intermediality

Of all the Total Conversion mods, *Counter-Strike* is perhaps the best known. Beginning life as a mod for Valve's *Half-Life*, *Counter-Strike* is a round-based, team action game where opposing groups adopt the role of terrorists and counter-terrorists. Missions are won by either completing the ostensible object or by eliminating the opposition forces. The immense popularity of the game certainly speaks of its success in encapsulating the pleasures of online play and has been an influential title with its fingerprints found on a number of subsequent mods and FPS games. However, it is *Counter-Strike*'s status that has made it something of a *cause célèbre* in the mod community and the focus of some scholarly attention (see Jenkins 2006; Dovey and Kennedy 2006, for instance). *Counter-Strike* originated as a Total Conversion mod for Valve's *Half-Life*. It is notable that *Half-Life* is itself built around the 'GoldSrc' engine, a heavily modified version of the *Quake* engine thereby further demonstrating the difficulty of defining modding because as Sotamaa (2003) observes, the high costs of developing game engines from scratch mean that code is frequently licensed and reused by commercial developers turning them into modders of sorts. Discussing his motivations for creating the mod, Minh 'Gooseman' Le stressed the independence of his vision:

> My initial motivation [for making mods] was probably the same as anyone else involved in the mod scene. I just wanted to customize the game to fit my vision of what a game should be. First and foremost, it is MY vision. not anyone else's. I don't spend 10+ hours a week working on a mod for free just to make a mod that satisfies everyone, I make a mod that I am happy with and if someone else happens to like it, then that's a bonus.
>
> ('rizzuh' 2000 [online])

What is particularly important about Minh 'Gooseman' Le's and Jess Cliffe's work on *Counter-Strike* is that its success prompted Valve to offer both of the amateur developers positions within the company and thereafter publish the mod as a standalone game. The extraordinary popularity and commercial success of *Counter-Strike* and Le and Cliffe's transition from enthusiastic amateurs personally motivated to work on projects they wanted to play themselves rather than with any specific commercial goal might lead us to overstate the mobility of modders and the innovation of the mod scene in general. Au (2002), for example, notes that, 'mods can come up with new gameplay elements that the industry is too conservative to implement, or too non-creative to come up with.' Certainly Total Conversion mods such as *Q3Pong* in which *Quake III Arena* is given a 1972 makeover and turned into a multiplayer version of the table tennis simulator (Sotamaa 2003: 13–14) and *Duffers Golf* that transforms FPS *Unreal Tournament 2004* into a 32-player pitch and putt course (Nieborg 2005: 7) lend weight to this position and present clear evidence of the dedication and inventiveness of modders. Similarly, politically motivated mods such as the *Political Arena* projects that turn *Quake III Arena* into a satire on the 2000 US election campaign demonstrate an engagement, topicality and desire to take risks that might be impossible in the mainstream industry (see Nieborg 2005: 10–11). However, in the face of this celebration of the innovation of mod culture, Dovey and Kennedy (2006) sound a rightly cautionary note. They resist the temptation to romanticize Minh Le and Jess Cliffe as lucky amateurs. As they explain, *Counter-Strike* production was, in fact, the result of a highly skilled, focused collective effort. Moreover, the team did not emerge from their garrets as struggling artists. While their effort should not be underestimated, they were far from unknown. Indeed, *Counter-Strike* was first showcased at the 'Half-Life Mod Expo', an event funded and supported by *Half-Life* developer Valve to publicise the innovative modifications of their game being made by their 'player creators' (Dovey and Kennedy 2006: 125).

Moreover, while we can highlight and showcase some of the more noteworthy creative endeavours such as *Counter-Strike*, we must be mindful of the fact that, as Sotamaa (2003: 6) suggests, most modding is an altogether more modest affair, 'a noteworthy share of the game add-ons consists of modest variations of game characters, weaponry and visual appearance of the game environment that barely can be interpreted as highly intellectual resistance of corporate media dynamics'.

This is hardly surprising given the levels of technical skill and amount of time required to produce mods of the size, scope and significance of Total Conversions such as *Counter-Strike*, for example. If we examine the more prevalent partial mods, we see the privileging of rather different sets of skills and the operation of different motivations. If Total Conversion teams embrace mod tools and software development kits as game development environments, those working on partial mods make a much more sparing use of the tools and typically leave the underlying mechanics of the game substantially unaltered and turn their attentions to editing or replacing media assets such as graphics and sound. Among the most common partial 'remix' mods are those that alter the availability or power of weaponry or the visual appearance of in-game characters. For Anne-Marie Schleiner, parallels with developments in music technology are inevitable. 'Like the hip-hop sampler or reggae dub mixer, the game patch artist manipulates the prefab semiotics of the game engine, a kind of "versioning" that reorganizes along both paradigmatic and syntagmatic axeses' (Schleiner 1999 [online]).

The allusion to remixing is useful here and draws our attentions not only to the position of the partial modder as an editor of material and creator of a final, playable experience rather than as an originator of assets (see also Manovich 2001), but also to the range of materials from which the modder might draw. Modifications based around remodelling in-game characters frequently reference other media texts and sit within complex networks of intertextuality. By appropriating the visual representations of *The Simpsons* or *Star Wars*, for instance, modders manifestly demonstrate their cultural frames of reference and situate videogames within a wider context of cultural production and consumption. The reliance on textual material as diverse as Lego, Tux the Linux mascot and Clippit the Microsoft Office Assistant, moves Sotamaa (2003: 8) to term *Quake III Arena* mod production 'radically intermedial'.

Of course, while we might celebrate the media literacy of these radical intermedial modders as poachers, participants and co-creators, the situation is not unproblematic. Interestingly, while we have noted a respect for intellectual property and copyright in other areas of amateur and fan production, here we see a wholesale and often unattributed incorporation of characters, representations and properties and the orientation of mods around this textual appropriation. As Dovey and Kennedy (2006: 133) correctly note, 'The *Quake III Arena* mod world is populated by player-created avatars that turn the game into a cult playground, where Maximus from *Gladiator* can battle against the Terminator, Darth Vader or Dr Evil from the *Austin Powers* films.' It is unsurprising to learn that there are many instances in which these practices have not been frictionless. Nieborg (2005: 9) reports the case of a team developing a GI Joe-themed mod for the Battlefield franchise:

> The developers of a GI Joe Mod stumbled upon the boundaries of using existing IP. Lawyers of the Hasbro Corporation, a toy manufacturer and owner of the GI Joe IP, had contacted the mod team and issued a cease and desist letter.
>
> (Nieborg 2005: 9)

The situation will be more than familiar to scholars of and participants in media fan cultures (see Jenkins 1992, for a thorough discussion). Indeed, the phrase 'Foxing' has emerged to describe what is seen within the fan community as unnecessarily overbearing or overzealous legal action (Foxing derives from the actions of 20th Century Fox who have been seen to publicly pursue their rights in relation to fan production). Here, then, we note that the modder is in a curious relationship with the commercial media industries. On the one hand, the videogames industry appears to be extraordinarily supportive of the acts of amateur production and facilitates the creative endeavours of a community that is virtually brought under its wing while, simultaneously, modders are thrust into an arena in which the harsh commercial and legal realities of ownership and rights have to be encountered and dealt with. The irony of the situation is that it is both the productive possibilities and the visibility of the ultimate works of modding that emerge from the ease, formality and institutionalisation of distribution that create these tensions for the modder.

However, this again rather romanticises the situation and positions the modder as struggling, dedicated fan rather than potentially budding developer and unduly positions the legalities of rights and intellectual property as draconian impositions on a cottage industry of charmingly amateur production. Indeed, this is but one of the legal restrictions that potentially constrain the operations and activities of the mod community. To use the mod tools supplied with commercial FPS games such as *Unreal Tournament 2004*, *Quake* and *Battlefield*, modders must abide by a set of rules and guidelines laid out in the End User License Agreement (EULA).

EULAs: industrial relations and the institutionalisation of modding

We have noted elsewhere that the videogames industry has a somewhat peculiar relationship with its own cultural heritage seemingly preferring to fix gamers' eyes on the imminent future and the forthcoming release than on the present or past. It might come as something of a surprise, then, to note the willingness of developers and publishers of FPSs to embrace the practice. Drawing on Aarseth (2002), Sue Morris (2003: 7) notes the potential conflict. 'The most profitable games for the industry are those that are largely disposable – played once and abandoned for the next.' Accordingly, gamers dedicating their time to playing *Counter-Strike* years after its original release do little to drive sales of the upcoming products that we have seen the industry is so keen to focus our attentions on. As Morris (2003: 7) explains, 'This has led to some tensions in the industry, in which community building has been seen by some as being a little too successful.'

We might well ask how we should account for the time, effort and resource that goes into creating and supporting the mod tools and communities that utilise them given that their very use and existence appears to run contrary to the commercial imperative. One answer at least might be found in the EULA. Every user of commercially available mod tools is required to abide by the terms of the license agreement that sets out, among other things, the need to ensure standards of legality and decency in productions. As Nieborg (2005: 11) has noted, a number of politicised projects have moved to open source software to pursue development given the incompatibility of their aims with the terms and conditions of use for commercial mod tools which, in the case of *Unreal Tournament 2004*, for example, state that mods cannot include 'libellous, defamatory, or other illegal material, material that is scandalous or invades the rights of privacy or publicity of any third party' ('Unreal Tournament 2004 EULA'). For Nieborg (2005), the business model of the videogames industry and its use of proprietary engines and EULAs to police the boundaries between legitimate mods and the production of material deemed 'illegal' is a problematic one. In contrast with the claims of innovation and the matchless creativity of the modding community, Nieborg argues that the protocols, restrictions and regulations on the practice lead to a self-censoring, commodified culture. In addition to the impact on the richness of mods, the obligation to maintain standards of decency also potentially affects the diversity of production and the opportunities for political expression as it exerts its normative effects. Indeed, as Nieborg notes:

> Games with strong ideological and potential offensive content chose to use the open-source Genesis3D engine, instead of e.g. the more technological advanced Unreal Engine. Games such as the extreme-right Ethnic Cleansing, (National Alliance, 2002), the anti-Israel game Special Force (Hizbullah Central Internet Bureau, 2003), and the religious shooter Catechumen (N'Lightning Software, 2000) all use the same open-source game technology.
>
> (Nieborg 2005: 11)

More than this, however, and serving the commercial interests of the industry even more manifestly, modern EULAs usually insist that mods require the use of the original game in order to operate. In other words, the mod cannot exist as a standalone product but must be an add-on to the original title which remains a commercially and functionally integral part of the new production. For Henry Jenkins, this condition problematises the practices of modding as contexts for new and innovative production because the relationship with the original text as a commercial entity is not merely presupposed by but enshrined in the contracts of production and consumption. While Jenkins sees the potential for modding to occupy a special position in the participatory cultures of fandom in which new interactions with the game are created through reprogramming, he notes an important caveat. Although game developers and publishers might provide flexible tools and position their games as mutable, playable systems in which the creation of new experiences is a vital part of the gameplay, the situation is not one of unfettered production and creativity and the commercial industry continues to exert considerable control of the process. 'I can change the fundamental code of the game if I mod it, but at the same time, nobody can play my transformed version of the game unless they become a consumer of the original work' (Jenkins 2006: 163).

As Kushner (2003: 168–169) observes, the earliest *DOOM* mod tools were issued in a rather more open spirit without any such formal stipulations on the relationship of the mod to the original game. Sotamaa's analysis of the *Quake III Arena* EULA shows how far id's position and that of the industry in general has moved. The EULA states:

> ID grants to you the non-exclusive and limited right to create for the Software (except any Software code) your own modifications (the 'New Creations') which shall operate only with the Software (but not any demo, test or other version of the Software).

Importantly, however, the restrictions on distribution of mods go considerably further than this. Not only can modders not distribute the fruits of their labours without locking them into the code of the original game and ensuring that any gamer wishing to play with their work must be a consumer of the original game, but also modders are prohibited from directly receiving remuneration for their works:

> You shall not rent, sell, lease, lend, offer on a pay-per-play basis or otherwise commercially exploit or commercially distribute the New Creations. You are only permitted to distribute, without any cost or charge, the New Creations to other end-users so long as such distribution is not infringing against any third party right and is not otherwise illegal or unlawful.
>
> (*Quake III Arena* EULA 1999)

The terms of the EULA simultaneously ensure that mod makers do not manoeuvre themselves into a position of competition with the originating game developer, and that budding gamers keen to immerse themselves in the rich and vibrant communities and cultures of user-generated content and the innovations that the mainstream cannot or will not produce (if we follow the argument offered by Au 2002) cannot but be paying consumers. As Mactavish (2003) has rightly observed, the EULA is a tool that effectively polices the boundaries of this productive practice and that ensures that the creativity of modders and the eagerness of gamers continue to act as a brand loyalty and marketing device. Ultimately, the EULA might tempt us to consider the commercial videogame industry's support for modding in bleak terms. Sotamaa (2003: 16) notes that for the videogames industry, modders may constitute an inexpensive research and development team (see also Dovey and Kennedy 2006). Jenkins (2006) sees things rather more positively in his discussion of Raph Koster's work on engaging *Star Wars* fans during the production of *Star Wars Galaxies* and concludes that 'games companies have been able to convince their consumers to generate a significant amount of free labor by treating game design as an extension of the game-play experience' (Jenkins 2006: 165).

Without doubt, and regardless of whether they are willing and grateful participants, the EULA places the creative and productive act of modding into an institutionalised context that is heavily weighted in favour of the commercial developer. As we have suggested, the implications of the EULA affect those gamers wishing to play within the cultures of modding as their continued purchases and subscriptions are a necessary condition of entry. Regardless of the legalities and commercial ethics of this situation, the fact remains that the customisation that is privileged in modding is a vital part of the cultures of FPS gaming. Moreover, as we shall see in the final section of this chapter, the influence of modding is beginning to spill out of this genre and even beyond the PC as a gaming platform.

'Game 3.0': user-generated content

Although Morris (2003) has drawn our attention to a number of different creative and productive roles that do not necessarily require high levels of coding proficiency, Dovey and Kennedy (2006) are right to note that the production of mods is not an activity open to all. Interestingly, in this regard, the development of modding culture has seen a marked shift from its origins in the *Construction Sets* and level designers built into some commercially available titles of the 1980s. There, the ethos was one of inclusivity and accessibility and the game making process was very much centred on issues of experiential design with the technical and technological operations concealed behind the visible, manipulatable, 'user-friendly' toolkit. Of course, we should remember that the complexity of game technologies has been transformed in recent years as have the expectations of modders who have become increasingly accustomed to an extremely fine-grained control over the minutiae of the game engine and system. Moreover, while the *Construction Set* might have offered design opportunities to the non-adept, the ability to share these productions was severely limited compared with the heavily institutionalised systems of distribution that embed mod productions into the mainstream. With modding tools becoming ever more complex and requiring considerable levels of dedication, investment and support on the part of both commercial developers and modders alike, we might be tempted to consider the production of mods as becoming increasingly unevenly available and marginal activity. However, Sony Worldwide Studios president Phil Harrison's keynote speech at the 2007 Game Developers Conference signals an interesting turn. In outlining the company's vision for 'Game 3.0', Harrison alluded to a synthesis of the openness and accessibility of the *Construction Set* of old, with the community, collaboration and sharing of the contemporary PC/FPS mod scene. According to Harrison, Game 1.0 was characterised by the stand-alone, non-networked console with games made up of 'static' content. By static, Harrison refers not to a lack of dynamism or responsiveness in the simulations and models of the games but rather to the fact that the extent of the game is fixed and not usually extended. *Super Mario World*'s 96 levels, for example, are supplied, hardwired on the silicon in the game cartridge and are not, perhaps cannot be, easily updated. According to Harrison's history, Game 2.0 saw the move to Internet connectivity. This shift made it possible to download expansion packs and other officially sanctioned materials essentially making the static content available episodically. Content, however, remains created by the few and distributed to the many, from developers to gamers. Game 3.0 differs in centring on online collaboration and user-generated content:

> Suddenly the content is dynamic and, as Sony says, Game 3.0 'puts the spotlight back on the consumer.' Harrison explained that Sony was influenced by the ideas put forth by web 2.0 – sites such as MySpace and YouTube that are driven by user-generated content.
>
> (Radd 2007)

The situation of gaming within the collaborative cultures and practices of social networking sites such as MySpace or the user-generated content networks of YouTube marks the formal acknowledgement of the significance of the collective intelligence of gaming culture. Beyond merely being embedded within or facilitating networks for sharing comment and criticism or even the modifications of a comparative minority of technically-savvy gamers, Sony's plan for Game 3.0 are to leverage the connectivity of the PlayStation Network and the console's local connections to gamers' media. Of the titles Harrison demonstrated, *LittleBigPlanet* is particularly illustrative of the vision:

> The community-based game effectively lets players have a major say in the look and feel of their game and character via customisation and collaboration with other players. The game comes with an initial set of levels but it will be up to the players to take the game to the next step by generating environments themselves. Characters can move anything in the gameworld and build new objects and items without a level design tool – everything is handled by the in-game toolset and gameplay. And when players are done customising and changing the levels, they can share them with the world and let others play and rate the creations.
>
> (French 2007)

What we see in Media Molecule's creation is essentially a sandbox in the style of the *Construction Sets* but offering the sophistication of an environment replete with complex models of simulation and in which objects are subject to the effects of real world physics, for instance. Although there are some pre-made levels, the game is essentially a set of mod tools that primarily exist to facilitate the creation of new and original gameplay experiences. In a similar way to the PC game modding, here, we note that gameplay and game development are seamlessly integrated as Jenkins (2006) observes. In fact, this is perhaps not as innovatory as Harrison and Sony might want us to believe. We have seen with consoles such as the Xbox and the facility in games such as *Amped 3* to replace the provided soundtrack with music ripped from the gamer's own CD library, that customisation and personalisation have been gradually emerging beyond the PC platform. What is particularly interesting about *LittleBigPlanet*, however, is the means by which gamers create these original productions and the scope of the resources they can draw upon.

As a 'convergent' media device that incorporates the ability to upload, store and view digital photographs, music and video, the PS3 can interface with gamers' digital still and video cameras as well as their digital music collections. Where the console presently allows photo slideshows, home movies and music to be viewed and listened to in dedicated player applications that exist alongside but outside the gaming functionality of the console, *LittleBigPlanet* brings this content into its gameworld. By storing digital photos on the PS3's hard drive, for instance, or plugging a camera memory card into the card reader slots in the front of the console, these images become material that can become part of the game with a few clicks of the joypad. Photos may be wrapped around the in-game character models, warped, edited and modified as they become a seamless part of the malleable material of play. In this way, the gamer's personal digital media library becomes indistinguishable from the audiovisual resources and assets supplied by the developers with the game. Personalisation and customisation in *LittleBigPlanet*, then, go beyond the remixing and 'manipulation [of] the prefab semiotics of the game engine' (Schleiner 1999). It goes beyond the rearrangement and assembly of pre-existing assets such as character designs, textures and backgrounds that we have seen in the Construction Sets to afford the easy inclusion of rich media materials derived from gamers' digital media collections. Like PC-based modding, *LittleBigPlanet* encourages and facilitates the sharing of these highly personalised gamer creations which are uploaded to a central server where they may be downloaded, experienced and further played with by other gamers. In this way, *LittleBigPlanet* clearly situates itself within the contemporary media environment that has seen the veneration of user-generated content, sociality and networking and shares much in common with Web 2.0 applications such as FaceBook and YouTube.

None of the GDC Game 3.0 titles are commercially available at the time of writing though Sony's PS3 virtual community *Home* that similarly affords the personalisation and customisation of an avatar and a 'private' apartment has been available in beta version for some time and offers many of the rich social and creative opportunities that residents of Linden Labs' *Second Life* will recognise. Regardless of the success of these specific games and services, it is particularly interesting to observe the way in which the sociality, creativity and productivity of a community or interconnected gamers assume so central a position in the strategy of so significant a platform holder. In some sense, neither *LittleBigPlanet* nor *Home* are games, though they may include elements of games within them. Rather, they are systems and services, toolkits and suites of resources that may be adopted and adapted by the community of gamers. Indeed, to have any purchase, they have to be adopted and adapted and their resources have to be augmented and personalised. Were we to subscribe to the criticisms of Boris Johnson *et al.* that we noted at the beginning of this book, Game 3.0 simply could not work. Without the creativity, productivity and sociality of gamers, without their collaborative networks, the sharing of knowledge and information, the development of new practices of performance and environments to perform within, neither *Home* nor *LittleBigPlanet* would be conceivable. It is my hope that by demonstrating the rich and varied ways in which gamers already engage in precisely these activities regardless of whether it is easy, convenient or accessible, the wild assertions of the detractors of videogames may finally be silenced. In the cultures, communities and emergent practices of videogaming, we see a richly diverse set of activities that provide an eloquent rejoinder to arguments about the poverty of videogames as a form and gaming as a pastime. It has not been my intention in this book to simply offer an apologist's account of videogames and gaming cultures. We have noted a number of highly problematic areas of practice and there is no doubt that many of the activities we have seen here, like much of the stuff of media fandoms, dance dangerously close to illegality and copyright infringement, for instance. However, it is my hope that the reader of this book will be left with a view of videogame cultures that is somewhat more balanced and informed than that offered by the critics determined to ignore or simply unaware of its contours.

Notes

I Everybody hates videogames

1 'Shelf-level-event' is a term that has gained popularity and currency in game development circles and describes a puzzle, moment or sequence in a game that is too difficult or perhaps too obtuse for players who return the game to the shelf never to return to it again. 'GameFAQs' as we shall see in Chapter 5, is a community website dedicated to sharing player-produced guides, solutions, hints and tips for a wide range of videogames.

2 'Digital Rights Management' is a generic term used to describe a variety of electronic copy-protection systems. Most widely known in relation to digital music distribution, but also prevalent in the realms of digital video and games, DRM systems aim to restrict unauthorised copying and reproduction of media content and is intended to uphold the rights of the material's owners by eliminating piracy. For many, DRM is seen as an infringement of fair use and an example of the way in which media owners mistreat their legitimate customers. Anti-DRM sentiment runs high in certain circles and is a prime motivation for many of the hacking scenes such as that operating on the Sony PSP (PlayStation Portable) as we shall see in Chapter 7.

2 Talking about videogames

1 'Easter Eggs' are commonplace in DVD-video also where 'bonus' material such as blooper reels or outtakes is often 'hidden' from the casual viewer and is often accessible only through a series of counter-intuitive menu commands that are deliberately obfuscated and impossible to deduce. Knowledge of these Easter Eggs is frequently shared within communities of fans, in magazines or via websites (see 'The Easter Egg Archive', for instance).

2 'Sidequests' are commonplace in action adventure and role-playing games (RPGs) such as *The Legend of Zelda* series. They are elements of the game that are not essential to the primary narrative thread and while they may often be avoided altogether, they add richness and longevity to the gaming experience.

3 See 'Xbox360achievements.org' for more on the diversity of Xbox Live Achievements.

4 Region coding refers to a range of technical systems that disallow media from one territory to be used in hardware designed for a different territory. Videogames

software, like DVD-video, is intended to be played only within the territory within which it is officially supplied. A number of strategies exist to circumvent region coding that range from importing both hardware and software (i.e. running Japanese software on a Japanese machine outside Japan) or modifying the hardware to disable or work around the region coding system. Both approaches are problematic though platform holders adopt different strategies in asserting their legal position. Though the exact details of the case remain clouded by accusation and innuendo, videogames importer Lik-Sang ceased trading in a blaze of publicity with claims centring on the threats of litigation from Sony (see 'Lik-Sang out of business announcement' 2006). For their part, Sony deny responsibility for the importer's closure (see Gibson 2006).

5 Future Publishing's *Official PlayStation 2* magazine enjoys NRS readership figures of 973,000 for the period January–December 2006, for instance. See 'Official PlayStation 2 Magazine: Print|Future Advertising' (n.d.) [online].

6 The survey was conducted in September 2007 and examined *PSW* (*PlayStation World*), September 2007 covering PS2, PS3 and PSP; *Nintendo: The Official Magazine*, October 2007 (Issue 21) covering Wii, GameBoy, DS and GameCube; *Xbox World 360* October 2007 covering XBox 360. All three magazines are published in the UK by Future Publishing.

7 The videogames industry seems caught in a love–hate relationship with the word 'game'. What was once the 'Edinburgh Games Festival' has been re-branded twice in as many years as the 'Edinburgh Interactive Entertainment Festival' and now 'Edinburgh Interactive Festival'. At the same time, Sony have described their current strategy for PS3, and *PlayStation Home* in particular, as representing 'Game 3.0'. See Chapter 7 for more on Sony's initiative and note Sheff (1993: 1) on the industry's ambivalent relationship with the term and reverence of other media forms.

8 With an aggregate score of over 95 per cent on Game Rankings. See 'Half-Life Game Rankings'.

3 Videogames and/as stories

1 Interestingly, Ian Livingtone went from launching *Dungeons and Dragons* in Europe, founding Games Workshop, through writing many *Fighting Fantasy* 'interactive adventure' books to become Creative Director of Eidos, publisher of *Tomb Raider* among other videogame titles. Livingstone's career speaks of the synergies between videogames, table-top games, board games and fantasy role-playing.

2 While the typical gamer will, inevitably, lose out to an infinite game structure such as that of Tetris, it may be theoretically possible to play in perpetuity and 'beat' the game. John Brzustowski's (1992) M.Sc. thesis outlines the mathematical means by which this might be approached.

4 Things to make and do

1 FanFiction.net employs a ratings system that authors use to the classification of their work. See FictionRatings (2005) while among Starmen.net's guidelines for fanfic submissions is an explanation that, 'No fanfic may contain profanity, sexual content or be overly violent. Everything must be kept family friendly . . . All fanfics must be of a tasteful nature. For example nothing overly violent or stupid. Untasteful fanfics

will be rejected.' See 'Starmen.Net Submission Guidelines' (n.d.) [online]. A similar policy is in place for fanart submissions also.

5 Game Guides, walkthroughs and FAQs

1 By considering walkthrough production as a kind of reverse engineering exercise that deals with the discovery and documentation of patterns in game code, we might draw parallels with the creators of videogame remakes (see Chapter 7).

6 Superplay, sequence breaking and speedrunning

1 'Speedruns' are sometimes known as 'Speed Demos'. Indeed, the Web's foremost repository of such material and one of the most active hubs for participants is the 'Speed Demos Archive'. The soubriquet dates from *DOOM's* and *Quake's* native .DEM format for recording what developer id referred to as 'demos' within the game engine.
2 Similarly, there are many other pleasures to be found in FPSs and racing games that are not oriented around completion and instead focus on blowing up vehicles with grenades in *Halo*; see Newman (2005); Glass (2002) and Juggertrout (2004) on 'Warthog Jumping' in *Halo*. See also the use of Garry Newman's 'Garry's Mod' for building Rube-Goldberg machines and other non-game-oriented contraptions in *Half-Life 2*, for example.
3 See the *Quake done Quick* collection at the 'Speed Demos Archive' for a current list of *QdQ* projects and movies.
4 In fact, the music track was altered for the final piece as copyright clearance proved prohibitively costly. See the discussion of the production of the video on Chris Brandt's website for more information (Brandt 2005).

7 Codemining, modding and gamemaking

1 In fact, most 'hacks' operate by applying their modifications to the original, unaltered code. As such, the data of original 'ROM' image is not actually modified but rather its operation and the way in which it is interpreted is modified by the 'patch'.

References

Aarseth, E. (1997) *Cybertext: Perspectives on Ergodic Literature*, Baltimore, MD: Johns Hopkins University Press.

—— (2002) 'The Dungeon and the Ivory Tower: Vive La Difference ou Liaison Dangereuse?' *Game Studies* 2(1). http://www.gamestudies.org/0102/editorial.html

—— (2004) 'Genre Trouble: Narrativism and the Art of Simulation', in N. Wardrip-Fruin and N. Harrigan (eds) *First Person: New Media as Story Performance, and Game*, Cambridge, MA: The MIT Press.

Abanes, R. (2006) *What Every Parent Needs to Know about Video Games: A Gamer Explores the Good, Bad and Ugly of the Virtual World*, Eugene, OR: Harvest House Publishers.

About the film. (n.d.) *High Score Movie.com*. <http://www.highscoremovie.com/about-synopsis.html>

AC Kid (2006) 'Metal Gear Solid: Portable Ops: No Alert Speed Run Guide for Main Missions and Side Missions', Version 2.01 (18 January 2006). <http://db.gamefaqs.com/portable/psp/file/metal_gear_solid_po_speed.txt>

Accardo, S. (2001) 'Halo (Xbox)', *GameSpy Reviews*. (Posted November 2001) <http://archive.gamespy.com/reviews/november01/halo/>

Adams, E. (1998) 'Games for Girls? Eeeeewwww!', *Gamasutra Designer's Notebook* (February 13 1998). <http://www.gamasutra.com/features/designers_notebook/19980213.htm>

—— (2007) 'Will Computer Games Ever be a Legitimate Art Form?', in A. Clarke and G. Mitchell (eds) *Videogames and Art*. Bristol: Intellect Books, pp. 255–264.

Alex (2007) 'The Legend of Zelda: Four Swords: A Link to the Past', Version: Final (15 July 2007). <http://db.gamefaqs.com/portable/gbadvance/file/zelda_four_swords_g.txt>

Aldrich, C. (2004) *Simulations and the Future of Learning: An Innovative (and Perhaps Revolutionary) Approach to e-Learning*, San Francisco, CA: Pfeiffer.

—— (2005) *Learning by Doing: A Comprehensive Guide to Simulations, Computer Games, and Pedagogy in e-Learning and Other Educational Experiences*, Chichester: John Wiley & Sons, Ltd.

Allen, G. (2004) 'Virtual Warriors Have Feelings, Too', *New York Times*, 4 November.

Allowable console changes (21 July 1997) *Quake Done Quick*. <http://speeddemosarchive.com/quake/qdq/articles/console.html>

An Introduction to Sequence Breaking (2002) *Metroid2002*. <http://www.metroid2002.com/sequence_breaking_introduction.php>

Apathetic Aardvark (2007) 'Final Fantasy VII: Complete Game Walkthrough'. Version Lucky 7s (27 June 2007). <http://db.gamefaqs.com/console/psx/file/final_fantasy_vii_l.txt>

ariblack (2007) 'Internet Hook-Ups of the Non-Sexay Kind!!!! Post #6 Betareaders and Coauthors, anyone?' *FanFiction.Net*. (Posted 4 June 2007.) <http://www.fanfiction.net/topic/31462/2079214/1/>

Au, J.W. (2002) 'The Triumph of the Mod' *Salon.com*. (Posted 16 April.) <http://dir.salon.com/story/tech/feature/2002/04/16/modding/index.html>

AvidWriter (2007) 'Halo Fan Fiction Contest'. *Halo Wars Heaven*. <http://halowars.heavengames.com/cgi-bin/forums/display.cgi?action=st&fn=6&tn=46&st=recent>

Bacon-Smith, C. (1992) *Enterprising Women: Television Fandom and the Creation of Popular Myth*. Philadelphia, PA: University of Pennsylvania Press.

Bailey, A. (1997) 'Zigzagging Through a Strange Universe'. *Quake Done Quick*. (Posted 12 October 1997.) <http://speeddemosarchive.com/quake/qdq/articles/ZigZag/>

Barker, C. (2007) 'The Interactive Parallel Universe'. Keynote speech delivered at the *2nd Annual Hollywood and Games Summit*. Renaissance Hollywood Hotel, California, 26–27 June. Information available at: <http://www.hollywoodandgames.com/conference/keynote.htm>

Barker, M. and Petley, J. (eds) (1997) *Ill Effects: The Media/Violence Debate*, London: Routledge.

Barthes, R. (1973) *Mythologies*, New York: Hill and Wang.

Baym, N.K. (2000) *Tune In, Log On: Soaps, Fandom, and Online Community*, Thousand Oaks, CA: Sage.

Ben (2007) 'Re: About the Time of the Track', *Bizarre Creations: Project Gotham Racing 4 Discussion Board*. (Posted 27 July.) http://www.bizarrecreations.com/forum/viewtopic.php?f=30&t=14802&p=

Benjamin, W. (1935) 'The Work of Art in the Age of Mechanical Reproduction', in W. Benjamin (1999) *Illuminations*, London: Pimlico.

Benwell, B. (ed.) (2003) *Masculinity and Men's Lifestyle Magazines*, Oxford: Blackwell.

Bisqwit interview (2004) (Original interview at GameCritics.com.) Now archived at *TASvideos* <http://tasvideos.org/Interviews/Bisqwit/GameCritics2004.html>

Black Light Princess (2005) 'Forums » Resident Evil: The Best Survival Horror Game » Dead Plot Bunnies?' *FanFiction.Net*. (Posted 18 December 2005.) <http://www.fanfiction.net/topic/2338/5710/1/>

Brandt, C. (2005) 'Dance, Voldo, Dance: A Machinima Music Video', *Bain Street Productions*. <http://www.bainst.com/madness/voldo.html> (See also <http://www.machinima.com/film/view&id=1234>)

Braun, C. and Giroux, J. (1989) 'Arcade Video Games: Proxemic, Cognitive and Content Analyses', *Journal of Leisure Research*, 21 pp. 92–105.

Bray, H. (2004) 'Inspired Animation Tools from an Uninspired Sitcom', *Boston Globe*, 17 March.

Brooker, W. (2002) *Using the Force: Creativity, Community and Star Wars Fans*, New York and London: Continuum.

Brooks, P. (1982) 'Freud's Master Plot', in S. Felman (ed.) *Literature and Psychoanalysis The Question of Reading: Otherwise*, New Haven, CT: Yale University Press.

Bryce, J., Rutter, J. and Sullivan, C. (2006) 'Digital Games and Gender', in J. Rutter and J. Bryce (eds) *Understanding Digital Games*, London: Sage, pp. 185–204.

Brzustowski, J. (1992) *Can You Win at Tetris?*, Masters thesis, University of British Columbia. <http://www.iam.ubc.ca/theses/Brzustowski/JBrzustowski_MSc_Thesis.pdf>

Buchanan, L. (2003) 'Underground Machinima Is Making Waves', *Chicago Tribune*, 9 August.

Buffa, C. (2006a) 'Opinion: Why Videogame Journalism Sucks', *GameDaily*. (Posted 14 July 2006.) <http://www.gamedaily.com/articles/features/opinion-why-videogame-journalism-sucks/69180/?biz=1>

—— (2006b) 'How to Fix Videogame Journalism', *GameDaily*. (Posted 20 July 2006.) <http://www.gamedaily.com/articles/features/how-to-fix-videogame-journalism/69202/?biz=1>

—— (2006c) 'Opinion: How to Become a Better Videogame Journalist', *GameDaily*. (Posted 28 July 2006.) <http://www.gamedaily.com/articles/features/opinion-how-to-become-a-better-videogame-journalist/69236/?biz=1>

—— (2006d) 'Opinion: The Videogame Review – Problems and Solutions', *GameDaily*. (Posted 2 August 2006.) <http://www.gamedaily.com/articles/features/opinion-the-videogame-review-problems-and-solutions/69257/?biz=1>

Burn, A. (2006a) 'Playing Roles', in D. Carr, D. Buckingham, A. Burn and G. Schott, *Computer Games: Text, Narrative and Play*, Cambridge: Polity Press, pp. 72–87.

—— (2006b) 'Reworking the Text: Online Fandom', in D. Carr, D. Buckingham, A. Burn and G. Schott (eds) *Computer Games: Text, Narrative and Play*, Cambridge: Polity Press, pp. 82–102.

Burn, A. and Carr, D. (2006) 'Motivation and Online Gaming', in D. Carr, D. Buckingham, A. Burn and G. Schott (eds) *Computer Games: Text, Narrative and Play*, Cambridge: Polity Press, pp. 103–118.

Bury, R. (2005) *Cyberspaces of Their Own: Female Fandoms Online*, New York: Peter Lang.

Buuk, R. (n.d.) 'A Day in the Life of MissingNo.' *Team Rocket's Rockin*. <http://www.trsrockin.com/missing.html>

C64Audio.com: The Commodore 64 Music Record Label. See <http://www.c64audio.com/>

Cahill, J. (2003) *Cosplay Girls: Japan's Live Animation Heroines*, Cresskill, NJ: Hampton Press.

Caillois, R. (2001) *Man, Play and Games*, trans. Meyer Barash, Urbana, IL: University of Illinois Press.

Cannon, R. (2007) 'Meltdown', in A. Clarke and G. Mitchell (eds) *Videogames and Art*, Bristol: Intellect Books, pp. 38–53.

Capcom (2006) *Resident Evil Archives: Umbrella's Virus Uncovered*, Indianapolis, IN: BradyGames.

Carr, D., Buckingham, D., Burn, A. and Schott, G. (eds) (2006) *Computer Games: Text, Narrative and Play*, Cambridge: Polity Press.

Carr, D., Campbell, D. and Ellwood, K. (2006) 'Film, Adaptation and Computer Games', in D. Carr, D. Buckingham, A. Burn and G. Schott (eds) *Computer Games: Text, Narrative and Play*, Cambridge: Polity Press, pp. 149–161.

Cassell, J. and Jenkins, H. (1998) *From Barbie to Mortal Kombat*, Cambridge, MA: The MIT Press.

Castranova, E. (2005) *Synthetic Worlds: The Business and Culture of Online Games*, Chicago: University of Chicago Press.

Center for Glitch Studies. <http://glitch.shorturl.com/>

Choquet, D. (ed.) (2002) *1000 Game Heroes*, Köln: Taschen.

Chung, D. (2005) 'Something for Nothing: Understanding Purchasing Behaviors in Social Virtual Environments', *CyberPsychology & Behavior*, 8(6): 538–554.

Church, D. (2000) 'Abdicating Authorship: Goals and Process of Interactive Design', *GDC 2000* (Game Developers' Conference), San Jose, Lecture 5403.

Clark, A. (2001a) 'Adaptive Music', *Gamasutra*. <http://www.gamasutra.com/resource_guide/20010515/clark_01.htm>

—— (2001b) 'Audio Content for Diablo and Diablo 2: Tools, Teams and Products', *Gamasutra*. <http://www.gamasutra.com/resource_guide/20010515/uelman_01.htm>

—— (2001c) 'An Interview with Darryl Duncan', *Gamasutra*. <http://www.gamasutra.com/resource_guide/20010515/marks_01.htm>

Clarke, A. (2007) 'An Interview with Brody Condon', in A. Clarke and G. Mitchell (eds) *Videogames and Art*, Bristol: Intellect Books, pp. 85–93.

Clarke, A. and Mitchell, G. (eds) (2007) *Videogames and Art*, Bristol: Intellect Books.

Conley, J., Andros, E., Chinai, P., Lipkowitz, E. and Perez, D. (2004) 'Use of a Game Over: Emulation and the Video Game Industry: A White Paper', *Northwestern Journal of Technology and Intellectual Property*, 2(2). <http://www.law.northwestern.edu/journals/njtip/v2/n2/3/Conley.pdf>

Consalvo, M. (2003a) 'Zelda 64 and Video Game Fans', *Television & New Media*, 4(3): 321–334.

—— (2003b) 'Cyber-Slaying Media Fans: Code, Digital Poaching, and Corporate Control of the Internet', *Journal of Communication Inquiry*, 27: 67–86.

—— (2004) 'Response To: Who Are Walkthroughs and FAQs For?', in J. Newman and I. Simons (eds) *Difficult Questions about Videogames*, Nottingham: Suppose Partners.

—— (2007) *Cheating: Gaining Advantage in Videogames*, Cambridge, MA: MIT Press.

Coppa, F. (2006) 'Writing Bodies in Space. Media Fan Fiction as Theatrical Performance', in K. Hellekson and K. Busse (eds) *Fan Fiction and Fan Communities in the Age of the Internet*, Jefferson, NC: McFarland and Company, Inc. Publishers, pp. 225–244.

Cosplay UK: Design, Create, Inspire. See <www.cosplay.co.uk>

Cosplay.com See <www.cosplay.com>

CosplayLab Look-alike Contest Winners', *CosplayLab.com*. <http://www.cosplaylab.com/contests/winners/index.asp>

Cragg, A., Taylor, C. and Toombs, B. (2007) 'BBFC Video Game Report', *British Board of Film Classification*. <http://www.bbfc.co.uk/downloads/pub/Policy%20and%20Research/BBFC%20Video%20Games%20Report.pdf>

Crawford, G. (2005) 'Digital Gaming, Sport, and Gender', *Leisure Studies*, 24(3): 259–270.

—— (2006) 'The Cult of Champ Man: The Cultures and Pleasures of Championship Manager/Football Manager Gamers', *Information, Communication and Society*, 9(4): 496–514.

Crawford, G. and Rutter, J. (2007) 'Playing the Game: Performance in Digital Game Audiences', in J. Gray, C. Sandvoss and C.L. Harrington (eds) *Fandom: Identities and Communities in a Mediated World*, New York: New York University Press, pp. 271–281.

Crimson Sky (3 March 2005) 'Doom3: Project Mars City', *TheBestCaseScenario. Custom Computer Community*. <http://www.thebestcasescenario.com/forum/showthread.php?t=1>

Criskah (2006) 'Reviews For: Ecco the Dolphin: Uniting of Times', *FanFiction.Net*. (Posted 29 October 2006.) http://www.fanfiction.net/r/2563685/

Cubitt, S. (1991) *Timeshift: On Video Culture*, London: Routledge.

Cumberbatch, G. (1998) 'Media Effects: The Continuing Controversy', in A. Briggs and P. Cobley (eds) *The Media: An Introduction*, Harlow: Longman.

—— (2004) 'Video Violence: Villain or Victim', *Video Standards Council (VSC)*. <http://www.videostandards.org.uk>

CyricZ (2007) 'The Legend of Zelda: Twilight Princess (Wii Version): A FAQ/ Walkthrough by CyricZ', 5 May 2007 (Version 1.2). <http://www.gamefaqs.com/ console/wii/file/928519/46241>

Daniel (2007) 'E3 2007: G4TV Assassin's Creed Live Demo', *Gaming Today: News for Gamers*. (Posted 13 July 2007.) <http://news.filefront.com/e3-2007-g4tv-assassins-creed-live-demo/>

Dark Angel (2003) 'Final Fantasy VII FAQ/Walkthrough', Version: Final (6 January 2003). <http://www.gamefaqs.com/console/psx/file/197341/16929>

dark-dragon101 (2006) 'Reviews For: Ecco the Dolphin: Uniting of Times', *FanFiction.Net*. (Posted 27 February 2006.) <http://www.fanfiction.net/r/2563685/>

Darkfury3827 (2006) 'The Legend of Zelda: Twilight Princess Full Walkthrough/In-depth Guide', Version 12.99 (21 December 2006). <http://db.gamefaqs.com/console/wii/ file/zelda_tp.txt>

David Wonn's Unique Video Game Glitches! <http://davidwonn.kontek.net/main.html>

Dawley (2005) 'Forums » Resident Evil: The Best Survival Horror Game » Dead Plot Bunnies?', *FanFiction.Net*. (Posted 18 December 2005.) <http://www.fanfiction.net/ topic/2338/5710/1/>

Deacon, D. (2003) 'Holism, Communion and Conversion: Integrating Media Consumption and Production Research', *Media, Culture & Society*, 25: 209–231.

Delaney, K.J. (2004) 'When Art Imitates Videogames, You Have "Red vs. Blue": Mr. Burns Makes Little Movies Internet Fans Clamor for; Shades of Samuel Beckett', *The Wall Street Journal*, 9 April 2004. <http://interactive.wsj.com/dividends/retrieve.cgi?id=/ text/wsjie/data/SB108145721789778243.djm&d2hconverter=display-d2h&template= dividends>

Dena, C. (2004) 'Current State of Cross Media Storytelling: Preliminary Observations for Future design', Delivered at 'Crossmedia communication in the dynamic knowledge society networking session', *European Information Systems Technologies Event*, The Hague, Netherlands, 15 November. <http://www.christydena.com/Docs/DENA_ CrossMediaObservations.pdf>

—— (2006) 'Writing Predictions for the Next Decade', *Cross-Media + Transmedia Entertainment*. (Posted 6 January 2006.) <http://www.cross-mediaentertainment. com/index.php/2006/01/06/writing-predictions-%20for-the-next-decade/>

—— (2007) 'Patterns in Cross-Media Interaction Design: It's Much More than a URL . . . (Part 1)', *Cross-Media + Transmedia Entertainment*. (Posted 10 March 2007.) <http://www.cross-mediaentertainment.com/index.php/2007/03/10/cross-mediainteraction-design-cmid/>

Denerstein, B. (2007) 'What for Art Thou?', *Kotaku*. (Posted 27 July.) <http://kotaku.com/gaming/feature/what-for-art-thou-283021.php>

Doerr, N. (2007) 'Fun Speculation: 80gb Ps3 to Come with Rumble Sixaxis?', *PS3 Fanboy*. (Posted 9 July 2007.) <http://www.ps3fanboy.com/2007/07/09/fun-speculation-80gb-ps3-to-come-with-rumble-sixaxis/>

Douglas, M. (1982) 'Goods as a System of Communication', in M. Douglas, *In the Active Voice*, London: Routledge.

Dovey, J. and Kennedy, H.W. (2006) *Game Cultures: Computer Games as New Media*, Maidenhead: Open University Press.

Dragorn (2002) '9 Day Challenge Walkthrough', Version .4 (29 March 2002). <http://db.gamefaqs.com/console/gamecube/file/pikmin_9_day.txt>

Dreamscape (n.d.) See <http://www.jettastarr.com/Dreamscape/DS_index.html>

Duchesne, S.K. (2007) 'Play vs. Presence in *Star Trek*', *Journal of Humanities and Social Sciences*, 1(2) <http://www.scientificjournals.org/journals2007/articles/1181.pdf>

du Gay, P., Hall, S., Janes, L., Mackay, H., and Negus K. (1997) *Doing Cultural Studies: The Story of the Sony Walkman*, London: Sage.

Duguid, P. (1996) 'Material Matters: The Past and Futurology of the Book', in G. Nunberg (ed.) *The Future of the Book*, Berkeley, CA: University of California Press, pp. 63–101.

Durack, E. (2000) 'Beta Reading', *Qui-Gonline*. <http://www.qui-gonline.org/fanfic/beta.htm>

Durkin, K. and Aisbett, K. (1999) *Computer Games and Australians Today*, Sydney, NSW: Office of Film and Literature Classification.

Ear Candy (2006) *360 magazine*, Imagine Publishing. Issue 6: 100–105.

EB Siege (n.d.) *Starmen.Net*. <http://starmen.net/ebsiege/>

Ebert, R. (2007) 'Games vs. Art: Ebert vs. Barker', Roger Ebert.com. (Posted 21 July 2007.) <http://rogerebert.suntimes.com/apps/pbcs.dll/article?AID=/20070721/COMMENTARY/70721001>

Eng, L. (2002) 'Otak-who? Technoculture, Youth, Consumption, and Resistance: American Representations of a Japanese Youth Culture', Research Seminar in Science and Technology Studies and Research Methods in Science and Technology Studies, Spring 2002. <http://www.cjas.org/~leng/otaku.pdf>

Eskelinen, M. (2001) 'The Gaming Situation', *Game Studies*, 1(1). <http://www.gamestudies.org/0101/eskelinen/>

Eurogamer. Available at: <http://www.eurogamer.net>

Faber, L. (1998) *re: play. ultimate games graphics*, London: Laurence King Publishing.

Facer, K., Furlong, J., Furlong, R. and Sutherland, R. (2003) *ScreenPlay: Children and Computing in the Home*, London: RoutledgeFalmer.

Falstein, N. (2004) 'Response To: Who Are Walkthroughs and FAQs for?', in J. Newman and I. Simons (eds) *Difficult Questions about Videogames*, Nottingham: Suppose Partners.

FanFiction.Net. <http://www.fanfiction.net>

Fiction Ratings. (2005). <http://www.fictionratings.com/guide.php>

Fiske, J. (1992). The Cultural Economy of Fandom', in L. Lewis (ed.) *The Adoring Audience: Fan Culture and Popular Media*, London: Routledge, pp. 30–49.

Floyd, J. (2005) 'The Boy Who Would Be El Rey', *The Dugout*. <http://www.thedugout.tv/community/showthread.php?t=16195>

FractalFusion (1 September 2007) 'Why and How', *TASVideos*. <http://tasvideos.org/WhyAndHow.html>

Frasca, G. (2001) *Videogames of the Oppressed: Videogames as a Means for Critical Thinking and Debate*, Masters thesis (Georgia Institute of Technology). <http://www.ludology.org/articles/thesis/>

—— (2003) 'Simulation versus Narrative: Introduction to Ludology', in M.J.P. Wolf, and B. Perron, (eds) *The Video Game Theory Reader*, New York: Routledge, pp. 221–235.

French, M. (2007) 'Sony and Media Molecule land on LittleBigPlanet', *Develop* (March 2007). <http://www.developmag.com/news/26008/Sony-and-Media-Molecule-land-on-LittleBigPlanet>

Frequently Asked Questions about Sonic 2 Beta, *The Sonic 2 Beta Page*. <http://s2beta.com/faq#s020>

Friedman, T. (1995) 'Making Sense of Software: Computer Games and Interactive Textuality', in S.G. Jones, (ed.) *Cybersociety: Computer-Mediated Communication and Community*, London: Sage.

—— (1999) 'Civilization and its Discontents: Simulation, Subjectivity and Space', in G. Smith (ed.) *On a Silver Platter: CD-ROMS and the Promises of a New Technology*, New York: New York University Press.

Fristrom, J. (2004) 'Some Notes on Half-Life 2', *GameDevBlog*. (Posted 29 December 2004.) <http://www.gamedevblog.com/2004/12/index.html>

Fron, J., Fullerton, T., Morie, J.F. and Pearce, C. (2007) 'Playing Dress-Up: Costumes, Roleplay and Imagination', *Women in Games*, 19–21April 2007, University of Wales, Newport. <http://www.ludica.org.uk/LudicaWIG07.pdf>

Fuller, M. and Jenkins, H. (1995) 'Nintendo®and New World travel writing: a dialogue' in S.G. Jones (ed.) *Cybersociety: Computer-Mediated Communication and Community*. Sage Publications.

Game Boy Game Pak Troubleshooting – Specific Games: 2. MissingNO/Pokémon 000. *Nintendo (US) support*. <http://www.nintendo.com/consumer/systems/gameboy/trouble_specificgame.jsp>

GameCity: International Interactive Entertainment Festival. <http://www.gamecity.org>

GameDevBlog. (Jamie Fristrom's game development blog.) <http://www.gamedevblog.com/>

GameFAQs. <http://www.gamefaqs.com>

Gardikis, A. (10 April 2007) 'Super Mario Bros.', Speed Demos Archive, <http://speeddemosarchive.com/Mario1.html>

Gee, J.P. (2003) *What Video Games Have to Teach Us About Learning and Literacy*, New York: Palgrave Macmillan.

—— (2007) *Good Video Games + Good Learning: Collected Essays on Video Games, Learning and Literacy*, New York: Peter Lang.

Giacquinta, J.B., Bauer, J.A. and Levin, J.E. (1993) *Beyond Technology's Promise: An Examination of Children's Educational Computing at Home*, Cambridge and New York: Cambridge University Press.

Gibson, E. (2006) 'Sony Denies Responsibility for Closure of Lik-Sang', *GamesIndustry.biz*. (Posted 24 October 2007.) <http://www.gamesindustry.biz/content_page.php?aid=20564>

Giddings, S. and Kennedy, H. (2006) 'Digital Games as New Media', in J. Rutter and J. Bryce (eds) *Understanding Digital Games*, London: Sage, pp. 129–147.

Gillen, K. (2004) 'The New Games Journalism', *Kieron Gillen's Workblog*. http://gillen.cream.org/wordpress_html/?page_id=3

Glass, R. (2002) 'Warthog Jump: A Halo Physics Experiment' (Machinima movie), *Machinima.com*. <http://www.machinima.com/film/view&id=204>

Gough-Yates, A. (2003) *Understanding Women's Magazines*, London: Routledge.

Graner-Ray, S. (2004) *Gender Inclusive Game Design: Expanding the Market*, Hingham: Charles River Media.

Gray, J., Sandvoss, C. and Harrington, C.L. (eds) (2007) *Fandom: Identities and Communities in a Mediated World*, New York: New York University Press.

Green, L. and Guinery, C. (2004) 'Harry Potter and the Fan Fiction Phenomenon', *M/C Journal*, 7(5). <http://journal.media-culture.org.au/0411/14-green.php>

Griffiths, M. (1999) 'Violent Video Games and Aggression: A Review of the Literature', *Aggression and Violent Behavior*, 4(2): 203–212.

Grossman, A. (ed.) (2003) *Postmortems from Game Developer: Insights from the Developers of Unreal Tournament, Black & White, Age of Empires, and Other Top-Selling Games*, San Francisco: CMP Books.

Grossman, D. (2001) 'Trained to Kill', *Das Journal des Professoren forum*, 2(2): 3–10.

Gunter, B. (1998) *The Effects of Video Games on Children: The Myth Unmasked*, Sheffield: Sheffield Academic Press.

Half-Life Game Rankings, *Game Rankings.com*. <http://www.gamerankings.com/htmlpages2/43362.asp?q=half-life>

Halliday, M.A.K. (1970) 'Relevant Models of Language', *Educational Review* 22: 26–37.

HappyPuppet (2007) 'Cave of Ordeals Minimalist Challenge Walkthrough. Version 1.51 (14 March 2007). <http://www.gamefaqs.com/console/wii/file/928519/46700>

Harris, J. (2001) 'The Effects of Computer Games on Young Children – a review of the research', RDS Occasional Paper No. 72, London: Home Office.

Heins, M. and Bertin, J.E. (eds) (2002) 'Brief Amici Curiae of Thirty-Three Media Scholars in Support of Appellants, and Supporting Reversal', United States Court of Appeals for the Eighth Circuit, Interactive Digital Software Association v St. Lois County, 24 September.

Hellekson, K. and Busse, K. (eds) (2006) *Fan Fiction and Fan Communities in the Age of the Internet*, Jefferson, NC: McFarland and Company.

Hermes, J. (1995) *Reading Women's Magazines: An Analysis of Everyday Media Use*, Cambridge: Polity.

Hill, A. and Palmer, G. (2002) 'Big Brother', *Television & New Media*, 3(3): 251–254.

Hills, M. (2002) *Fan Cultures*, London and New York: Routledge.

HLcomic (comic strip created in *Half-Life*) <http://www.hlcomic.com/>

Hockey, R. (2004) 'Response To: Who Are Walkthroughs and FAQs for?', in J. Newman and I. Simons (eds) *Difficult Questions about Videogames*, Nottingham: Suppose Partners.

Hodge, R. and Tripp, D. (1986) *Children and Television*, Cambridge: Polity.

Hodgson, D.S.J., Stratton, B. and Stratton, S. (2002) *Super Mario Sunshine: Prima's Official Strategy Guide*, Roseville, CA: Prima Games.

Holmes, T. (2006) 'Electronic Journalism and Electronic Publishing', in J. McKay, *The Magazines Handbook*, London: Routledge, pp. 149–160.

Huhtala, A. (2005) 'Interview: Sharing Snake with Hideo Kojima'. *ComputerAndVideogames.Com*. (Posted 11 March 2005.) <http://www. computerandvideogames.com/article.php?id=116014>

Hunger, F. (2007) 'The Idea of Doing Nothing: An Interview with Tobias Bernstrup', in A. Clarke and G. Mitchell (eds) *Videogames and Art*, Bristol: Intellect Books, pp. 107–115.

HVSC Administration (2007) 'The High Voltage SID Collection (HVSC) Info Page: The High Voltage SID Collection Release v47 – 07th of June 2007'. *HVSC*. <http://www.hvsc.c64.org/Info/index.html>

Ikaruga: Chapter 1 (gameplay video) (n.d.) *Ikaruga.co.uk*. <http://www.ikaruga.co.uk/downloads/vid_view.php?play=1p&mode=arcade&diff=normal&chap=1>

Into the Pixel: An Exhibition of the Art of the Video Game. <http://www.intothepixel.com>

Jackson, P., Stevenson, N. and Brooks, K. (2001) *Making Sense of Men's Magazines*, Cambridge: Polity Press.

Jansz and Martens (2005) 'Gaming at a LAN Event: The Social Context of Playing Video Games', *New Media and Society*, 7(3): 333–355.

Jenkins, H. (1992) *Textual Poachers: Television Fans and Participatory Cultures*, London: Routledge.

—— (1993) ' "X Logic": Repositioning Nintendo in Children's Lives', *Quarterly Review of Film and Video*, 14(4): 55–70.

—— (2003a) 'Transmedia Storytelling: Moving Characters from Books to Films to Video Games Can Make Them Stronger and More Compelling', *Technology Review*. (Posted 15 January 2003.) <http://www.technologyreview.com/Biotech/13052/>

—— (2003b) 'Why The Matrix Matters', *Technology Review*. (Posted 6 November 2003.) <http://www.technologyreview.com/blog/post.aspx?bid=293&bpid=15779>

—— (2006) *Convergence Culture: Where Old and New Media Collide*, New York and London: New York University Press.

—— (2007) 'Transmedia Storytelling 101'. *Confessions of an Aca/Fan: The Official Weblog of Henry Jenkins*. (Posted 22 March 2007.) <http://www.henryjenkins.org/2007/03/transmedia_storytelling_101.html>

Jensen, J. and Pauly, J. (1997) 'Imagining The Audience: Losses and Gains in Cultural Studies', in M. Ferguson and P. Golding (eds) *Cultural Studies in Question*, Thousand Oaks, CA: Sage, pp. 155–169.

Jessen, C. (1995) 'Children's Computer Culture', *Dansk Paedagogisk Tidsskrift*, No. 5. Also available at: <http://www.carsten-jessen.dk/childcomp.html>

Johnson, B. (2006) 'The Writing Is on the Wall – Computer Games Rot the Brain', *Telegraph.co.uk*. Last updated 28 December 2006. <http://www.telegraph.co.uk/opinion/main.jhtml?xml=/opinion/2006/12/28/do2801.xml>

Johnson, S. (2005) *Everything Bad Is Good for You: How Popular Culture Is Making Us Smarter*, London: Allen Lane.

Jones, G. (2002) *Killing Monsters: Why Children Need Fantasy, Super Heroes, and Make-Believe Violence*, New York: Basic Books.

Jones, M.B. (1984) 'Video Games as Psychological Tests', *Simulation & Games*, 15(2) June: 131–157.

Jones, R. (2006) 'From Shooting Monsters to Shooting Movies. Machinima and the Transformative Play of Video Game Fan Culture', in K. Hellekson and K. Busse (eds) *Fan Fiction and Fan Communities in the Age of the Internet*, Jefferson, NC: McFarland and Company, pp. 261–280.

Juggertrout (2004) 'Halo Warthog Jumping FAQ', Version 1.40 (24 February 2004). <http://db.gamefaqs.com/console/xbox/file/halo_warthog_jump.txt>

Juul, J. (2001) 'Games Telling Stories? a Brief Note on Games and Narratives', *Game Studies*, 1(1). <http://www.gamestudies.org/0101/juul-gts/>

—— (2004) 'Response To: Can You Cheat in a Videogame?', in J. Newman and I. Simons (eds) *Difficult Questions about Videogames*, Nottingham: Suppose Partners.

Karpovich, A.I. (2006) 'The Audience as Editor: The Role of Beta Readers in Online Fan Fiction Communities', in K. Hellekson and K. Busse (eds) *Fan Fiction and Fan Communities in the Age of the Internet*, Jefferson, NC: McFarland and Company, pp. 171–188.

Kazephyr (2007) 'Would It Look Okay If I Lengthened FFVIII Selphie's Dress?', *Cosplay.com* forum discussion. (Posted 14 August 2007.) <http://forums.cosplay.com/showthread.php?t=122826>

Keizer Xilian (2006) 'Forums » Resident Evil: The Best Survival Horror Game » Dead Plot Bunnies?', *FanFiction.Net*. (Posted 6 June 2006.) <http://www.fanfiction.net/topic/2338/5710/1/>

Kelly, R.V. (2004) *Massively Multiplayer Online Role-Playing Games*, Jefferson, NC: McFarland & Company.

Kemps, H. (2005) 'Sega's Yuji Naka Talks!' *Gamespy Xbox*. (page 4 of 5.) <http://uk.xbox.gamespy.com/articles/654/654750p4.html>

Kent, S. (n.d.) 'Hideo Kojima: Game Guru, Movie Maniac', *Gamers Today: World Tour of Games*. <http://www.gamerstoday.com/world_tour/kojima/index.html>

Kent, S. and id Software (2004) *The Making of DOOM 3*, Emeryville, CA: McGraw-Hill/Osborne.

Kenter, K. (2004) 'Response To: Who Are Walkthroughs and FAQs for?', in J. Newman and I. Simons (eds) *Difficult Questions about Videogames*, Nottingham: Suppose Partners.

Kerr, A. (2006) *The Business and Culture of Digital Games*, London: Sage.

Kinder, M. (1991) *Playing with Power in Movies, Television and Video Games*, London: University of California Press.

King, B. and Borland, J. (2003) *Dungeons and Dreamers: The Rise of Computer Game Culture from Geek to Chic*, Emeryville, CA: McGraw-Hill/Osborne.

Kirriemuir, J. and McFarlane, A. (2004) 'Literature Review in Games and Learning', *NESTA Futurelab Literature Reviews*, No. 8. <http://www.futurelab.org.uk/resources/documents/lit_reviews/Games_Review.pdf>

Klein, M.H. (1984) 'The Bite of Pac-Man', *The Journal of Psychohistory*, 11: 395–401.

Kline, S. (1997) 'Pleasures of the Screen: Why Young People Play Video Games', *Proceedings of the International Toy Research Conference*, Angouleme, France, November.

—— (1999) 'Moral Panics and Video Games', paper presented at the *Research in Childhood, Sociology, Culture and History Conference*, University of Southern Denmark, Odense, November.

Kojima, H. (2002) 'World Exclusive: Hideo Kojima Looks to the Future', *ComputerAndVideogames.Com*. (Posted 18 January 2002.) <http://www.computerandvideogames.com/article.php?id=24175>

Konzack, L. (2006) 'Geek Culture: The 3rd Counter-Culture', Presented at FNG2006, 26–28 June 2006, Preston, England. <http://www.vrmedialab.dk/~konzack/GeekCulture.pdf>

Korrekt (2005) 'While The Cat's Away . . .', *The Dugout Community*. (Posted 9 March 2005–2 January 2007.) <http://www.thedugout.tv/community/showthread.php?t=1041>

Koster, R. (2005) *A Theory of Fun for Game Design*, Scottsdale, AZ: Paraglyph Press.

Krzywinska, T. (2002) 'Hands-On Horror', in G. King and T. Krzywinska (eds) *Screenplay: Cinema/Videogames/Interfaces*, London and New York: Wallflower Press, pp. 206–223.

—— (2006) 'The Pleasures and Dangers of the Game Up Close and Personal', *Games and Culture*, 1(1): 119–122.

Kushner, D. (2003) *Masters of DOOM: How Two Guys Created an Empire and Transformed Pop Culture*, London: Piatkus.

Lake, M. (2001) 'Luigi's Mansion: Preview', *NintendoWorldReport*. (Posted 23 August 2001.) <http://www.nintendoworldreport.com/previewArt.cfm?artid=3401>

Lamarre, T. (2004) 'An Introduction to Otaku Movement', *Entertext: Animation Special Issue*, (4)1. <http://www.brunel.ac.uk/4042/entertext4.1/lamarre1.pdf>

LateNiteSlacker (2004) 'Aishiteru', *FanFiction.Net*. (Posted 23 December 2004.) <http://www.fanfiction.net/s/2186636/1/>

Legal Information (Copyrights, Emulators, ROMs, etc.), (n.d.) *Nintendo* (US) corporate website. <http://www.nintendo.com/corp/legal.jsp>

LethalLink99 (2007) 'A FAQ/Walkthrough for Animal Crossing: Wild World for the Nintendo DS', Version 4.00 (15 April 2007.) <http://db.gamefaqs.com/portable/ds/file/animal_crossing_ww_g.txt>

Lévy, P. (1997) *Collective Intelligence: Mankind's Emerging World in Cyberspace*, New York: Plenum.

Lik-Sang Out of Business Announcement (2006) <http://www.lik-sang.com/>

Lin, S. and Lepper, M.R. (1987) 'Correlates of Children's Usage of Video Games and Computers', *Journal of Applied Social Psychology*, 17: 72–79.

Lister, M., Dovey, J., Giddings, S., Grant, I. and Kelly, K. (2003) *New Media: A Critical Introduction*, London and New York: Routledge.

Livingstone, I. (2004) 'Response to: Who Are Walkthroughs and FAQs for?', in J. Newman and I. Simons (eds) *Difficult Questions about Videogames*, Nottingham: Suppose Partners.

Livingstone, S. (2002) *Young People and New Media*, London: Sage.

Lowood, H. (2005) 'Real-Time Performance: Machinima and Game Studies', *International Digital Media and Arts Association Journal*, 1: 10–17.

—— (2007) 'High-Performance Play: The Making of Machinima', in A. Clarke and G. Mitchell (eds) *Videogames and Art*, Bristol: Intellect Books, pp. 59–79.

Mactavish, A. (2003) 'Game Mod(ifying) Theory: The Cultural Contradictions of Computer Game Modding', paper presented at *Power Up: Computer Games, Ideology, and Play*, Bristol, UK, July 14–15, 2003.

Malone, T. (1980) *What Makes Things Fun to Learn? A Study of Intrinsically Motivating Computer Games*, Palo Alto, CA: Xerox.

Manovich, L. (2001) *The Language of New Media*, Cambridge, MA: MIT Press.

Marino, P. (2004) *3D Game-Based Filmmaking: The Art of Machinima*, Scottsdale, AZ: Paraglyph Press.

Marshall, P.D. (2002) 'The New Intertextual Commodity', in D. Harries (ed.) *The New Media Book*, London: BFI, pp. 69–82.

Martin, B. (2007) 'Should Videogames be Viewed as Art?', in A. Clarke and G. Mitchell (eds) *Videogames and Art*, Bristol: Intellect Books, pp. 201–210.

McKay, J. (2006) *The Magazines Handbook*, London: Routledge.

McLoughlin, L. (2000) *The Language of Magazines*, London: Routledge.

Megura, K. (2000) 'Final Fantasy VII FAQ', *The Spoiler*. <http://www.the-spoiler.com/RPG/Square/final.fantasy7.2.html>

Metroid Guide. <http://www.metroidguide.com/>

Metroid2002 (speedrunning community). <http://www.metroid.2002.com>

Miles McCloud (2002) 'What Is an Action Adventure Game?', *Sonic the Hedgehog Area 51 Messageboard*. (Posted 8 February 2002.) <http://ssrg.emulationzone.org/area51/cgi-bin/ikonboard/topic.cgi?forum=1&topic=434&start=0> [accessed November 2003, currently offline]

Miller, K.A. (1998) 'Gender Comparisons within Reenactment Costume: Theoretical Interpretations', *Family and Consumer Sciences Research Journal*, 27(1): 35–61.

Missing Sonic 2 Levels. (n.d.) *Sonic Area* 51. <http://ssrg.emulationzone.org/area51/sonic2.html> [accessed November 2003, currently offline].

Mitchell, G. and Clarke, A. (2003) 'Videogame Art: Remixing, Reworking and other Interventions', in M. Copier and J. Raessens (eds) *Level Up: Digital Games Research Conference Proceedings*, University of Utrecht (CD-ROM).

Miyamoto, S. (2003) 'Miyamoto Interviews', <http://www.miyamotoshrine.com/theman/interviews/081403.shtml>. (Original interview: 14 September 2003, *Official Nintendo Magazine* (UK), EMAP).

Mochan (2001) 'The Evil Summoner FAQ v1.0 "How to Be a Cheap Ass"', Version 1.0 (28 May 2001). <http://db.gamefaqs.com/console/ps2/file/summoner_evil.txt>

Montfort, N. (2005) *Twisty Little Passages*, Cambridge, MA: MIT Press.

Morris, D. and Hartas, L. (2003) *Game Art: The Graphic Art of Computer Games*, London: Collins.

—— (2004a) *Role Playing Games*, Lewes: Ilex.

—— (2004b) *Strategy Games*, Lewes: Ilex.

Morris, S. (2003) 'WADs, Bots and Mods: Multiplayer: FPS Games as Co-creative Media', in M. Copier and J. Raessens (eds) *Level Up: Digital Games Research Conference Proceedings*, University of Utrecht (CD-ROM).

Moulthrop, S. (2004) 'From Work to Play: Molecular Culture in the Time of Deadly Games', in N. Wardrip-Fruin and N. Harrigan (eds) *First Person: New Media as Story Performance, and Game*, Cambridge, MA: The MIT Press, pp. 56–70.

MrShotgun (2007) 'The Legend of Zelda: Twilight Princess FAQ/Walkthrough', Version 1.32 (26 July 2007). <http://db.gamefaqs.com/console/gamecube/file/zelda_tp_g.txt>

Murray, J.H. (1997) *Hamlet on the Holodeck: The Future of Narrative in Cyberspace*, New York: The Free Press.

Noobz! Homebrew Without a Clue. <http://www.noobz.eu/joomla/>

Nader, M. (2004) 'The Secret of MissingNo', *Team Rocket's Rockin*. <http://www.trsrockin.com/missingno_fic.html>

—— (n.d.) 'Tales From the Glitch 1: MissingNo . . . the Phantom of the Pokedex!', *Team Rocket's Rockin*. <http://www.trsrockin.com/missingno.html>

NeoGAF (2007) 'New Super Mario Galaxy Famitsu scans', *NeoGAF*. (First posted 18 July 2007.) <http://www.neogaf.com/forum/showthread.php?t=172172>

NES Hacks. (n.d.) *Zophar's Domain*. <http://www.zophar.net/hacks/nes.html>

Newman, J. (2002a) 'In Search of the Videogame Player: the Lives of Mario', *New Media and Society*, 4(3): 407–425.

—— (2002b) 'The Myth of the Ergodic Videogame', *Game Studies: The International Journal of Computer Game Research*, 2(1). <http://www.gamestudies.org/0102/newman/>

—— (2004) *Videogames*, London and New York: Routledge.

—— (2005) 'Playing (with) Videogames', *Convergence: The International Journal of Research into New Media Technologies*, 11(1): 48–67.

Newman, J. and Oram, B. (2006) *Teaching Videogames*, London: BFI Publishing.

Newman, J. and Simons, I. (2003) 'All Your Base Are Belong to Us: Videogame Culture and Textual Production Online', in M. Copier and J. Raessens (eds) *Level Up: Digital Games Research Conference Proceedings*, University of Utrecht (CD-ROM).

—— (2007) *100 Videogames*, London: BFI Publishing.

—— (eds) (2004) *Difficult Questions about Videogames*. Nottingham: Suppose Partners.

Nieborg, D.B. (2005) 'Am I Mod or Not? – An Analysis of First Person Shooter Modification Culture'. Presented at *Creative Gamers Seminar – Exploring Participatory Culture in Gaming*. Hypermedia Laboratory (University of Tampere). <http://www.gamespace.nl/content/DBNieborg2005_CreativeGamers.pdf>

Nintendo (2007) 'Revolution Has a New Name', *Nintendo* (US) corporate website. <http://www.nintendo.com/revolution>

Nintendo (US) corporate website. <http://www.nintendo.com>

Nintendojo. <http://www.nintendojo.com/>

NintendoLand. <http://www.nintendoland.com>

Norman, D.A. (1988) *The Invisible Computer*, Cambridge, MA: MIT Press.

Official PlayStation 2 Magazine: Print|Future Advertising, (n.d.) *Future Advertising*. <http://www.future-advertising.co.uk/ads/portfolio/print.jsp?brand=30&print=40>

Oldschool (2007) 'Crisis Core: FF7 to be 30 to 100 hours long! WOW!', *NeoGAF Forums*. (Posted 27 May 2007.) <http://www.neogaf.com/forum/showthread.php?t=159096>

Our Unique History (2004) *Twin Galaxies*. (Posted 16 April 2004.) <http://www.twingalaxies.com/index.aspx?c=17&id=332>

OverClocked ReMix FAQ (2007) *OverClocked ReMix*. <http://www.ocremix.org/info/Frequently_Asked_Questions>

OverClocked ReMix Mission (2007) *OverClocked ReMix*. <http://www.ocremix.org/info/Mission>

OverClocked ReMix Tutorials (2006) *OverClocked ReMix*. <http://www.ocremix.org/info/Category: Tutorials>

OverClocked ReMix: Unofficial Game Music Arrangement Community. <www.ocremix.org>

Owston, M. (n.d.) 'Peach, Warrior Princess', *NintendoLand Fan Art Gallery*. <http://www.nintendoland.com/art_gallery/mario/view.htm?mandy_peach.jpg>

Papert, S. (1980) *Mindstorms: Children, Computers and Powerful Ideas*, New York: Basic Books.

Peace Flower (2005) 'Reviews for: The Perfect Wall', *FanFiction.Net*. (Posted 6 April 2005.) <http://www.fanfiction.net/r/2136013/>

Pearce, C. (2002) 'The Player with Many Faces: A Conversation with Louis Castle by Celia Pearce', *Game Studies*, 2(2) <http://www.gamestudies.org/0202/pearce/>

—— (2006) 'Productive Play: Game Culture from the Bottom Up', *Games and Culture*, 1(1): 17–24.

Pepperidge (2002) 'Re: It's Buzzbomber's Horribly Flawed Chaos Emerald Theory!', *The Mobius Forum*. (Posted 31 March 2002.) <http://pub12.ezboard.com/fsonichqcommunityfrm10.showMessageRange?topicID=1867.topic&start=1&stop=20>

Perron, B. (2003) 'From Gamers to Players and Gameplayers: The Example of Interactive Movies', in M.J.P. Wolf and B. Perron (eds) *The Video Game Theory Reader*, New York and London: Routledge, pp. 237–258.

PHWonline. (comic strip created in *Half-Life*). <http://comics.phwonline.com/archive/>

Pikachu 4 President (2003) 'Animal Crossing Guide', Version X.1 (6 May 2003). <http://db.gamefaqs.com/console/gamecube/file/animal_crossing_c.txt>

Play! A Video Game Symphony. See <http://www.play-symphony.com/>

Play-Asia.com. <http://www.play-asia.com>

PlayStation Pro 2: Fan Fictions. <http://www.playstationpro2.com/fanfics.html>

Poole, S. (2000) *Trigger Happy: The Inner Life of Videogames*, London: Fourth Estate.

Prensky, M. (2006a) 'Presentation at the 2006 EDUCAUSE Learning Initiative Annual Meeting, January 30, 2006, San Diego, CA.' <http://www.educause.edu/upload/presentations/ELI061/GS01/Prensky%20-%2006-01-Educause-02.pdf>

—— (2006b) *Don't Bother Me Mom—I'm Learning!*, New York: Paragon House.

—— (2007) *Digital Game-Based Learning*, New York: Paragon House.

Press Play On Tape: The Commodore 64 Revival Band. See <http://www.pressplayontape.com/>

Prince Battles Video Games, *BBC News Online*, 11 July 2001. <http://news.bbc.co.uk/1/hi/entertainment/new_media/1433290.stm>

Provenzo, E. (1991) *Video Kids: Making Sense of Nintendo*, London: Harvard University Press.

PSP Fanboy. <http://www.pspfanboy.com>

Quake Done Quick. (QdQ). <http://speeddemosarchive.com/quake/qdq/>

Quiggin, J. (2006) 'Blogs, Wikis and Creative Innovation', *International Journal of Cultural Studies*, 9(4): 481–496.

Radd, D. (2007) 'Gaming 3.0. Sony's Phil Harrison Explains the PS3 Virtual Community, Home', *Business Week*, 9 March. <http://www.businessweek.com/innovate/content/mar2007/id20070309_764852.htm?chan=innovation_game+room_top+stories>

Raddatz, B. (2005) 'MISSINGNO. Guide for Pokemon Red and Blue'. <http://db.gamefaqs.com/portable/gameboy/file/pokemon_missingno_a.txt>

Raph Koster's Website. <http://www.raphkoster.com/>

Resident Evil: The Novels. (n.d.), *Resident Evil Fan: A New Blood*. <http://www.residentevilfan.com/novels/default.asp>

Richards, T. (1997) *The Meaning of Star Trek*, New York: Doubleday.

Rickard, D. (2006) 'Half-Life "in 45 Minutes Und 45 Seconds . . ."', *Rebel.at Games*. (Posted 19 January 2006.) <http://www.rebell.at/?cnt=artikel&id=728>

rizzuh (2000) 'cs year 1', *CS-Nation: Covering the Future of Counter-Strike*. (Posted 18 June 2000.) <http://www.csnation.net/articles.php/1/>

Romhacking dot net. <www.romhacking.net>

Rubin, S. (2004) 'Response to: Who Are Walkthroughs and FAQs for?', in J. Newman and I. Simons (eds) *Difficult Questions about Videogames*, Nottingham: Suppose Partners.

Rutter, J. and Bryce, J. (eds) (2006) *Understanding Digital Games*, London: Sage.

Ryoga Masaki (2002) 'What Is an Action Adventure game?', *Sonic the Hedgehog Area 51 Messageboard*. (Posted 8 February 2002.) http://ssrg.emulationzone.org/area51/cgibin/ikonboard/topic.cgi?forum=1&topic=434&start=0 [accessed November 2003, currently offline].

Salen, K. (2002) 'Quake! DOOM! Sims! Transforming Play: Family Albums and Monster Movies', Exhibit. Presented at the Walker Art Center October 19, 2002. <http://www.walkerart.org/gallery9/qds>

Salen, K. and Zimmerman, E. (2004) *Rules of Play: Game Design Fundamentals*, Cambridge, MA: MIT Press.

San, J. (2004) 'Response to: Who Are Walkthroughs and FAQs for?', in J. Newman and I. Simons (eds) *Difficult Questions about Videogames*, Nottingham: Suppose Partners.

Sanders, J.L. and Brown, R. (1994) 'Glossary of Fanspeak', in J. Sanders (ed.) *Science Fiction Fandom*, Westport, CT: Greenwood Press, pp. 265–269.

Sandvoss, C. (2005) *Fans: The Mirror of Consumption*, Cambridge: Polity Press.

—— (2007) 'The Death of the Reader? Literary Theory and the Study of Texts in Popular Culture', in J. Gray, C. Sandvoss and C.L. Harrington (eds) *Fandom: Identities and Communities in a Mediated World*, New York: New York University Press, pp. 19–32.

Sandford, R. and Williamson, B. (2005) 'Games and Learning: A Handbook from Futurelab', NESTA Futurelab. <http://www.futurelab.org.uk/resources/documents/handbooks/games_and_learning.pdf>

Savin-Baden, M. (2003) *Facilitating Problem-based Learning: Illuminating Perspectives*, Buckingham: Open University Press/SRHE.

Savin-Baden, M. and Major, C. (2004) *Foundations of Problem-based Learning*, Maidenhead: Open University Press/SRHE.

Saxe, J. (1994) 'Violence in Videogames: What Are the Pleasures?', Paper presented at the *International Conference on Violence in the Media*. St John's University, 3–4 October. <http://web.archive.org/web/20000815110856/http://www.media-awareness.ca/eng/issues/violence/resource/reports/gamedoc.htm>

Schleiner, A-M. (1999) 'Parasitic Interventions: Game Patches and Hacker Art', *Opensorcery*. <http://www.opensorcery.net/patch.html>

—— (2007) '"Cracking the Maze" Curator's Note', in A. Clarke and G. Mitchell (eds) *Videogames and Art*, Bristol: Intellect Books, pp. 80–81.

Schott, G. (2006) 'Agency in and around Play', in D. Carr, D. Buckingham, A. Burn and G. Schott (eds) *Computer Games: Text, Narrative and Play*, Cambridge: Polity Press, pp. 133–148.

Schott, G. and Burn, A. (2007) 'Fan-Art as a Function of Agency in Oddworld Fan-Culture', in A. Clarke and G. Mitchell (eds) *Videogames and Art*, Bristol: Intellect Books, pp. 238–254.

Schott, G. and Horrel, K. (2000) 'Girl Gamers and their Relationship with the Gaming Culture', *Convergence: The International Journal of Research into New Media Technologies*, 6(4): 36–53.

Scott, D. (1995) 'The Effect of Video Games on Feelings of Aggression', *The Journal of Psychology*, 129(2): 121–132.

Seiter, E. (1999) *Television and New Media Audiences*, Oxford: Oxford University Press.

Sequence Breaking (2002) *Metroid2002*. <http://www.metroid2002.com/sequence_breaking.php>

Serengeti Lioness (2006) 'Reviews for: Ecco the Dolphin: Uniting of Times', *FanFiction.Net*. (Posted 29 December 2006.) <http://www.fanfiction.net/r/2563685/>

Shaffer, D.W. (2007) *How Computer Games Help Children Learn*, Basingstoke: Palgrave Macmillan.

Sheff, D. (1993) *Game Over: Nintendo's Battle to Dominate an Industry*, London: Hodder and Stoughton.

Shen, L.F. (2007) 'Anime Pleasures as a Playground for Sexuality, Power, and Resistance', Presented at *MiT5, Media in Transition: Creativity, Ownership, and Collaboration in the digital Age: International Conference*, 27–29 April. <http://web.mit.edu/commforum/mit5/papers/Shen_fullPaper.pdf>

Shinan (2007) 'The Commune', *FanFiction.Net*. (Posted 27 September 2007.) <http://www.fanfiction.net/s/2073522/1/>

Simon Silvertongue (2004) 'A Game', *FanFiction.Net*. (Posted 16 October 2004.) <http://www.fanfiction.net/s/2096694/1/>

Sjöberg, L. (2002) 'The Geek Hierarchy', *Brunching Shuttlecocks*. <http://www. brunching.com/geekhierarchy.html>

Smith, G.M. (2002) 'Computer Games Have Words, Too: Dialogue Conventions in Final Fantasy', *Game Studies*, 2(2) <http://www.gamestudies.org/0202/smith/>

Smith, H. (2001) 'The Future of Game Design: Moving Beyond Deus Ex and Other Dated Paradigms', *IGDA*. <http://www.igda.org/articles/hsmith_future.php>

Sonic the Hedgehog Area 51 Messageboard. <http://ssrg.emulationzone.org/area51> [accessed November 2003, currently offline].

Sotamaa, O. (2003) 'Computer Game Modding, Intermediality and Participatory Culture'. <http://www.uta.fi/~olli.sotamaa/documents/sotamaa_participatory_culture.pdf>

Southard, B. (1982) 'The Language of Science-Fiction Fan Magazines', *American Speech*, 57: 19–31.

Speed Demos Archive FAQ. (n.d.) Speed Demos Archive. <http://speeddemosarchive. com/faq.html>

Speed Demos Archive. <http://speeddemosarchive.com/>

Speed Freaks. (syndicated from *Edge* magazine) *Next-Generation: Interactive Entertainment Today*. (Posted 26 August 2007.) <http://www.next-gen.biz/index.php?option= com_content&task=view&id=6957&Itemid=51&limit=1&limitstart=1>

Starmen.Net (formerly 'Earthbound.Net'). <www.starmen.net>

Starmen.Net Staff (2007) 'The EarthBound Anthology', *Lulu.com*. (see also <http:// starmen.net/ebanthology/>)

Starmen.Net Submission Guidelines (n.d.) *Starmen.Net*. <http://starmen.net/fanfics/>

Starmen.Net's Mother 3 Petition (n.d.) *Starmen.Net*. <http://classic.starmen.net/ petition/mother3/>

strawhat (2006) 'Pokemon Fire Red/Leaf Green (GBA) Speed Walkthrough', Version 1.2 (21 November 2006). <http://db.gamefaqs.com/portable/gbadvance/file/pokemon_ frlg_speed.txt>

stuckgamer.com: Streaming Enlightenment. <http://www.stuckgamer.com>

Super Saiyan Zero (2003) 'Metroid Fusion 1% Challenge Guide v1.1', Version v1.1 (2 January 2003). <http://db.gamefaqs.com/portable/gbadvance/file/metroid_fusion_ 1_percent.txt>

Surman, D. (2007) 'Topic: IGDA Sex SIG Wiki: Make Your Voice Heard!', *GayGamer.Net Forum*. (Posted 25 April 2007.) <http://gaygamer.net/forum/index. php/topic,1709.0.html>

Surowiecki, J. (2004) *The Wisdom of Crowds: Why the Many Are Smarter Than the Few*, London: Abacus.

Swalwell (2006) 'Multi-Player Computer Gaming: "Better Than Playing (Pc Games) with Yourself"', *Reconstruction*, 6(1). <http://reconstruction.eserver.org/061/swalwell. shtml>

Tales From the Glitch: MissingNo Visitor Accounts (n.d.) *Team Rocket's Rockin*. <http://www.trsrockin.com/missingno2.html> and <http://www.trsrockin.com/ missingno3.html>

Tales From the Glitch 4: MissingNo Mystery Solved (n.d.) *Team Rocket's Rockin*. <http://www.trsrockin.com/missingno4.html>

TASvideos (Tool-Assisted Speedruns). <http://tasvideos.org/>

Tavares, G. (2004) 'Response to: Who Are Walkthroughs and FAQs for?', in J. Newman and I. Simons (eds) *Difficult Questions about Videogames*, Nottingham: Suppose Partners.

Taylor, T.L. (2003) 'Multiple Pleasures: Women and Online Gaming', *Convergence: The International Journal of Research into New Media Technologies*, 9(1): 21–46.

—— (2006) *Play Between Worlds*, Cambridge, MA: The MIT Press.

Team Rocket's Rockin fanart', *Team Rocket's Rockin*. <http://www.trsrockin.com/glitch_fanart.html>

Team Rocket's Rockin' (n.d.) 'Super Mario Bros. Series Glitches and Tricks', *Team Rocket's Rockin*. <http://www.trsrockin.com/smb_glitches.html>

Tetris: From Russia with Love (2004) BBC4 Television, first broadcast 6 July 2004.

The Easter Egg Archive. <http://www.eeggs.com/>

The Frogger. *Seinfeld*, episode 174 (Season 9), NBC Television, first aired 23 April 1998.

The GameSpy Staff (2001) 'GameSpy's Top 50 Games of All Time', *GameSpy.com*. <http://archive.gamespy.com/articles/july01/top502ase/index3.shtm>

The High Voltage SID Collection – Commodore 64 Music for the Masses (HVSC). <http://www.hvsc.c64.org/>

The Hylia (2007) 'Topic: Do You Think the Fs Games Count?', *The Hylia*. Available at <http://www.thehylia.com/forums/do-you-think-the-fs-games-count-t3170.0.html>

The Machinima FAQ. (8 March 2005) *Academy of Machinima Arts and Sciences*. <http://www.machinima.org/machinima-faq.html>

The Sonic 2 Beta Page' (v4.96) (n.d.). <http://www.s2beta.com>

The (Unified) Mother 3 Fan Translation. (n.d.) <http://mother3.fobby.net/>

The Virus AJG (2003) 'Re: Sort-of proof for Sonic being 15', *The Mobius Forum*. (Posted 9 April 2003.) <http://pub12.ezboard.com/fsonichqcommunityfrm10.showMessageRange?topicID=3238.topic&start=21&stop=40>

Thompson, C. (2005) 'The Xbox Auteurs', *New York Times*, 7 August.

Trautman, E.S. (2004) *The Art of Halo: Creating a Virtual World*, New York: Del Rey.

Tulloch, J. and Jenkins, H. (1995) *Science Fiction Audiences: Watching 'Dr Who' and 'Star Trek'*, New York: Routledge.

Turkle, S. (1984) *The Second Self: Computers and the Human Spirit*, New York: Simon and Schuster.

Tushnet, R. (2007) 'Copyright Law, Fan Practices, and the Rights of the Author', in J. Gray, C. Sandvoss and C.L. Harrington (eds) *Fandom: Identities and Communities in a Mediated World*, New York: New York University Press, pp. 60–71.

Unsworth, G. and Ward, T. (2001) 'Video Games and Aggressive Behaviour', *Australian Psychologist*, 36: 184–192.

Vader's First 501st Legion. See <http://www.501st.com/>

Valve (2004) *Half-Life 2: Raising the Bar*, Roseville, CA: Prima Games.

Verba, J.M. (1996) *Boldly Writing: A Trekker Fan and Zine History, 1967–1987*, Minnesota: FTL Publications.

Video Nasties (Dispatches series) 3BM for *Channel 4 Television* (UK), first broadcast 23 March 2000.

Whetmore, E.J. and Kielwasser, A.P. (1983) 'The Soap Opera Audience Speaks: A Preliminary Report', *Journal of American Culture*, 6: 110–116.

Wilonsky, R. (2002) 'Joystick Cinema: It's Man vs. Machinima When Video Games Become, Ahem, Movies', *Screen Entertainment Weekly*, 14 August.

Winet, J. (2007) 'In Conversation Fall 2003: An Interview with Joseph DeLappe', in A. Clarke and G. Mitchell (eds) *Videogames and Art*, Bristol: Intellect Books, pp. 94–106.

Wolf, M.J.P. and Perron, B. (eds) (2003) *The Video Game Theory Reader*, London: Routledge.

Wonn, D. (n.d.) ' "Minus World". Nintendo 8 bit Glitches'. *David Wonn's Unique Video Game Glitches!* <http://davidwonn.kontek.net/nes.html#S>

Wright, T., Boria, E., and Breidenbach, P. (2002) 'Creative Player Actions in FPS Online Video Games: Playing Counter-Strike', *Game Studies*, 2(2). <http://www.gamestudies.org/0202/wright/>

Writing Tips (n.d.) *NintendoLand* <http://www.nintendoland.com/fanfics//writingtips.htm>

Xbox 360 Achievements <http://www.xbox360achievements.org/index.php>

Xbox360 Fanboy <http://www.xbox360fanboy.com>

Z (2006) 'Reverence Through ReMixing', *Hipster, Please!* <http://www.hipsterplease.com/2006/08/reverence-through-remixing.html>

Zelda Guide: Zelda Fan Fiction. <http://www.zeldaguide.com/fanfiction.htm>

Zzap! 64 Newsfield Publications Ltd. (1985–1992) (See also <www.zzap64.co.uk/>)

Index

Related titles from Routledge

Restyling Factual TV
Audiences and News, Documentary and Reality Genres

Annette Hill

News and current affairs, documentary and reality TV are part of a turbulent time in broadcasting as the boundaries between fact and fiction are pushed to the limits. *Restyling Factual TV* addresses the wide range of programmes that fall within the category of 'factuality', from politics, to natural history, to reality entertainment. It looks at ways viewers navigate their way through a busy, noisy, and constantly changing factual television environment.

Focusing on contemporary trends in the world of television, primarily in the UK and Sweden (both countries with a public service tradition), but with reference to other countries such as the US, Annette Hill investigates complex issues such as the truth claims of factual television, knowledge and learning, and fair treatment in factual programming. Audience research highlights how people engage with and reflect on various representations of reality, and by looking at factuality in this way, we can see how audiences are centre stage in the transformation of factual television.

ISBN13: 978-0-415-37955-7 (hbk)
ISBN13: 978-0-415-37956-4 (pbk)

Available at all good bookshops
For ordering and further information please visit:
www.routledge.com

Related titles from Routledge

Media and Cultural Theory

Edited by James Curran and David Morley

Media & Cultural Theory brings together leading international scholars to address key issues and debates within media and cultural studies including:

- Media representations of the new woman in contemporary society
- The creation of self in lifestyle media
- The nature of cultural globalisation
- The rise of digital actors and media

These subjects are analysed through the use of contemporary media and film texts such as *Bridget Jones* and *The Lord of the Rings* trilogy as well as case studies of the US and UK after 9/11.

ISBN13: 978-0-415-31704-7 (hbk)
ISBN13: 978-0-415-31705-4 (pbk)

Available at all good bookshops
For ordering and further information please visit:
www.routledge.com

Related titles from Routledge

Introduction to the Theories of Popular Culture
Second Edition

Dominic Strinati

Praise for the first edition:

'An excellent introduction to popular culture. Complex theories are presented in a clear and concise manner.' Stephen Dawkins, *Park Lane College*

An Introduction to Theories of Popular Culture is a clear and comprehensive guide to the major theories of popular culture. Dominic Strinati provides a critical assessment of the ways in which these theories have tried to understand and evaluate popular culture in modern societies.

Among the theories and ideas the book introduces are mass culture, the Frankfurt School and the culture industry, semiology and structuralism, Marxism, feminism, postmodernism and cultural populism. Strinati explains how theorists such as Adorno, Barthes, Althusser and Hebdige have grappled with the many forms of popular culture, from jazz to the Americanization of British popular culture, from Hollywood cinema to popular television series, and from teen magazines to the spy novel. Each chapter includes a guide to key texts for further reading and there is also a comprehensive bibliography. This new edition has been fully revised and updated.

ISBN13: 978-0-415-23499-3 (hbk)
ISBN13: 978-0-415-23500-6 (pbk)

Available at all good bookshops
For ordering and further information please visit:
www.routledge.com

Related titles from Routledge

Television Entertainment

Jonathan Gray

Television entertainment rules supreme, one of the world's most important disseminators of information, ideas, and amusement. More than a parade
of little figures in a box, it is deeply embedded in everyday life, in how
we think, what we think and care about, and who we think and care about
it with.

But is television entertainment art? Why do so many love it and so many
hate or fear it? Does it offer a window to the world, or images of a fake
world? How is it political and how does it address us as citizens? What
powers does it hold, and what powers do we have over it? Or, for that
matter, what is television these days, in an era of rapidly developing technologies, media platforms, and globalization?

Television Entertainment addresses these and other key questions that we
regularly ask, or should ask, offering a lively and dynamic, thematically
based overview that offers examples from recent and current television,
including *Lost*, reality television, *The Sopranos, The Simpsons*, political satire,
Grey's Anatomy, The West Wing, soaps, and *24*.

Communication and Society
Series Editor: James Curran

ISBN13: 978-0-415-77223-5 (hbk)
ISBN13: 978-0-415-77224-2 (pbk)

Available at all good bookshops
For ordering and further information please visit:
www.routledge.com

Related titles from Routledge

The Media Student's Book
Fourth Edition

Gill Branston and Roy Stafford

The Media Student's Book is a comprehensive introduction for students of media studies. It covers all the key topics and provides a detailed, lively and accessible guide to concepts and debates. This fourth edition, newly in colour, has been thoroughly revised, re-ordered and updated, with many very recent examples and expanded coverage of the most important issues currently facing media studies. It is structured in four main parts, addressing key concepts, media practices, media debates, and the resources available for individual research.

Individual chapters include: Interpreting media * Narratives * Genres and other classifications * Institutions * Questions of representation * Ideologies and power * Industries * Audiences * Advertising and branding * Research * Production organisation * Production techniques * Distribution * Documentary and 'reality TV' * Whose globalisation? * 'Free choices' in a 'free market'?

Chapters are supported by case studies which include: Ways of interpreting * *CSI: Miami* and crime fiction * J-horror and the *Ring* cycle * Television as institution * Images of migration * News * The media majors * The music industry, technology and synergy * Selling audiences * Celebrity, stardom and marketing * Researching mobile phone technologies * Contemporary British cinema.

The authors are experienced in writing, researching and teaching across different levels of pre-undergraduate and undergraduate study, with an awareness of the needs of those students. The book is specially designed to be easy and stimulating to use with:

- marginal terms, definitions, references (and even jokes), allied to a comprehensive glossary
- follow-up activities, suggestions for further reading, useful websites and resources plus a companion website to supporting the book at www.routledge.com/textbooks/0415371430/
- references and examples from a rich range of media forms, including advertising, television, films, radio, newspapers, magazines, photography and the internet.

ISBN13: 978-0-415-37142-1 (hbk)
ISBN13: 978-0-415-37143-8 (pbk)

Available at all good bookshops
For ordering and further information please visit: www.routledge.com

Related titles from Routledge

Media, Gender and Identity
An Introduction
Second Edition

David Gauntlett

Popular media present a vast array of stories about women and men. What impact do these images and ideas have on people's identities?

The new edition of *Media, Gender and Identity* is a highly readable introduction to the relationship between media and gender identities today. Fully revised and updated, including new case studies and a new chapter, it considers a wide range of research and provides new ways for thinking about the media's influence on gender and sexuality.

David Gauntlett discusses movies such as *Knocked Up* and *Spiderman 3*, men's and women's magazines, TV shows, self-help books, YouTube videos, and more, to show how the media play a role in the shaping of individual self-identities.

The book includes:

- A comparison of gender representations in the past and today, from James Bond to *Ugly Betty*
- An introduction to key theorists such as Judith Butler, Anthony Giddens and Michel Foucault
- An outline of creative approaches, where identities are explored with video, drawing, or Lego bricks
- A website with extra articles, interviews and selected links, at www.theoryhead.com

David Gauntlett is Professor of Media and Communications at the University of Westminster, London. He is the author of several books on media audiences and identities, including *Moving Experiences* (1995, 2005) and *Creative Explorations* (2007). He produces Theory.org.uk, the award-winning website on media, gender and identity.

ISBN13: 978-0-415-39660-8 (hbk)
ISBN13: 978-0-415-39661-5 (pbk)

Available at all good bookshops
For ordering and further information please visit:
www.routledge.com

Related titles from Routledge

Watching with The Simpsons
Television, Parody, and Intertextuality

Jonathan Gray

Using our favourite Springfield family as a case study, *Watching with The Simpsons* examines the textual and social role of parody in offering critical commentary on other television programs and genres.

In this book, Jonathan Gray brings together textual theory, discussions of television and the public sphere, and ideas of parody and comedy. As a study, including primary audience research, it focuses on how The Simpsons has been able to talk back to three of television's key genres – the sitcom, ads, and the news – and on how it holds the potential to short-circuit these genre's meanings, power, and effects by provoking reinterpretations and offering more media literate recontextualizations.

Through examining television and media studies theory, the text of The Simpsons, and the show's audience, Gray attempts to fully situate the show's parodic humor within the lived realities of its audiences. In doing so, he further explores the possibilities for popular entertainment television – and particularly comedy – to discuss issues of political and social importance.

Communication and Society
Series Editor: James Curran

ISBN13: 978-0-415-36203-0 (hbk)
ISBN13: 978-0-415-36202-3 (pbk)

Available at all good bookshops
For ordering and further information please visit:
www.routledge.com